CORFU ON MY MIND

THE AUSTRALIAN FAMILY GREECE

'Crikey, that's us!'

ELIZABETH PAPPAS

A catalogue record for this book is available from the National Library of Australia

Disclaimer

This autobiography is to some extent, loosely based on actual events and told to that extent as truthfully as recollections from long ago permit. However, some individuals and events are creations and bear little or no resemblance to actual events or individuals alive or dead, having been created by me. Some names have been changed and identifying characteristics altered to respect the privacy of persons the subjects of this story.

Copyright © 2023 Elizabeth Pappas
All rights reserved.
ISBN-13: 978-1-922727-74-9

Linellen Press
265 Boomerang Road
Oldbury, Western Australia
www.linellenpress.com.au

Dedication

First and foremost, I dedicate this book to the brothers I didn't grow up with. I also dedicate this book to my courageous mother who suffered for love and paid far too heavy a price, and my father for his many years of devotion to her. I also thank my husband Mark, my daughter Naomi Alexandra and son-in-law Tristan Xavier. Your love and faith have kept the dream of this book alive.

Contents

Disclaimer ii

Dedication iii

Contents iiv

Acknowledgements vii

Corfu, a Poem viii

Chapter 1 - Lulled by the wing of *Morpheus* 1

Chapter 2 - The Peak of *Pantocrator* 9

Chapter 3 - Pyrgi Palace 21

Chapter 4 - Marietta 27

Chapter 5 - The Tricky Dicky Chicken Ticker Story 34

Chapter 6 - Demythologizing Greek Villas 47

Chapter 7 - Idols in the Market Place 59

Chapter 8 - Lentils and Beans Saved Greece 69

Chapter 9 - I Have a Little Lamb, and My Name Isn't Mary 79

Chapter 10 - Serenading Chickens 83

Chapter 11 - Bread and Tomatoes 88

Chapter 12 - A Wheel Within a Wheel, Within a Wheel 92

Chapter 13 - Judas at their Table 101

Chapter 14 - Shorelines of the Nile 109

Chapter 15 - Bouboulina 117

Chapter 16 - Sweet As 124

Chapter 17 - Let's Talk About Sex, Baby 135

Chapter 18 - Troubles in the *Kafeneon*   145

Chapter 19 - Villa Kapodistria   158

Chapter 20 - Book Him   166

Chapter 21 - Mullet Returns   175

Chapter 22 - Catching-up   186

Chapter 23 - The Pillars of Greek Society - you like-e-fakelake?   194

Chapter 24 - Stick and Took   207

Chapter 25 - Tickling Time Bombs   218

Chapter 26 - Easter Sunday   226

Chapter 27 - The Day is but a Pup   237

Chapter 28 - Easter Sunday Afternoon   245

Chapter 29 - Letters from the Edge   257

Chapter 30 - Momma Mia   268

Chapter 31 - In the Driver's Seat   275

Chapter 32 - The Christening   280

Chapter 33 - Written Off   290

Chapter 34 - The Vice Consul's Function   294

Chapter 35 - Hail to the Mail - The Australian Family Greece   301

Chapter 36 - Before the *Gamos*   312

Chapter 37 - The *Gamos*   327

Chapter 38 - The Night of the Flying Typewriter   338

Chapter 39 - In the Hands of *Hebe*   348

Chapter 40 - Giving Up the Ghost   355

Chapter 41 - Pebbles from Pyrgi   366

About the Author   372

Acknowledgements

I thank Helen Iles as both publisher and chief editor of *Corfu on my Mind* for making the process both possible and enjoyable. I also thank fellow writers and friends Lacey June Healey and Pamela Mistilis for kindly editing the first drafts of my book and for their invaluable input and enduring support. Gratitude also to Christine Spagnuolo for her flair and imagination in designing the front cover of my book. I express enormous gratitude to Xuan-Gnuyen Unsplash for the use of the image of the doorway on the front cover of this book. Also, many thanks to Michael Mistilis for his invaluable ideas and feedback.

Enormous appreciation also goes to my dear friends and mentors, Professor Byron and Valarie Kakulas, and Lynette-Kay Lewis for encouraging me to write stories about my childhood on Corfu. What started as a couple of fun accounts about Greek island life, slowly evolved into a substantial collection of anecdotes about the Corfu years culminating into this collection of childhood memories.

It is important to note that in autobiographical works, recollections from so long ago are inevitably, by their very nature, filled with subjectivities and diverse memories because each family member experiences life differently. This has long been a dilemma for writers but, by listening to those often-smaller voices that in the past may have been silenced or dismissed, these can often contribute to a much deeper understanding of the way we were. Indeed, if anything is to be gained by the sharing of these recollections, then it is paramount that never again should silence be weaponized and used against women and girls to maintain toxic ideas and policies that harm them and their precious children. Nor should their loved ones or others be discouraged from telling those stories. Let us not forget that it takes enormous courage to question the past and reflect on the pain it has caused. Nevertheless, by attempting to understand the past, healing can begin.

Sadly, with the passing of time, many of my family and friends have died. Even so, I express my heartfelt thanks to my parents, siblings and Sourayya Frick-Azam and sons, Vivienne Pittendrigh, Dimitri Sinardinos, Paul Handley, Kester Berwick, Harriet Guggenheim, Nathalie Herman, Roger and Ines Furse, Gordon Leeder, George and Nina Kaloudis, the villagers of Pyrgi and Saint Marcos and many others. You filled my life with countless, enduring memories of Corfu and for this I will be forever grateful.

Corfu, a Poem

Beyond our reach at eventide, the artist paints a vanishing point upon the landscape. Its mirroring distant hues of misty clouds. The image edges the eye, cupping it as if captured in the click of a wide-angled lens, shot by the mind. It records forever the arches of the Liston near the Palace of Saint Michael and Saint George.

Here the image rests beside the eastern side of the Spianada where the cricketers pause for winter. The canvas is sequenced in lines of curves so fine it plays tricks on my pooling eye, making the landscape shimmer. Here the image descends with a stroke stretched and bathed in the islands surrounding tides, moving in motion with the moment.

Soothed by a hand, the setting in which the ebb and flow moves, mimics memories with trembling sweeps. They give no undisclosed moment a home to hide. Long oars plunge, pushing through ripples on a mirrored surface near the lagoon behind Pontikonosi. They plunge deep into the depths to flex this luminous pool.

It's a place that was once filled with Ulysses' audacious spirit. His submerged watery world now breaks free from the rocks. These liquid lines evoke another spellbinding moment. It is here the Sirens chorused to entice sailors long silent.

Adrift on this pallet, two figures merge through a cloud of colonnade arches to reach that shimmering moment with a distant eye on time. Then floating on the horizon, sighs for stasis move in refracted mists as the day's final rays fall upon this place.

We are bound in the sweet bliss of youth, hammock seated in a cove of salted sails, flapping colonnades of cloth curling in the wind. A cotton-covered world moving beside a tear-filled lagoon as church bells ring loud and doves soar. With hands in a pose of connecting, the moment passes then moves on.

Now the dappled light of a last scene floats in dreamy strokes upon this ethereal scape, sitting on a reserved wall in my heart. For a masterpiece long ago stroked by an artist's loving hand, must fade into dreams, stilling at last, this portrait as it takes its final breath.

Elizabeth Pappas

Corfu, April 1970

Chapter 1

Lulled by the wing of *Morpheus*

The first day of my new life ends and I drift into an uneasy sleep lulled by the haunting sound of the *Maestro* wind racing through the ancient narrow alleyways of Corfu town's crumbling Venetian townhouses. Our guesthouse, very much an elegant old lady, whispers tales of the past through her thick white-washed walls as she breathes in and out in rhythm with the wind. Her shutters crack like whips lashing flesh. Back and forth they go against her walls, echoing hollow thumps into the spring night. It guarantees our finances are not the only reason our stay in this accommodation will be brief.

My troubled sleep is fanned by the rhythmic fluttering of *Morpheus*, the winged god of sleep and dreams. As I'd sat in the *plateia* near the *Liston* with my family of six others earlier in the day, I'd read about *Morpheus*, a messenger who heralds from famous stock. Though still a child, I find this information fascinating. *Morpheus's* father is a god too, and a god of sleep. Funny how things run in families. Known as *Hypnos*, his name is the same word the Greeks use today to refer to '*sleep*'. I didn't know this until today. The truth is, I didn't know a lot of things until today.

Portrayed as a gentle soul with a fascinating fetish for well-groomed hair, *Morpheus* has control over a quarter of our lives.

I reckon that's worth knowing. It's said he has wings protruding from his temples and shoulders. He'd stand out at a party. Unlike *Hypnos*, recently I've seen sculptures of *Morpheus* in museums and contrasting with his father, he's distinguished from other gods with one ear primed to listen to our dreams and the other ear, which is winged, designed to fly messages on our behalf to the omnipresent gods. My dad, David, a man whom I reckon has a brain like a satellite dish about to explode with information overload, tells me 'Our past, present and future are revealed in our dreams, and as the gods determine our daily lives, they need to stay informed. If for these reasons alone, dreams come easily to those who sleep in Greece.'

'Really, Dad?' I ask, captivated, clinging to his every word.

'Absolutely, Possum. Haven't you noticed that since we've been travelling through Europe, our lives have become filled with all sorts of magnificent gods, myths and magic?'

Delighted by his unwavering focus and intriguing comment, I nodded in wonderment. But it was Dad's conversation with the welcoming Spartilas waiter much earlier in the day that directed my mind's slumber. It's driven meandering back in time and space to Melbourne – Melbourne so long ago yet, in reality, only a few months. In my half-conscious mind, even in the misty world of dreams, I concede all ideas, good or bad, have to come from somewhere. I wonder who gives us our ideas? Dad was right, I suppose ... well, in a way. Of late, I've become used to saying the gods, of course. Yes, the ancient Egyptian, Greek and Roman gods guiding our lives in ways that are beyond the control of us mere mortals.

The Corfiot waiter and Dad ... what were they saying earlier today? Ah, that's it, the waiter asked him why we've moved to Greece. Dad responded, floating a mix of frothy fabrication into the air like bubbles with incredible ease. So much so, I was startled by his comments. More surprisingly they went un-popped. He'd made it seem so easy, but in truth it wasn't.

Now in a deep sleep, *Morpheus* helps me recollect the past. Dad's various configurations of truth distortion are separated from other information. The filtering of facts, determining what's important and what's not, my mind works like an efficient filing system. Yes, that's it. A crisp clear Melbourne starry night responsible for an idea that was hatched in a moment, then rapidly dispatched. It was an idea that came completely left of field and struck like a note from a tuning fork with a pitch that was so penetrating, it would resonate through the rest of our lives.

Through a haze of blurry frames and willowy images, these begin to unfold slowly. They reveal the upstairs lounge room of our recently renovated hip urbanite Edwardian terrace home in North Carlton. 194 Amess Street. Yes, there's the old place. It's as clear as day in my mind's eye. Dad's put the mocker on any chance of us kids lazily swanning around after dinner and watching our usual array of snowy resolution, black and white television chestnuts. Now: I recall, family pleasers like our all-time favourite Graham Kennedy's 'In Melbourne Tonight.'

Dad's imposing body looms in the lounge. He's told the neighbours to 'Stuff off and mind your own bloody business.' No one's going to stop him booming his favourite songs from our portable record player as loudly as he can legally. He's drinking heavily. With little else to do because our telly chances have been dashed, we children, who are as far removed from the pristine Von Trapp children as you can possibly get, sit intrigued by his performance. He's as charismatic as ever, especially now he's had a few. Taking centre stage, he's primed and proceeds to move about the lounge room with a glass filled with cognac. He's showcasing his own version of Anthony Quinn dancing to Zorba's theme.

While I'm no expert and have yet to be formally initiated into the not-so-subtle art of Greek dancing, I am however, sure his pastiche parody is amateurish by anyone's standards. But Dad, as happy as Larry, is not bothered by anyone or anything. He stumbles, steps and leaps his way through his theatrical Antipodean version of that Greek dance classic, void of inhibitions. I watch as curls of smoke from a cigarette wedged tightly between his lips mimics his moves and he sinks his teeth tightly down onto its soft spongy filter-tipped end. Squinting against the intervals of thick smoke that rise around him like Comanche smoke signals, he enthuses around the room. But try as he may as he circles the coffee table again and again like an unhinged earth rotating the sun, this novice doesn't have a chance in hell of ever usurping the magnetic Zorba. He's the true master of the *sirtaki* which I've seen many times in the movie classic *Zorba the Greek*.

With him now in full flight, ignited and spurred on by the booze and booming bounce of the bouzouki, and we kid's clapping along intrigued by his exaggerated Greek *horepsi, dance* moves, he carries out an aeronautical leaping *sirtaki* step. This is accompanied by a few bold below the belt gyrations. He hits the carpet 'bang' with his feet, and continues his caricature of Zorba for they have morphed into one. Then, seemingly for effect with clicking fingers less the flying hanky and souvlaki, he suddenly rises up again and makes a mid-air declaration that comes completely left of field. He quickly grabs the cigarette from his gaping mouth. As if in a hypnotised state, he sends ash flying about him spraying a fine layer of unwelcome soft grey flakes onto one of Mum's favourite antique rugs. He cries, 'We're all moving to Greece.

Your mother and I have decided to sell everything. I'm going to become a writer.'

He thrusts the now almost bent-beyond-repair cigarette back into his mouth with his large nicotine-stained fingers. As if imitating Houdini, he bends it even further into a crooked, on the verge of collapse, battered bit of Benson and Hedges. This movement is hurriedly followed by a hissing sound through his teeth. Continuing unobstructed by our looks of dismay, he yells, *'Opa!'* Clicking his fingers once again in rhythm to the music, he moves his head into a deliberately defiant and proud pose leaving his cigarette perched precariously on his lower lip. Dad lands on the ground again this time with a thump, and continues to dance about the room with a stagger, slopping his drink from side to side. His large fair frame in a stupor, he's not bothered to look up or gauge our response. With globules of sweat pouring from his forehead, Dad's set a resigned expression on his red, reticulated face. There's no turning back now.

Just like that, without so much as a flinch from my mother Jo, who sits suspiciously quiet on the sidelines with a fixed look infused with both relief and red wine, our lives are suddenly switching direction. We are being thrown onto a new and dizzy path bound for the Greek islands. It's as far away from the relative predictability and everyday inner suburban city order, rhythms and sounds of downtown Melbourne as you can possibly get. So far as I know it's also the fastest baptism known to man, via bouzouki into Greek culture. Crikey, do we need our craniums read for allowing ourselves to be so easily led? After all, Dad's brain is heavily impacted by the powerful fog of grog.

I wonder about this for I suddenly have visions of a land clotted with gargantuan Greek Gods and saints called Nectareous and Nicholas, not to mention heroes called

Hector, Homer and Hercules. I foresee all the remaining days of our lives moving in rhythm to the slow, tinkling but very pleasant sounds of melodious mountain sheep bells in some far-off white-washed simple sun-speckled spot like Santorini. I suppose Dad putting it to us in such a casual, even dismissive way has the intended effect of taking some of the edge off our panic. Well, mine anyway. After all, what he's suggesting is no mean feat. We're going to be on the move again, and this time going against the vast tide of daring diasporas in the 1960s and early 1970s. Most Greeks are leaving Greece and heading to Australia these days. Very few, if any Aussies, are heading the other way seeking to find a home on the Greek islands. That is unless they're loaded. Aussie Onassis's, and that firmly swipes us off the list of likely contenders. Or nuts because the country's in the midst of a military coup d'état. Surely, it can't be a good idea moving there whilst others are fleeing – I mean, what about the perils and practicalities?

There are seven of us and what will we all do there ... and why so suddenly? I know Mum has become fascinated with brave run-aways, bohemians absconding from what she called 'The stifling drab of post-war Melbourne.' Germaine Greer, Clive James, Barry Humphries and Robert Hughes and many more 'unconventional others' to London. Or people like Charmain Clift and George Johnson to Greece. Forerunners who'd spread the word about the Greek dream, the joys of simple village life. A life that could be hypnotising ... for a while. They'd returned to Australia successful writers showing it could be done. Beacons of hope for uninitiated writers like my father and quirky unconventional types like my mother. But unlike my parents, they had always planned to return to Australia. And what about the Durrell's to Corfu? But that was long ago. Nor was Papadopoulos in control when they lived on the island.

Then as the moment falls away and catching me by surprise, my concerns can't be contained and surface, bubbling like simmering lava. I panic – might it get lonely being reverse rebels, trend turners of a type? I mean, who can we talk to until we learn the language? Can Greeks in Greece speak English? Such is the extent of my ignorance about that far-off land.

My heart pounds in my chest. Merging now with Melbourne in my dream are visions of Greek soldiers, guns borne by young men barely old enough to handle their menacing killing machines. I see my grandmother, her portrait embedded in my mind; her words, her warnings about 'The Collapse of Democracy' dismissed out of hand as preposterous codswallop by Mum.

'Mere exaggerations by the press,' she retorts defensively.

Dad, now captured by the spellbinding idea of following his muse before taking her in his arms and relenting, agreeing to become a writer and in so doing fulfilling her fantasy. And now his? But I sense all is not what it seems and for some reason she's reaching for the panic button. Why would my mother want leave Australia?

Still my heart pounds as I realise now in this restless sleep there is more to our moving to Greece than my parents are revealing. This is something I've sensed since we left Melbourne months ago. It's in the stringy fraying mesh that holds their volatile marriage together. It's an unsettling shadow that hovers along with us wherever we go and my dream is pressing the issue. No one travels to the other side of the world to a country in the midst of a military coup d'état, risking the lives of their five children as my parents have done unless, unless …

I wait for an answer to come but suddenly as the answer is

about to be revealed, I'm thrust into consciousness by *Morpheus*.

As my mind centres on the present; it recalibrates. His message is loud and clear. I must find the real reason as to why we are here. We are Australians, not Greeks. What's the purpose of this spur-of-the-moment move to Corfu? A lingering aching feeling of dread fills my gut. I know the dream is right. I have been misled, lied to. We all have. I close my eyes once again and press *Morpheus* to tell me more. To take me back into the land of sleep and dreams. But he's winged his way into the morning light, disappearing through the old town, and beyond the mountain slopes dotted with ancient olive groves to far-off places where the sun is beginning to depart the sky. He's left me with more questions than answers. I blast the gods for lighting only part of our paths. They leave us to stumble our way through life, clinging to a few cryptic fragments of truth that have been cast at us like random quatrains scribed by Nostradamus. '*Morpheus, Morpheus,*' I whisper, 'please come back. Don't leave me like this.' But there's only the sound of the *Maestro*. I lower my head further into my pillow and silently weep, urging *Hypnos* to also weave his magic. But he too, like his son, has vanished. How can I discover the truth when it's locked in the remote spheres of my parents' hearts?

Chapter 2

The Peak of *Pantocrator*

We've arrived on this beautiful island at a dangerous time. There's an edge in the air. Yet, winter's weeping parasols of suspended mist lift, and the land of the ancient gods reveals blue skies filling the soul with hope and expectation. On the steepest peak of Corfu sits *Mount Pantocrator*. This imposing presence, impossible to ignore, symbolises its name; the powerful, all-seeing and all-knowing God the Creator. Locals believe that from his divine throne he casts a vigilant gaze, like a fishing net, over all the mortals below.

On one side of this vast mountain range nestles the village of Spartilas. The atmosphere on the slope around the village is occupied with anticipation and awakenings. Here, woollen jackets and raincoats are being removed and stowed like loyal but temporarily abandoned friends until next winter. Amongst the rock-strewn soil and no longer troubled by the cold, spring flowers shift with the sea breeze in a chaos of chromatics. Among these swaying stems crowd the mysterious and sacred *wild windflowers*. In this ancient place, their name spools easily off the tongue but are moved to mind for these are the blooms of the bloodshot poppies that were once white anemones Now transformed from bud to flower, they stand erect as if drawing in the incandescent scarlet flames of a renewed sun, and the inhumane violations covertly enacted behind stinking prison doors in secret places away from prying eyes.

Locals believe these sacred blooms were fashioned by the Goddess Aphrodite to symbolise the stain of Adonis's blood upon this land. He was her mortal lover. Now in the modern era, the floral complexion of these blooms continues to signify blood. It's the vermillion dye that fails to dry or fade. That of dead and wounded bodies, the result of millennia of unrest. Yet, even today in the crosswind, the anxious spirits of these ancient god's whisper. They are transferred through the ether like shards of light and dance in an annual dalliance with Chloris. She is the goddess of flowers. Chloris is responsible for all the mesmerising perfume that's emitted into the air from the wild blooms and resilient herbs that cover this beautiful yet apprehensive land.

Through the silvery green olive trees, the steeple of a white-washed church and village houses rooted deep in this landscape ease into view. We are making our way up the narrow pot-holed road of twenty-six hairpin turns from the coast. Terrified, my family counts each tight curve as our two cars screw-drive up the steep slope. Anchored and layered between tiered stone walls in this grand gradient, groves of twisted and contorted olive trees stand casting cooling shadows over the earth. The locals say if you look long and hard into the trunks and branches of these sinuous heroes, you can imagine bent bodies and unworldly beings, bulbous and distorted. Yet, these are the superstars of this fruitful land and herald back to the Venetian period spreading their splendour to the valley below. They pause where the land meets the sea. In the far-off distance, the grey and pink mountainsides of Albania lie semi-submerged. Their tops sit laden beneath snow while the steep, curved base of this alien landscape emulates the hard hide of a hippopotamus playing in the reflection of a deep gentian Ionian Sea. A cloudless sky offers a sample of the summer to come.

Upon reaching the mountain village, my family gather in front of a small *kafenio, café* and stretch our legs. New to this land, we have been touring the island all morning and pause to take stock of what we have seen. It's thirsty business. The sun seeks with ravenous appetite our insipid skin. It's been a lengthy journey by sea from Melbourne to England, then by car across a snow-covered Europe to Greece. Our destiny was always Corfu. In this spring sunshine, it's here that we hope to begin a new life. I pause beside my towering father.

'Are you okay, Dad? You look worried. We're going to be okay in Greece, aren't we?'

With furrowed brow, he doesn't answer. A pulse flickers on the side of his neck. His mind is elsewhere brooding about how, months earlier in Melbourne, his Greek friend George berated him in his stern, sophisticated Athenian modulation:

'You want to move to Greece and become a writer? But you haven't written anything, ever. Anyway, Greece is already full of writers, Greek ones. Granted, most of the very good ones are in exile, or in Greek concentration camps being tortured by the fascists. So, take it from me, *filos, friend*, you're going the wrong way. Besides, Aussies rarely move to Greece to live, and Greeks always settle here. It's logical, no? Australia is a safe country. In this place socialist, fascist, communist ... who cares? This is a fact ... it's in the Greek Australian encyclopedia of common knowledge.'

With shining eyes, George laughs unconsciously, his dry Greek humour getting the better of him. Feeling compassion for his Australian friend, he pauses to offer him a cigarette then, with a quick flash of fire, lights his own and his friend's with a personalised gold lighter. As the moment subsides, George goes back to sipping his warm Greek coffee, allowing his comments to percolate in the air between the two men.

Swanston and Lonsdale Streets are full of Greek cafes like this. They spill onto footpaths and into the surrounding suburbs, distilling the rich intoxicating tastes of European flavours and cosmopolitan awakenings into a yearning postwar Melbourne. Shopfronts decorated with the blue and white key of Greece tiles, symbolic magnets drawing in Melbourne's Greeks, philhellenes and the curious. They offer sanctuary from the stark Melbourne heat with their cool, urbane European '60s cafe chic, each café showcasing aligned rows of displays gorged with shiny glass shelves layered with Greek *glikia, sweets, sesame halva,* trays of *baklava,* wide rounds of *kataifi,* and almond and pistachio nougat boxes. Greek newspapers stretch athletically across tables, and cosmopolitan Greeks speaking *Katharevusa* and *Demotiki,* can be heard intermittently through steady clouds of smoke, city traffic and laughter. A transistor radio swings nonchalantly past in the hand of a thin-faced, long-haired pedestrian, booming Beatles music into the air. He passes quickly, momentarily drowning the café's piped *bouzouki* music. Seconds after an indiscreet lingering slurp of his coffee, George casts a serious, but kind surveying eye over my anxious father. He raises his hands as if to more effectively communicate his message, his face galvanized with a look of Solomon.

'Going to Greece now would be like slipping into my mother's *tzatziki dip* and drowning. And with a wife and five children, *po, po, po!* The whole country is in the midst of a military coup d'état. And you can't speak the language – none of you can! Let me tell you ... if you go, let it be on all your crazy heads. Don't you read the newspapers? They say it's the "End of Democracy in Greece!" Seriously, *filos,* take my advice. I know a very good doctor; he's an expert in nut cases like you. Let me make an appointment today. And of course, he's Greek. His name is Costas from Corfu.'

Back in Melbourne, Dad tilted his blond head back, his military haircut an obvious contrast to the other men around him as he nervously laughed at his friend through their rings of swirling tobacco smoke and the rich aroma of good coffee. He wasn't a nut case. He was simply a man trying to gratify his wife, pacify her by looking for a cheap place to live. For months she'd become agitated, obsessed with leaving Australia. He didn't know why she felt so strongly about abandoning our comfortable life, except she reckoned if we stayed in Melbourne, we'd live a stiflingly empty existence of keeping up with the Jones's and the Dame Edna Everages of the world. Could anything be worse, more soul destroying? He had to admit, the idea of Greece was tempting.

After the Korean War, the Vietnam War was yet another unnecessary catastrophe. Now a disillusioned regular army officer, my father derives little, if any, joy instructing conscripts and volunteers to fire high-power hoses to extricate conscientious objectors from the nation's streets. It was below his dignity to do so. Anyway, what of his own sons? Did he want them enmeshed in some stinking, unwinnable war? Had he not seen enough in Korea? Maybe Mum's idea was not a bad one after all. Get their young sons out of the country before they are called to action. That might be years off ... but ... Mmm, he could try and write; give it a go.

In her busy head, she'd worked it all out, calculated that now he could retire, he could access his small army officer's pension. He was forty-seven; it was time to grab life by the throat and go to a place where he could become a writer. Could he not see himself as one? – a Truman Capote, an Ian Fleming, or Ernest Hemmingway – her eyes shining, hoeing through the doubts in his mind. How hard can it be? As if this wasn't sufficient, she'd stir him up; she'd challenged him by scoffing at our safe, comfortable inner-city life. He knew she'd enjoyed Charmain Cliff's columns in the Melbourne Herald over the years and that she was shocked by her overdose. Now with Mum's mind fixed on overseas horizons, her reasons to leave Australia seemed insurmountable. In the end, it was a lesser evil to abandon Australia, proving his love for her, show he wasn't a "bloody bore" than deal with the effects of her swipes at his character and her unpredictable moods, repercussions that were so telling about their complex relationship because on bad days they fired armed missiles above our heads wounding one another. When the blows didn't hit the mark, there'd be collateral damage: us kids. A wooden broom broken over a back, the stinging flicks of the metal end of a belt on a thigh, kicks that bruised shins. In this odd covenant between couples, on good days when Dad was open to ideas, they rattled different countries in their heads until moving to Greece popped into hers.

Mum calculated, 'Even in a political crisis, Greece will remain the seat of democracy, the CIA will ensure it. And what's not to love about the Greek islands with their cheap food, plonk, cigarettes and fascinating old villas ... well once you have swept aside the spiders and scorpions. And don't forget the friendly natives. The Queen Victoria Markets are full of them. The kids mightn't need to go to school. The Greek islands should be enough education for them; for anyone. If Johnson and Clift can do it, so can we. Anyway, don't worry, we can sort out any residual problems when we get there.'

That was typical – she could so easily dismiss the concerns or needs of others if they didn't slot conveniently in with hers. Looking outward from our bird's eye view from the *kafeneo* across the Spartilas ridge, he wonders if he's made the right decision for our family? He's done everything his friend George told him not to do – sold the only home we've ever owned and, with not enough money to buy another one, our future security surges like unpredictable waves in his brain breaching upon fatigued grey matter.

He moves to a chair; he needs to pause. Above his head braced by ancient twisted trunks, grapevine-leaves spread and nestle top dressed in the secure arms of a shady pavilion. He sits and steadies himself. With his signal like a waving bear's paw, we follow suit. I lunge into the seat beside him and look into his striking blue eyes. I'm impatiently waiting for a reply to my question. 'Dad, you haven't answered me?'

As if being drawn reluctantly back into the arms of the present, he absently pauses, reaches across the table to jumble my hair with his wide hand. 'What was that, dear?'

I jolt my head back and scramble to rearrange my shock of blonde tresses. A bald spot on my scalp needs camouflaging. Mum tells me I'm a nervous child – I need to toughen up otherwise ...

'Yes, of course we'll be happy here. We'll be as snug as seven little bugs in a rug. You'll see. Now, Possum, what would you like to drink? Something fizzy? I don't think they sell Fanta in Greece. How about trying something else?'

Leaning back into the wooden chair, he raises his hand for the waiter. He's hoping a Greek cognac will settle his nerves, make his head stop pounding. A good stiff drink always makes him feel better. The Greeks make excellent cognac. It's cheap too. The Greek cigarette clasped between his fingers tastes pleasant, sustaining his gripping addiction. A soft pack of 25 filter-tipped Pallas retail at five drachmae. The same price as a loaf of local village bread. Five cents in Australian currency. A bargain compared to Australian prices, but will they find a cheap villa to rent? The question thumps in his head like a relentless drum beat.

Remaining silent, he inhales deeply on his cigarette as we, his five children, order food and drinks. Mum joins him in ordering a good cognac, a Metaxas Seven Star. The waiter, impressed and keen to please, enquires about our nationality and sighs with relief when he's told we are Australians. A broken conversation of sorts ensues between the two men as they are rapidly engulfed and bound in a visible, unguarded beautiful verbal dance between Greek host and *xeni, foreigner*. Their lives are condensed into uncomplicated lines of conversation that flow in harmony with a tide of simple smiles and gestures. After the conversation has run its inevitable course, the waiter disappears, only to return soon after with drinks and a *meze, appetizer* of sliced meats, tomatoes, cucumbers and olives harvested from the surrounding hills. It's in this moment that a collision between the canned foods we had been eating in sufferance across Europe, fades like a smile at a funeral into the distant plains of our minds as the organic qualifications of this food skreich at us. It's a fresh feast drizzled in rich green olive oil topped with feta and sprinkled with oregano. Generous chunks of bread still warm from the village baker's oven accompany this delightful spread. We smile curiously at the unfamiliar combination of foods, then dive in. Our palettes sing in silence with this delicious adjustment in Greek feasting.

Tapping the marble table top with her long fingernails, Mum breaks the silence between herself and my father.

'We need to find a home as soon as possible. Corfu town is too dusty, busy and infuriatingly expensive. As you know, I'm not impressed with the villas we've seen so far. I reckon we need a place close to the coast. It has to be cheap. Perhaps the villa I saw as we drove along the Ipsos seafront? There was a sign advertising a villa for rent. Did you see it as you passed along the waterfront? It's certainly not the Ritz, but let's stop on the way to town and make enquiries? All I can say is, I hope to God someone speaks the Queen's English and can translate for us. You know, I have absolutely no intention of ever learning Greek. It's far too complicated for me to digest. As for the alphabet, well need I say more? If Greeks want to talk to me, they'll have to learn English.'

Satisfied she's made her point; she doesn't engage us except to slow our attack on the *meze* with one hand and caress my young brother's shoulders with the other. He is her masterpiece. With troubled hazel green eyes, she continues, 'Perhaps I'm wrong but, I think properties on the south side of the island will be too expensive. Maybe this side of the island is cheaper?'

The aromatic cognac kickstarts Dad's insides. His face shifts from milky white to a vegetable stain pink as its therapeutic powers send hot electrical signals to his brain. He smiles an optimistic smile, but his heart is thrashing.

'Yes, dear, you're probably right. The sooner we settle somewhere the better. Yes, I saw it. Like you I haven't been impressed with the villas we've seen so far. Way too expensive. But the villa on the coast looked compact, basic. But it's right on the beach, it could be ideal for the kids.'

Moments pass and a few sips of cognac later, her mood mutates. Mum moves anxiously in her chair as an underbelly of irritability travels, exiting through her nails. She taps her cigarette impatiently like a drumstick on a drum. It resonates through the cheap plastic Pallas ashtray, marking time. She recoils, 'Of course, it's not the grand villa I'd envisaged, but we need somewhere to live. This could be a temporary solution until we find something more fitting, more us. If we decide on the villa, it can't be a permanent solution. I won't tolerate it. We haven't come all this way to live in a Greek sweat box.'

Having picked up on her mood, he instinctively treads carefully. To top it off, she's put on that new accent of hers, the one she's assumed in her reimagining of herself. The same one that goes from slinging full-bodied Australian lingo to something akin to a pastiche, upper-class British accent. Self-ordained now as a citizen of the Continent, her duopoly of accents moves with her moods and is carefully adjusted to coincide with the company she's in. Dad disregards the superior edge in her voice. Raising his arm, he orders another round of drinks. Yes, cognac always helps. It softens life's jagged edges. He leans back in his chair. The intense Greek sun tingles. It dances challengingly on his fair freckled skin through a gap where the grapevine leaves have yet to spread.

Soon the sun's rays will sear cruelly into the rich earth of this ancient land. Knowing this, bright-eyed swallows fly low overhead seeking shade. They are searching for insects to take back to their young in snug mud nests as locals open businesses in anticipation of the approaching tourist season. Their endeavours will not stop until the late autumn storms bend challenging the minarets of the tall cypress trees.

A faint breeze stirs the air and my family chats. My brothers and sister tease one another, slap backs and laugh. After we have had our fill of food and beverages, we clamber the crumbling sides of the peak seeking a better view of the scene across the straits to the mainland. I soon fall behind deciding the ground is unsteady, and the day too hot to not return to the *kafeneo*, and cocoon myself beneath its shady pergola. I park myself out of sight not far from where my parents remain seated but within safe ear shot of their conversation.

I sit, not knowing what I am listening for, and then it comes, the outpour. They speak with surprise about the simmering political crisis brewing around us and now more horrifyingly, they admit that if things don't work out in Greece, we are marooned on this island. The reality explodes in my head. We don't have the money to return to Australia and rebuild our lives if things go wrong. Far too much is riding on our finding a cheap place to live and the Australian dollar rising in value against the weak and volatile drachma. A feeling of dread overwhelms me as our future is much more precarious than I had ever imagined.

When my siblings return, I say nothing to them of what I have heard and, like them, join my parents as they contemplate the stunning Corfu vista of the plummeting green valley below and the expanse of the Ionian Sea. We are all occupied with our thoughts. I imagine it's running away from us, this vast wide tide of water to Albania, the mainland of Greece, Italy, perhaps home? If only I could get a grip on a wave and go with it. But no, I'm a child and must remain with my family and think serious thoughts. If, when and where will I start school? I'm twelve years old and the next school I attend will be my fifth in seven years. I act as if everything is fine but it's not, I'm prone to injury, the kind that comes from a life of unsteadiness, a life that resonates from an undercurrent of family rage – one that won't stop morphing. And no matter how many times I go through this tense re-emergence, my insides ache because I'm infused with fear. I'm apprehensive because there are problems with the dates on my birth certificate and passport, both are incorrect. My parents insist its nothing and anyway, they can't be rectified. But somehow, I'm not convinced. There is a malevolent cloud that hovers above me pressing me to hold my tongue, not make waves. Even before we left Australia, it had been made clear to me that my silence, my irrelevance in the overall scheme of things, is essential when crossing international borders and in the presence of any officials. I feel like a fish out of water: I don't speak Greek and don't understand the culture or why everyone is in everyone else's line of fire. Dad's is the only comforting arm that reaches out to me but even that depends on what's brewing. Picking the right side in our daily family battles is too important to him and to all of us.

Now in a land of raging strikes, violent political upheaval, tanks and soldiers, gone are my anchors: my friends, grandparents and homeland in one fell swoop. I wonder how much further we can go before my parents stop raging, reach a truce or part? This has to be the edge. There's nowhere else to go. And if things go wrong and we topple off Greece's sides, will it hasten forth the remote and impenetrable schism that lies between them? Between all of us? The one that has kept us moving and circling each other like suspicious strangers ever since I can remember. Yes, perhaps here the mystery will reach its climax amid the uncertainty, restrictions on basic civil liberties, the stench of Greek gun powder blended with the delicate scent of spices and spring flowers. Then, maybe this new life we are creating will declare itself in the full light of the sun, take root and grow in nourishing Greek soil if and when peace returns to this land? To us? Or will we become insignificant crushed castaways left to rot on the rugged rocks of *Pontikonisi*, our demise sung to us in mocking scores by the ancient Sirens?

Chapter 3

Pyrgi Palace

Imitating an aloof bystander, Mum's positioned herself defensively with arms vaulted stubbornly across her slim chest. She's mirroring the cocky actions of young soldiers armed with heavy weapons we see strutting or lounging on the streets of Corfu town, only she's not holding a gun. If she had one, she'd probably shoot Dad. Her attractive face critically surveys the garden of the property we are considering leasing in Pyrgi. She tosses her head to one side – not a happy possum.

Spying her stance, Dad contemplates the worst so offers an olive branch, hoping to shift her disappointment. 'She'll be right, Darl. Good things come in petite packages. Give the bonzer little place a go. It's only short term; you'll see. With luck, rents will go down, the Aussie dollar up and when they do I promise we'll move into a bigger villa. So, don't worry.'

With arms still folded, her hands burrow firmly under her arms. 'It's all very well for you to say that now, but it's not the grand Venetian villa you promised in Australia, is it? Open your eyes, man ... the shack's got a serious dose of size deficit.' She swipes him with a menacing look. 'We must be insane considering this excuse for a villa. It's woefully more than a few pillars short of the acropolis. Christ, man, it resembles the ruins of Stonehenge. Actually, no ... the truth is I'm having difficulty describing what it is!'

Wincing then scratching his head as if a mosquito had just

taken a liberal bite out of his scalp, he gulps greedily the mesmerising salty Pyrgi sea air. It smells wonderful. He's hooked. But here we go again. Her moods change as fast as a racing-car cuts and burns on a straight stretch of road. He'd made no such promise about grand Venetian villas back in Australia. And anyway, she's the one who suggested this villa on the coast, but she's not listening.

In the months before we'd left Australia, Mum buried her nose in European real estate magazines. She'd sniffed out gorgeous Greek villas and imagined us living in them. Reaching to where Dad sat in his leather armchair, she'd poke him in the arm and flash pages of white-washed minimalist possibilities at him, prod him with palatial palaces pointing to the ones she liked the best. His mind on the cryptic crossword puzzle, 'Mmm, looks very nice, dear, but this could be a crash course in cutbacks. I'm only on a modest army officer's pension now. Things might get tight with you, me and five children to feed.'

But his words were of no consequence. Her mind was bored by their implications and so she simply compressed them until they disappeared into the air. She was off in that other world of hers, the happy one planning elaborate cocktail parties in luxurious villas as she mooched with wealthy thoroughbreds – people like the Onassies, European aristocracy and Hollywood movie stars, no less.

Eyeing the villa in front of us she releases an agonising groan. Back in the real world it's not an alluring apparition by any stretch of the imagination. Armed with her strong Australian accent, she pitches it like an Aussie fast bowler determined to knock out the batsman. 'Oh, for Christ's sake, David, come on, give me a break. You must be delusional. Even you have to admit it lacks the famed Greek Golden Ratio. I should have known this trip to Europe was gunna be one of those gunna-be life changes and it's not gunna be anything like I imagined! The villa's the size of a rear-end suppository. Talk about paring our lives back to the crack.'

Hands shaking, her long slender fingers reach into her handbag seeking her trusty Oroton cigarette-case. Clicking open its top, she extracts one. Lighting it goes some way toward taking the edge off her litany of frustration and disappointment.

Not wanting to debate the issue further, Dad lowers his head, deciding collision is not the best course of action. Choosing his battles wisely, he resolves today's not the day to remind her that it was her idea to leave Australia, not his. As an ex-military man, he's painfully aware that all around us death lurks under this military coup, snarling at our feet without aggravating the situation further, and so lets the moment pass without comment.

But she's right. Under closer examination, the villa has few charms of an Onassis oasis. Still, for its faults in size and aesthetic impact, this tiny unassuming villa packs a modest punch. Honey-coloured terracotta tiles crown a simple grey cement structure. Hand-woven curtains, cool terrazzo floors and white shutters add a level of simple appeal and character. Its location is the real draw-card. Anchored on a strip of blue seafront, there is only a wisp of a narrow road between it and a wide pebbled beach. This means we kids can harness ourselves to the coast, conjure up disappearing acts all day long on the forever shore line of Pyrgi and Ipsos Bay. Now, for parents, that must be a bonus. To the east across the bay, the villa has spectacular vistas of the long-veiled mountains of Albania and Greece. If we rent the place, every morning like clockwork the sun will magically lighten this part of the northern hemisphere as it rises over the undulating mountains. With this spectacular view, each daybreak will bring forth a sunrise you're never likely to forget. All for a peppercorn rent. A couple of curious local women stop to chat in broken English. They inform us that the traffic in winter along this east coast road is light with just a few donkeys, the occasional car, bus, motorbike and gypsy wagons. Traffic increases only slightly during the summer – it's perfect.

Keen for us to take on the lease, the women smile with welcoming delight as their strong milk chocolate-coloured arms soar skyward. They are effortlessly clasping large water jugs gracefully balancing upon their proud and sturdy white scarved heads.

The villa, while chipped and tarnished around the edges from previous party-loving tenants, this we ignore, as the place has running water unlike the homes of the women we have just seen. It also has a functioning bathroom, electricity, a tiny kitchen with a marble sink and a new shiny primus stove sitting proudly on a very narrow stunted marble counter. There are three bedrooms but no sitting room. If we take on the lease, in summer our lounge, dining area and Dad's office will be in the front garden where it's agreed a long table will be placed beneath the shady boughs of the old, knobbly and gnarled olive trees. Foot traffic along the road could prove to be an open invitation to disruption for a writer. Dad will have to find a way to overcome this potentially distracting detail if he wants to be a successful author. This will be fascinating to witness because he loves people and any excuse to socialise.

In winter, when the rain falls in torrents, it's arranged we'll all hunker down in my parent's front bedroom. It will serve as the lounge and Dad's office if we stay in this villa through to next summer. During the day, beds will be miraculously contortioned into seating. It's proposed we browse Corfu town and purchase a few colourful peasant rugs and reserve them for seating throws along with a selection of colourful traditional kilim cushions. Dad reckons this should do the trick, but Mum's not convinced. Incensed, she thinks they will make our makeshift lounge look like the crammed interior of an Anatolian brothel.

'Kids, your father's finally gone batty ... scattered cushions indeed. What a stupid idea! No sum of rugs or Greek peasant cushions chucked onto beds with those hideous headboards will ever look like a conventional sitting room.'

She has a point, but looking like the guilt-ridden caterpillar that stole a chunk out of Newton's apple, Dad smiles seeking redemption. Keeping everyone happy is becoming his moment-to-moment mantra. Well, hasn't it always been the case until he can take no more? But not today, there's too much at stake. He realises our survival in the long term is reliant on his retaining harmony. In the meantime, his guts churn.

While the villa is Spartan with only a few strewn mismatched pieces of scruffy furniture, on our income it could be a lot worse. With a wide optimistic smile, he makes light of it. 'Ok, everyone, take a deep breath in and then slowly exhale out and relax. Do what the Greeks do: stop worrying and get into a mindset of keeping everything simple from now on. We don't need much to live a happy life, now, do we? I mean, when you add up the villa's positives, it's an absolute sanctum by the sea. As far as I'm concerned, it's perfect.'

Mum sniffs the air, releasing a smile set in aspic. This is not her idea of a Grecian bull's-eye. 'The person who coined the phrase "the simple life" has a lot to answer for. I feel queasy. Yes, I'm going to vomit. There's no laundry, or washing machine. It's positively primitive. I can't cope without a washing machine. The very idea is repugnant. I'm not a peasant woman!'

Moaning, she bends forward, going through the motions of dry retching. We stand back embarrassed and uncomfortable by her dramatic reaction. Dad moves forward, taking her elbow. 'Well, of course it's primitive, and God only knows you have enough on your plate. Let's think of a solution.'

Chapter 4

Marietta

If the dramatic gravity of Mum's repugnancy towards the clothes washing facilities at the Pyrgi villa was deliberate, then she achieves her goal. She makes it a condition of entry that Dad needs to hire someone to do the laundry; if he doesn't, we are not moving in. With no other suitable cheap villa on the horizon, and both of them partial to quick fixes, especially ones offering an inexpensive reprieve from domestic duties, he studiously arranges to engage a helper.

In the time it takes to throw open and spread a Corfu fishing net, a local from Saint Markos becomes the solo contender for the job. Marietta is transformed from a village *yiayia, grandmother* into our official much-loved Washer Woman. This is made possible because an affable local called Pythagoras generously translates and negotiates the lease on the villa and Marietta's working arrangements. It's decided Marietta will work every Friday from 7am until the family's washing is done. She will receive 100 drachmas, lunch, a loaf of bread to take home and a full bottle of her favourite tipple, ouzo. We will supply the soap and bleach and all the other washing equipment. With smiles on all sides, they shake hands to seal the deal.

Dad beams glowingly, imitating a friendly firefly on a warm spring night and reckons, 'Now we'll be just a quick flick of an olive pip from the sea. Life doesn't get much better than this. See kids, I knew we'd solve our domestic hiccup, our

Pericles pickle.'

We laugh more with relief than anything else ... We certainly didn't want to be burdened with the washing. Mum occasions a smile too because the thought of having a servant of sorts to supervise cheers her up immensely. It's the only bright spot she can see on the horizon until Dad clicks the sides of a couple of mis-matched glasses he's found in the kitchen and suggests they buy a chilled bottle of *Retsina* to celebrate.

On the Thursday before Marietta starts her Friday visits to our humble hive, and with chest puffed with pride, she arrives at our villa dressed in her finest clothing; her outfit consists of a white blouse, red velvet bolero jacket boasting gold Byzantine eagles on each breast, and a wide black skirt. A crisp white apron, hitched high upon her waist serves as a precarious substitute bra of sorts, supporting her substantial breasts. Plucking a red geranium from an old olive tin that functions as a rusty flowerpot, she pops the jaunty bud into her hair. Vainly pausing, her white head scarf is adjusted as she checks her reflection in the front window of our villa. Before her departure, Ajax, her dependable donkey, is lassoed to our mulberry tree. She ensures his straw hat, dressed with ribbons and colourful tassels, is set straight, delivering further shade. He'll remain beneath the tree for the duration of her absence. Finally satisfied, she's ready to go to Corfu town on the first green bus of the day. Mum has given her plenty of drachmae, enabling her to purchase the products needed to carry out her new washing duties.

The green bus returns in the late afternoon with the blare of three different radio stations playing simultaneously accompanied by the loud squealing of brakes across the road from our villa. Crying out '*Adio*' to the bus driver, Marietta precariously descends its steps. Struggling to appear sturdy, she chuckles to herself recalling a private joke. Recovering from her fit of giggling, she manages to haul a huge metal wash tub, a heavy-duty wooden scrubbing board, a wooden whacking stick, a bag of green olive oil soap, and two bottles of bleach. She resembles a circular shaped juggler practicing her circus act. We soon discover these bottles of bleach will be used on almost everything my brothers wear, and everyone's underwear irrespective of colour. With the fortitude of a female version of Hercules, she lugs her purchases the short distance from the bus stop to our front door refusing our assistance. There is an unmistakable smell of ouzo and fermenting *tzatziki dip* emanating from her breath and pores as we crowd around her in curious anticipation. She leans forward on the old door-frame of our villa ready to knock but I ignore her protocols.

I bellow with urgency, 'Mum, get a look at this! You should see what Marietta's brought home with her. She's got half the shop and there's even green soap.'

Reaching the front door, Mum's eyes widen. She stands fascinated as Marietta proudly displays her purchases. Who'd have thought washing clothes demanded so many gadgets and contraptions? Now, leaning slightly from her ouzo and *tzatziki* consumption, Marietta cheerfully imitates an orchestra conductor communicating via sign language with a few more discombobulated combustible hiccups.

Her cheeks now rosy-red, she giggles, 'I'll be back with Ajax at 7am tomorrow to start work.'

Leaving the purchases stacked on the front veranda, a gregarious backward wave of her hand is flung into the air as she cries out '*Adio sas,*' *goodbye to you*. Then she lunges with an upward thrust of an effectual swish of her skirt and flash of petticoats hurling herself assuredly onto the back of Ajax. Settled at last on her wood and leather tasselled saddle, away they go in a hasty trot as she confidently waves a stick victoriously in the air of the rising afternoon heat. Soon the pair evaporate like shifting spooks through the cooling allure of the shade of the nearby olive groves.

After her departure, and taking a contented deep breath, Dad relaxes, flopping like a rag doll into one of our newly purchased foldup directors' chairs. Enthusiastically he pours himself and Mum more celebratory drinks. He says he's 'relieved because finally we can settle into village life, tap into the rhythms and less chaotic pace of this rural locale with the convenience of a servant, well, of sorts.'

In fact, from then on wherever we go Mum, duplicating a vocal British radio broadcaster, publicizes for all to hear, 'Oh, my Marietta this,' and 'Oh, my Marietta that,' in her pastiche accent.

Dad chuckles, 'I reckon Marietta will work harder than any motorised washing machine known to man. She may be as wide as a bus, rattle and roll a bit, but by gee, I reckon she'll purr like the engine of a Merc once she gets going on the washing. I'd say the old gem is guaranteed never to rust! What do you reckon, dear?'

'Oh, come on,' chuckles Mum, raising her glass in the air for a top-up. 'She'll never rust. She runs on olive oil like the rest of us! I don't think we'll ever squeak or creak again either with all the oil in our diet lubricating our bits and pieces. I have to admit, she's put a new spin on my life.'

Now, every Friday morning Marietta makes the trip side-saddle on old Ajax from the village of Saint Marcos to our villa. For years, throughout the cold winters and long summers under the thin canopy of ancient grapevines that slope over a pergola next to the well, she sets up shop. Using the new wash tub that dazzles in the sunlight, and rippled wooden scrubbing board, she works resolutely for our family, labouring without complaint, her stumpy arms reaching deep into the washing tub, back arched; always aching. No tide or current of suds is too deep for her. No ancient relic of a stain unsalvageable or fabric unfathomable. She's Mum's dream machine.

On hot afternoons, Marietta sits and eats lunch chatting to Anna our neighbour, their bottoms planted and expanded like soft dimpled Greek dough, rising in the warmth on the side of our well. The women laugh, chatting above an orchestral accompaniment of cicadas.

Some days, feeling the tumultuous complexities of being a twelve-year-old, a soon-to-be teenager, I feel a deep sense of loneliness and so I join them. Quickly we become friends. As our bonds thread and weave into each other's lives, they fill the void in my life that missing my grandmothers in Australia has created. Stretching out the day with the skilled ease that requires centuries of mastering, they portion wonderful stories about their lives, and so fill and fortify the elongated moments of our Friday lunch breaks. In this way, my mother is no exacting timekeeper, content as she is to linger with Dad over lunch under the trees with my siblings looking out over the bay. The hardships of Anna and Marietta's lives, even the war years, have ironed out any bitterness in this fold of female survivors. Acceptance of what they have now has led to an enviable inner serenity.

Like clockwork, at the end of her long working day, you can't miss Marietta's rich, deep belly laugh as it resonates through the oleanders and bougainvillea surrounding our villa. All of our clothes have been draped and top-dressed over these plants until they dry as we have no clothes line. Our garden does a convincing job of imitating a refugee camp on Friday afternoons with all our unmentionables on full display. When Mum pays her wages, tipsy from ouzo, Marietta holds a dry bleached sheet to Mum's keen nose for her to judge the quality of her work. It's her way of a laundry quality evaluation test. She claims, Greek women have what she calls a *three-pillar* test. To do this you must conduct the touch test. A viewing, or fabric inspection test. And finally, a smell test. This should be the most delicious and exotic test of the three as you sink your nose deep into the delights of newly washed sun-drenched fabrics. It allows the infectious freshness emanating from dried cotton sheets and other washed delights, sunbeam-kissed from the garden, to explode in your nostrils. This completes the *three-pillar* test to a delightful orgasmic sensory conclusion. At this juncture, Mum releases a satisfied smile. Marietta with a twinkle in her eyes and the verve of the victorious, tells her in Greek, 'You see, Mrs Jo; my sheets always smell very nice; always the best. The best in all Corfu. Nobody washes clothes like me!'

Mum, not understanding the bulk of the conversation simply smiles in harmonious retaliatory ignorance. It's a weekly ritual between the two women and it's true, Marietta's sheets seem to dazzle more brilliantly than anyone else's.

Every week, upon receiving the wages for her tenuous labours, Marietta takes the 100 drachmae note and rolls it so it becomes so tiny you can hardly see it. She places it into the centre of a crisp bleached white cotton handkerchief which she knots securely for safe keeping. Lifting her layers of starched white petticoats until she finds the one closest to her body, ties the handkerchief into its layers high-up for safety. Her monetary reward entwined round and around by a pale pink ribbon, almost impossible to undo, as if seeking sealed and promised memories from long ago, she bends forward, eyes closed in reverence, lips to hand to kiss her hard-earned hoard while mouthing a prayer. She then crosses herself three times in a ritualistic blessing. The bound ribbon and its contents are then released from her hand to be consumed and lost in the folds of her petticoats. Safe in its remote location away from daylight, it's unlikely anyone would find her secret stash.

Still, I can't but wonder if any of it gets lost as it's enfolded by so much fabric. But for all her funny ways, even when she's tipsy from far too much ouzo at lunch time, Marietta knows what she's doing. Her days of soaking and scrubbing other people's cruddy cotton crutches with hands red raw, sore and bleached to the bone, makes every drachma she earns for her family precious. With back bent till it's brittle over a scrubbing board, imitating a benevolent worshiper in the searing heat of the day, she'd never risk losing her hard-earned wages under her petticoats. Her stash of Hellenic cash is as safe as the Bank of Greece. I only wish ours was as safe as hers.

Chapter 5

The Tricky Dicky Chicken Ticker Story

Our first few months on Corfu speed by. They are a reminder that time is brief even in a villa where we have none of the usual distractions like a telephone or television to hasten the passing of our days. Chronos, the god of time, knows all about *ora*. He reminds us with each *kalo mina, good month* that chronology can be a destructive force. Time passes irrespective of how it is used; it can't be halted. The wheels of the military coup keep grinding as my parents' hair begins to grey and wrinkles remain fixed in the corners of their bright eyes even when the sun has run its course for the day. Because of these obvious physical changes, I'm quickly learning that my parents, whom I'd always considered immortal, are indeed mortal and, like me, are not made to resist the ravages of time. In our world by the sea, the papers are full of news about Mikis Theodorakis going into exile in France. A private airport belonging to Onassis was used to fly him out of Greece to safety. While his music is still banned by the regime, irrespective of this, my father often plays the theme from Zorba the Greek loudly from our portable record player in our garden for all the world to hear. So far, we haven't been arrested.

While we may think time is slipping away too quickly on this tense but tourist and sun-drenched island, unlike the god Chronos, none of my brothers are so bored as to collaborate to castrate and depose our father for being foolish and challenging the political system. Today, however, Mum might be tempted to put Dad out of action by applying Chronos's ruthless methods. There she goes flooring us with one of her disdainful looks. She stops our incessant childish chatter by saying, 'I hate to break it to you children but I think your father's done an Elgin on us.'

'What does that mean?' I ask baffled.

She shakes her head worriedly. 'Well he's lost his marbles, hasn't he? He's like the rest of the Greeks without those stolen Parthenon thingamajigs; something's missing. In your father's case, it's his bloody brains! He's gone and got self-sufficient all of a sudden. His Hippocratic oath to write a novel has been flung in favour of a fetish for a strap-on tool kit. He's out there wearing a pair of ridiculous steel caps and a knotted checked hankie; the thing is arranged like a tradie's on his head. Looks like Tom the bloody Tool Twit.'

Hands shaking, mumbling something indecipherable while lighting a cigarette, her pessimistic eyes squint and water from its grey snake-like trail of smoke. 'I know your father loves to dress for the occasion but crikey, kids … I think he's gone too far. He looks bloody ridiculous. And he still hasn't done anything about the electric shocks we get every time we take a shower. What about the rising damp? It's taken on a life of its own, morphing in mossy cancerous colonies up the walls of this old villa as I speak, thanks to this humidity.'

In any conventional family, self-sufficiency might be considered a wise economic decision, especially living in the Greek countryside with five ravenous children and a wife to feed on a less than adequate income. Yet, Mum's responding to Dad's novel dithering like a bull to a red flag. 'I'm not sure if you kids are aware of this but your father and a hammer are a lethal combination. He'd knock down a wall as soon as lean on it. I see this all going pear-shaped; in fact, I'm just waiting for the wheels to fall off his latest idea no matter what it is.'

His recent career change is worrying. Our only income is his tiny pension and a small, ever-decreasing amount of savings that are supposed to be squirrelled in the bank for extreme emergencies. However, this stash of cash regularly gets raided. With no novel on the horizon as yet, Mum is right to be concerned. She rattles, her voice choking from smoke, 'Your father is fine huffing and puffing on his director's chair under the olive trees, going on about how the Trojan War was won, or lost, with villagers and random walk-in tourists he meets along the front path. The truth is, even a blind man can see he wouldn't know the difference between chook wire, barbed wire, or fly wire.'

With unsteady hands reaching to pour a cognac to settle her jittery nerves, she continues, 'The truth is your father is cerebral and not in the least manual.'

Dad, however, walking in on our conversation reckons, 'Ah, ye who hath such little faith, I'll show you! Before you know it, we'll have our own olive oil and wine flowing through our veins.'

'Really,' scoffs Mum, pushing aside a coil of salt and peppered black hair that's shifted from its usual position tucked tightly behind her right ear.

'Yes, really. And while I'm creating this new life, I'll erect a fence to end our landlady's nomadic sheep and goats meandering across the garden … bloody pests defecating everywhere. I ask you, who communes with sheep while tucking into breakfast, or lunching on the lawn? Reckon it's stretching neighbourly relationships too far. And another thing, how can anyone, even the most experienced olive picker, tell the difference between a sheep pooh, and a ripe black olive lying on the ground until they pick it up and squeeze the thing?'

He has a point; who indeed? And if he's switching careers so readily, redirecting our lives to making a living from the land by olive picking our way to prosperity, we need to find this out fast. Dad erecting a fence is a practical start, even if most of the villagers aren't into overt borders and boundaries. They seem to rely on word of mouth or instinct to determine such things. Some locals even roll a few boundary rocks to the right or to the left depending on where their neighbours fruit falls, gaining a sneaky claim over the bounty. The problem is sheep, chickens and goats don't understand rocks or invisible borders, waving arms and Greek superlatives. Come to think of it, neither do we.

Mum moans in despair about the prospect of olive picking as we congregate around the table. 'I refuse to hand press every olive we pickle to make sure it's not a sheep or goat's dropping. But either we do that, or do what the ancient Romans used to do and invest in a few well located vomitories around the garden.'

'Well, that brings a whole new meaning to a touch test,' Dad replies, scratching his chin and contemplating the rest of his days squeezing with us the guts out of olives to determine their place or orifice of origin. 'Mm ... I wonder if they sell rubber gloves in town? Put them on the shopping list, will you, Love?'

Over the next few days Dad sticks to his idea of making the 'Good life' our new mode of living.

'Life of strife, you mean. There are not enough olives in our garden to put a plate of *meze* together for morning munchies, let alone feed us for a year,' protests Mum.

She has a point. Not only that, collectively we are hardly the toiling agricultural type. But undeterred by her pessimism, Dad sets off like a man on a mission. Dressed in farmer's gear, he wanders the village inspecting a few small local farm holdings. After ending up at the *kafeneo* with some of the local farmers and fishermen, arms threaded around shoulders, he eventually sways his way home under the moonlight and is kindly deposited at the front door with a head full of cognac and self-sufficiency strategies.

A few days later, he heads to Corfu town in our old scruffy car to a hardware store down the end of a winding noisy laneway near the New Port. Our other car has been officially abandoned at the port because of engine problems which we can't afford to fix and, as we know we won't be able to pay the ridiculously high car import taxes that will soon be imposed on it, there it will stay. This is because there is the annual government levy on all foreign cars – you either pay the taxes on your car, or take it out of the country for the day, and then bring it back into Greece again. With funds being so prohibitive, there's no hope of us ever saving Dad's car from its inevitable demise. With the loud slam of a paper stamp onto an official looking document that's then stamped with an ink stamp from customs, he's washed his hands of it. We quickly learn Greek officials love miniscule paper stamps which always cost a small fortune to purchase and these administrators derive enormous satisfaction stamping these tiny stamps with a force that if you were the initiator, you'd end up being charged with assault. As it is, we stretch the drachmae to maintain one car. But in this way, we are still fortunate because even with our only just functioning solo jalopy, it's still considered a luxury by local standards.

With his new buddy Spyros, a man who looks like a cross between Pierce Brosnan and Tom Hanks, he joins Dad on his shopping trip to town. Spyros, liking the idea of a day away from his land-holdings reckons, 'I need a break. Escape my wife Nina's rumblings in the olive groves. *Theo mou, my god*, she's driving me crazy.'

It's one of life's intriguing experiences watching these two men in action as they communicate via sign language and an extremely bad mix of high school French. They augment their conversations with scratchy diagrams on paper. This is most helpful and between them they seem to understand one another. Over a few cheeky ouzos the two of them reckon they can patch up the Parthenon, redevelop Delphi, and expand the Corinth Canal all in one go. These are lofty claims indeed, as are their assertions that they've only had a few ouzos.

Later in the day and after hearing a loud horn blaring and then a thump, Mum looks through the shutters of our villa and spies our old car scrunched as if in an intimate embrace with the unyielding mulberry tree in the garden. Stumbling and laughing, the two men get out of the car and attempt to stand. Back in San Rocco Square near the *kafeneo* on the corner, without much thought, they'd thrown their purchases untidily in the car. The chaos and distraction of loud horns, the pulse of pedestrians on cracked paths, the tourist traffic, crammed departing buses and the rising heat had done nothing to improve their rushed and disorderly stacking skills, nor the racing car speed of their departure from town back to the coast. The car looks like a caricature of the ACME truck in a Road Runner cartoon. Planks, wire and poles poke in every direction.

Horrified, Mum shakes her head in despair and confronts them. 'Bloody idiots. Why are brakes always considered an optional extra in this country, and a horn essential? You knew the tree couldn't move out of the way. Look what you've done to my car! You can't tell me the wood poking out the back, and all the windows of the car is legal? Sometimes I think you are *terra* bloody *nullius* on top. You've made a first-class idiot out of yourself. And you're not off the hook either,

Spyros.'

Heads down like disobedient children, they follow her inside where she slams mugs of bull ant black coffee down with a thump onto the old kitchen table. 'Drink,' she orders.

Soon they are snapped back into action but only after much slapping of shoulders, laughter and filling an ashtray with the burnt remnants of smouldering cigarette butts. Submissively the pair remove the contents of our car and stack the purchases on a cleared area alongside our villa. That night sitting in the kitchen, I watch my parents argue. What Greek *terra firma* we have is suddenly looking very wobbly. But then this beautiful ancient land is renowned for its earthquakes.

The next day Mum, looking depressed, moans, 'You don't have to be a meteorologist to work out which way the wind blows in this country. I can see your father darting off to play cards or *tavli, backgammon* all day, every day at the tavern with that annoying little Spyros character ... the two of them slowly pickling themselves to death on ouzo. Yes, while we toil the soil like the rest of the exhausted women in the village pickling olives and vegies.'

It's a gloomy thought. But against her barrage of criticism, in no time he and his buddy have, in between frequent ouzo and cognac breaks, managed to erect a chook house. Even on a good day it's as lopsided as their crooked fence. Upon completion, Dad courageously asks Mum what she thinks. 'For heaven's sakes, man, they're teetering on the brink of disaster. Look, the fence sags because you've used chook wire, and you can flick the chook house over with your fingers. Mark my words, just one strong gust of a roaring *Maestro* and over they'll go.'

But being the stoic type, he refuses to be punctured by her negativity. His next self-sufficiency proposal is to purchase chickens and ducks to augment our precarious food supply. He adds a couple of air guns to the shopping list; these are intended for my brothers. They will be shown how to use them safely; in that way they can join in with the village lads on hunting trips into the hills around Saint Marcos and Spartilas. Mum is ropable, and foreshadowing doom and disaster. But he's not swayed.

'She'll be right, dear; they're growing lads. This will teach them responsibility, help them fit in with the local hunters. You want them to fit in, don't you? Trust me on this, and just let the duck fart.'

Over the next few weeks our newly acquired feathered friends settle in. Daily our chooks and ducks are released from their wobbly lop-sided pen to do the free-range rounds of our garden. Even the plump olives that fall from the ancient trees onto the ground are yummy pickings for our plucky poultry. More savvy than us, they are genetically blessed to know the difference between olives, sheep and goats' droppings.

A few days later, Mum is peering through the paint peeled wooden frame of our small kitchen window. Admiring the gnarled and twisted trunks of the ancient olive trees dotted around our villa, quite by surprise her gaze becomes an eerie stare as her eyes meet my grandmother's face as an unsettling, distorted resemblance emerges from the bark and looks back at her from the morphed shape in the olive tree's trunk. Sending shivers down her tanned slim body, she's left momentarily mute.

It's an unnerving reminder of my grandmother's parting expression as we left Australia, her face strewn with a look of despair as we said our goodbyes; my grandmother unable to disguise the anguish in her eyes knowing we were leaving Australia forever and entering of all things "a potential war zone." But beyond this, Mum knew my grandmother guessed the true motive for our departure. It wasn't so much the news headlines about the political crisis in Greece, as if that wasn't bad enough, it was the other headline in all the Australian papers, headlines that could blow my mother's life apart. Gran saw the connection and caught on the moment Mum mentioned moving – the coincidence was obvious. Gran could always see through her daughter. But my grandmother is a wise woman and so said nothing.

Leaning against the cool of the old marble kitchen sink, Mum's stomach churns as her long slender fingers grip the edge of the counter. Yet, even more disconcertingly, the image of her mother is reminiscent of the tormented look the world's finest artists capture in their depictions of the universal mother. It's the visage of fear shooting from the haunted eyes of the Madonna as she clasps the Christ-child possessively in her arms. It's that look, the one that captures the exact moment when she foresees the death of her child. How many times has my mother seen this look in her mother's eyes and the eyes of the Madonna? And for my mother, all those times when she appealed to God for help? But God ignored her pleas as did the doe-eyed Madonna. They'd abandoned her, those pitiless idols and she'd learnt her lesson. She'd pledged before her impotent god and the Madonna that she'd never appeal to either of them again. Far too many times they'd ripped her heart apart, even when she pledged her soul to them. Swore she'd never do it again. But she did, time and time again and never learnt from the regret and pain that assuredly followed. To her, it seemed unnatural to stop. Anyway, she reckoned, Gods and saints were all created to make fools of the living. She'd decided long ago when death comes and the hypnotic scent of graveside frankincense has been swept aside by the winds, there can be no thereafter, for once the earth gobbles lustily upon our rotting flesh, nothing remains; there is nothing more. Just like all the sins we accumulate throughout our lives, they will evaporate into the ether, wolfed down by ravenous worms, ignorant of what they are consuming. Therefore, life is essentially meaningless and she secretly despises the stupidity of those who think otherwise.

The morphed image of her mother cradled in the old olive tree's bark makes her turn her head away. Her eyes squint then quickly return back to accurately pinpoint its location. She wipes hot moist sweat from her upper lip with the back of her hand. Having marked with her keen eye the morphed image in the plot next door, she will endeavour never to look upon the old olive tree again. It's an unwanted boobytrap, no different to a hand grenade thrown by some impervious assassin into a room and he's fled the chaos oblivious of the pain he's caused. After all, what's the point of dwelling on the past when it drives you careering toward that thin line between sanity and insanity.

Mum suddenly speaks in a faraway voice, 'Look at the chickens and ducks in the garden, kids, aren't they having a lovely time? Don't they look healthy? I hate to eat my words, but in retrospect, perhaps your father's idea of being self-sufficient wasn't such a bad idea. Now hopefully he can get on with his book…'

Hearing her comments as he enters the steamy throb of our kitchen, Dad thrusts his chest upward into a rooster-style pose. After all, it isn't often she pays him a compliment. But within seconds the air is sucked out of his chest as he spies my brother in the garden with his new air gun. The boy takes aim with surprising precision, fires and shoots one of our chickens. It flutters to its death. My brother then aims selecting another random feathered target and fires once again. From where Mum is now standing by the window, she hasn't seen my brother, so is stumped as to why our chickens are suddenly dropping to the ground.

'Are our chickens alright?' she asks. 'Oh my God, David, you better get out there. See what's going on … we can't afford to lose all our chickens to some dodgy Greek chicken disease.'

No sooner had the words left her mouth than Dad's racing down the hallway sliding on the terrazzo floor and rugs as he goes. 'Yes, stay there while I find out what's going on. Could be contagious…!'

'You might have to consider mouth to mouth …'

Moments later he's outside pulling my brother roughly aside and grabbing the gun. 'What the hell are you doing? You can't use chickens for target practice. Don't do that again … don't tell your mother what you've done or you'll cop it from me, do you hear?'

'I was only practicing.'

'Just practicing? Your mother reckons you and your brothers with guns are nothing more than a collective coalition of the bloody killing, our own home-grown nasty little partisans, and I think your mother's right. Now, you little monster, yours is confiscated until further notice.'

My brother's body collapses like a deflated balloon.

'Well, long may you hang your head in shame, young man. Now get your backside inside and remember … Mum's the word.'

Devastated by the fact he's losing his gun and newly acquired power and independence, he scuttles head down into the villa. After cautiously disposing of our pelleted pullets, Dad goes back inside, shaking his head.

'Struth, dear, it must be a case of the Dicky Chicken Tickers disease. Spiros and his mate warned me about Greek chooks being prone to heart attacks; it's a disease of sorts … if they're exposed to too much excitement and stress, that is. Now you can't tell me living with us isn't like Hiroshima and Naga bloody Saki bombs going off right, left and centre with our five kids charging like maniacs around the place. No, dear … I reckon it's too much excitement for the poor little feathered fellows, we'll have to keep them locked up in the chook pen from now on.'

But Mum's smelt a rat. 'You never mentioned this before. I've never heard of anything so ridiculous in my life. Are you sure they're not faulty fowls and you've been taken for a ride? Maybe that Spiros fellow's dodgy? You could report him to the tourist police. We have some rights, you know.'

Knowing she's no fool and this could blow out, he promptly intercedes, 'Now I don't think we need to go that far, Jo. No, I think you're being hasty. I swear I heard there's been a chicken ticker bug going around the village. Yes, and just the other day too.' But to avoid the situation escalating further, he agrees to make enquiries about chicken diseases that cause heart conditions with his local taverna mates.

'Well, you better, otherwise you and the rest of the local population are all mad. The very idea of Greek chickens suffering from some stress disease and prone to coronary heart failure; it doesn't make sense. I think you're all as nuts as … as … squirrels!'

The idea had on occasion entered his mind. 'Well, dear, stranger things have happened at sea, now trust me on this, please.'

Conscious of her threat however, like a clever strategist he cuts her off at the pass. He may not be handy with a hammer but he can't get to Hoppy's *kafeneo* quickly enough to tell his new pals about the pellets in pullets incident. Sitting and drinking with a translator, the local farmers, fishmen and shepherds think his story is hilarious. Enjoying the opportunity to mock the stupidity of women, especially foreign ones, they all promise to play along with the tricky dicky chicken ticker disease story. With prevailing bonds of masculine comradeship so deeply embedded in the Greek male psyche, Mum doesn't stand a chance of ever discovering the truth.

From now on it's our chickens and duck's destiny to be ferreted into the wobbly back chook-pen where my brother is warned to stay away. Every now and then when all's quiet on the home front and my brother is out for the day, the birds are allowed to range freely. In the meantime, Mum with her little bag of left-over kitchen scrappy birdie delights does a daily delivery service right to their doorstep. Mindful of their disposition, she always approaches our chickens with the utmost consideration, oozing soothing words full of inflated compliments; the kind chickens and ducks like to hear. Never again any surprises or sudden movements for our fowls. After all, they're fragile feathered friends and every effort must be made to mollycoddle them. Indeed, pluck them gently from the hard knocks of life, especially living with our family.

Chapter 6

Demythologizing Greek Villas

We soon discover we are not the only expats living on Corfu. Sadly, in the very early days there were no Australian families with children. A few years later another Australian family arrives from Samos, but in the meantime among the British and European mix, there is an eccentric American neighbour called Hilary. She has three children. Her eldest daughter Star fell in love with a Corfiot soon after her family moved to the island. A while later, they became engaged. But a year or so passes and her daughter has announced that their congenial connubial bliss has collapsed a few days before her wedding. The news comes as one hell of a shock. Hilary's wringing her hands in despair as she arrives at our villa to have a good cry on my parents' shoulders.

She sits under the olive trees with tears reddening her eyes, threatening to murder her daughter. My parents offer comfort in the form of a generous supply of cigarettes and cognac.

In her deep Texan accent she grumbles, 'Shit, what am I going to do? I have aeroplane loads of friends and relatives arriving on the doorstep. I've got unsettling visions of maggots with Stetsons and alligator suitcases, merging and breeding on my front veranda as I speak!'

She reaches for a cigarette, squints her eyes as she lights it, adding more tears to the shower already bathing her cheeks. Having surrounded herself with pale smoke, she appeals to her audience by thrusting in our direction her large breasts, currently on show in a low-cut top. 'I know I can't avert an aborted wedding, but what am I going to do about my villa? It's too small to accommodate everyone, and God damn it, my only toilet is, as you Aussies say, "dodgy." If the wedding was on, it would distract everyone. But now ... holy shit! The bookings have been stuffed up because of some ridiculous administration error. Now it's high season and all of the hotels are booked out with British package deals and yodelling Germans stripping off their leather lederhosen and letting it all hang out.'

'Shit indeed!' Dad responds, expressing his overt dislike for Germans, and then he does what he does in any crisis by reaching for the cigarette packet. He manages to crack a weak smile through the rapidly accumulating cloud of smoke above our heads. 'People will understand, Hil's – she'll be right. You couldn't demythologise a cancelled wedding and a dodgy Greek dunny if you tried. Yes, the Greeks may have invented democracy but their plumbing leaves much to be desired. I suggest you joke about it and make the most of the situation.'

He lifts the brandy bottle, shaking it temptingly in the air, offering to pour her another cognac. She nods encouraging him to pour her a large one by signalling with two chubby fingers. However, she's not convinced by his solution.

'There's nothing amusing about a cancelled wedding, a tiny Greek villa or my, as you call it, "dodgy dunny." I don't know how I'll cope. God damn it ... I need solutions to my ablutions.' She smiles a weak smile.

She's right. The situation is complex. Her daughter's ex-fiancé won't get the hint and hovers, moping around her villa. Periodically he declares his undying passion for Star, who's fled the scene. She's on another Greek island having masterly escaped the drama of the unfolding calamity. But back on the home front, every so often her upset ex throws himself in the ocean. Before he does, he declares to the world he's going to kill himself. Each time Hilary spots him so much as sticking a toe in the ocean, she panics and alerts anyone close at hand to dive in and save him irrespective of his motives. He's been put on permanent suicide watch. But for Hilary, it's her lousy loo that's particularly perplexing. That's in between feeding queues of guests who have already arrived and now expect free food and accommodation for the duration of their Greek island holiday. Meanwhile, Hilary's latest lover, Paddy, a Dubliner with a passion like hers for expensive art and "the drink," is under the olive trees in her garden. He's running Greek dance classes for her guests as he generously tops up everyone's glasses with cheap plonk at her expense.

At close range Hilary projects brandy breath into my ear, 'Can my life get any more complicated? Isn't the loo already too small for my family of four to cope with? Now I've got rampant relatives and friends using it? To top it off, I caught that suicidal maniac, the ex-fiancé yesterday hovering suspiciously in the bathroom. Caught him fossicking around with my Gillette razor blades. Had his eyes on my sleeping tablets too. And he must have done a swifty on my haemorrhoid suppositories, cos they're missing. But hey, guys, that's not the worst of it.'

'Gee, Hilary I don't know what could be worse .... Mmm ... a person in a disturbed state stealing razor blades, and with the potential to nick your haemorrhoid suppositories. I don't know about you but I'm visualising a messy death scene here ... especially if he inserts your suppositories into multiple orifices. Crikey, I hate to be a pessimist but anything could happen,' counsels Dad.

'Yes, and that won't re-tify his problem, or yours,' laughs Jo.

Looking doomed, Hilary moans, 'But hey, that's not the

worst of it. Yesterday Star's ex, drunker than I've ever seen him, threw himself fully dressed in the ocean again. This time Paddy did an Olympic dash and rescued him. He dragged him inside. When he'd dried him and changed his clothes, he found great wads of wet drachmae and American dollar notes in his pockets.'

We look on intrigued as Hilary continues.

'We had no idea the guy carried so much cash. I mean, we knew he was loaded but, there's loaded, and there's loaded. Paddy put him to bed to sleep it off, leaving me with the huge stash of mullah. Well, what could I do with it? I don't have a clothes dryer like I had back in the States. My only option was to use great care unfolding the notes and separating them. Then I carefully pinned the tips of the money on my make-do clothes line. You know, down the side of my villa with those ridiculously big wooden dolly clothes pegs. Let me tell you, that was quite a task. I got to say, they looked outlandish hanging there. Anyway, as the rows of notes fluttered gently in the afternoon breeze, I fell asleep on my deck chair in the garden. Then I had the weirdest dream.'

Intrigued, we move our seats closer. Assured she's captivated her audience, she pauses and uses the opportunity to take a generous slug of cognac, and light another cigarette before continuing. 'In my dream, Anna my neighbour walks by the next day, an early riser by habit and notices the money flapping in the wind. Startled at the sight of cash pegged on the line, suddenly terrified, she screams like a mad woman and sends her sheep scattering all over the hamlet, "Oh, my God … it's a miracle, a miracle" blowing the whole situation out of proportion. By the time my cleaning lady Maria arrives, she's met by half the neighbourhood. Cautiously, they stand some distance from my clothesline in absolute amazement of the vision before them. I reckon they must have been confused

… not sure if it's the devil's doing or a most wonderous miracle executed by a very generous God. Then Maria, racing as fast as her plump little legs can carry her up the steps of my villa, bursts into my kitchen to tell me about the miraculous sight on the clothes line. As I'd just risen and not got my head around my first cup of coffee for the day, I was in no mood for shenanigans from anyone, let alone Maria.'

'Wow, now that's a dream if ever there's a dream,' I say in wonderment.

'I know, so I venture outside pulled by an excited Maria; I see a crowd staring at the clothesline. The next thing, Father George arrives, his stove pipe hat secure on his head … I reckon it's his direct line to heaven. He'd been summoned from Saint Marcos to make haste to my villa and behold the strange vision. He arrives dressed in full ecumenical attire ready to tackle any situation. With arms held aloft, he's gripping a tall shiny cross. On either side of him … two nervous altar boys.'

Wide eyed and wondering what Hilary will say next, Dad intervenes, laughing, 'You can't be serious!'

'Sure am,' continues Hilary. 'Some dream, isn't it? The kids had been conscripted from the village to quickly dress, each grab a large processional icon from the church and follow him. Standbys for Father George if he needed extra spiritual backup. You know, the kind only sacred icons like theirs can proffer.'

Mum interrupts, 'Come on, Hils! Admit you were on magic mushrooms, or that whacky tabacki stuff?'

'Yeah, yeah, I wish,' laughs Hilary. 'There they were, all three of them standing armed with enough consecrated power to blow the socks off the devil himself. Even so, Father George is an adaptable guy, ready to accept a charitable donation on behalf of the church. After all, for all he knows, it could be a miraculous gift from God. Priests have been known to be very supple when it to comes to gifts.'

We nod and smile.

Having slipped off her shoes and curled her feet under her generous bottom like a nesting bird, Hilary continues. 'In the dream I'm standing on my front porch, and call out to everyone, "OK, settle down folks ... the show's over. No miracles today. So, please everyone, go home." With a twinkle in my eye, I tell them, "The reason the notes are on the clothesline is because I've been worried about infections since a recent illness. I stupidly washed the money to make sure it was sanitary, not contaminated with nasty bugs so my visitors won't catch anything while staying with me. I hope no one's offended or inconvenienced by this, upon reflection, rather a crazy idea of mine, but let me assure you folks, it won't happen again. So please everyone, vamoose." Look, I gotta admit it was one hell of a mixed-up dream, but then dreams are like that, aren't they? And the way the dream concluded meant no one finds out that the ex-fiancé tried to kill himself.'

We all smile in agreement.

'By the time I awoke, the money had dried and when Star's ex emerged, the money was returned to him, dry, crisp and counted. I didn't even apologise that it wasn't ironed. I told him never to pull a stunt like that again, Buddy.'

'Wow, what a dream, Hils,' laughs Dad as we continue to sit hanging onto her every word.

Now looking serious, Hilary continues. 'Ever since that suicidal maniac left to go home to his mother, that useless lover of mine has been prancing around the garden squawking about the money on the line. You should have seen Paddy this morning, blowing the story out as he led a troupe of booze-infused guests around my garden. Looks like a Russian Cossack dancer if you ask me ... using improvised steps stolen from the Celts. He's treating my guests like mugs, and in truth ... they probably are. Half of them are hillbillies ... from my ex-husband's side of the family, of course, cos they sure aren't from my side.'

She pauses and laughs, rocking like a cradle in her creaky chair. 'I bet none of them have noticed that they're not even dancing a proper Greek dance. Hell, folks, I don't know what the world's coming to.'

But in true stoic style, Hilary's trying to make the best of a difficult situation. As for accommodation shortages at her villa; she's moved some of her guests into the houses of local friends, while others are billeted into tents and sleeping bags in her garden. While her guests find this unpleasant, especially with sheep roaming through her garden, she, unlike us, hasn't thought to erect a fence until now, but at least this way everyone gets a bed of some description, even if they wake up in the arms of one of Leonidas's lambs surrounded by sheep deposits. I suppose such an unenviable sensory source only adds to her guests overall Greek holiday experience.

Hilary points out, 'I've become quite partial to the sound of sheep's bells ringing in my ears on those mornings when I've greeted the sunrise after discovering myself beneath the arms of an olive tree. But back to my toot issue ... the overriding problem is everyone merges outside the loo at the same time during peak hours and causes traffic jams. Then they complain to me, "How do you put up with it?" and roll their eyes, moan, groan and holding their noses, reluctantly submit themselves to my bathroom. Of course, they're right. It's primitive! With no lock on the loo door, it is operation keep your knickers on. Or close at hand, even under the shower. The whole bathroom situation is embarrassing and without exaggeration, you'd be lucky to get out alive – if you can get in in the first place. I have to warn everyone, "First in best dressed. If you want a hot shower; get in early."

Hilary pauses to light yet another cigarette, and Dad, sympathetically in tune with his guest's thoughts, pours more cognac. Smiling gratefully at his generosity, she continues. 'Yeah, it's a miracle the Corfu Health Department hasn't moved in and shut down my villa because of queues of cross-legged crowds flowing out the front door onto the porch. With the potential to be a serious health hazard, my shitty, not so funny, "dunny" as you Aussies call it, often heralds the sounds of someone crying out, "The loo's blocked again!"

Poor Hilary's right. Her loos on road performance at staying unblocked is nothing to rave about. I know from past experience. It bubbles, gurgles and blocks just like ours. While she's used to her loo and its revolting anomalies such as the: "no flushing loo paper in the loo" rule, or any other unmentionable disposables that end up in a toilet bowl in the West, it's hard for her guests to conform. Hilary continues to grumble.

'Why can't people respect the golden Greek "no flushing rules"; these not only apply to my toilet. They apply to every toilet in Greece. How many times do I have to say, never flush toilet paper in the loo? Disposable materials like toilet paper must go into the designated toilet paper basket next to the loo. I know my convenience is a real inconvenience, but hello folks, that's Greece. So, get over it.'

Hilary stops to catch her breath, butt out her cigarette and sip more cognac. 'I say to my guests, "Listen up everyone! When my toilet blocks, I gotta call Greece's magic loo master blaster. He's my charming toilet un-blocker, my drain deity. Perhaps I should erect a shrine in his honour? The man deserves the Hellenic Award for Bravery for his patriotic duty keeping Corfu's loos fresh and flushing. Yes, let me tell you he's the plumber that packs a powerful punch in my shitty potty. In fact, I think he could retire on the money he's made unblocking my toilet in one summer alone!" So, I warn everyone, "Don't block my loo!" But do they listen? Of course not!'

She's right. With targeted precision her plumber jump starts her toilet with suction cups, fangled attachments and long bits of hose. I've seen him in action. He unblocks ours on a regular basis too. The smell fells, so everyone evacuates to the designated muster point on the beach, opposite her villa while he performs the unpleasant deed. After he's completed his task, he pushes and promotes optional extras at discount prices. It's his way of a loyalty program for his regulars. Hilary's children are like us, and laugh, then whinge, "Boy, are we regular. Too many beans and continental lentils."

Hilary's plumber flashes bathroom defoggers, mounted exhaust systems, rear view mirrors, even extra deluxe new, one-pull, single stroke chains at her. Apparently, the cogs on what she calls his "Antikythera pressure mechanism" are truly something to behold. I wonder what she means by this as she simultaneously gives Mum a suggestive wink? While she reckons his sales pitch is fine, much to her disappointment, he has yet to come up with a solution for the foul toilet paper basket with its daily tissue build-up.

Hilary tells us that at other times her loo blows. From a poised throttle position on her loo, she says you can end up like a quadbike rider being flung by dung, anywhere and everywhere in her cubicle-sized toot of many horrors. She reckons it's like mounting volcanic Vesuvius when it's poised to blow. Added to her wet room woes, her water supply flows from a well at the back of her block. From time to time there's a 24-hour ban on its use. When this happens, she and her children bucket water in from their neighbours well on the other side of her property, all because some desperado's been caught urinating near the well, resulting in a shutdown.

"That's it!" Hilary bellows, her face contorted into an ugly imitation of a raging cyclops. "Didn't anyone inform that son of a bitch on the dangers of urinating near wells, and the health problems associated with seepage? Sorry, folks, but, gee ... I get real pissed off."

I wait for steam to escape from her ears.

She's not wrong about water problems. While her guests are still with her, summer ends and the island's beautiful crystal-clear well water shrinks to disturbingly low levels from overuse. Each time a tap is turned on, water is drawn from deeper into the ground water table to access what little fresh water remains. As they draw water from closer to the seawater level, the occasional unwelcome visitor pops out. Tiny raw prawns or other seaside creatures thrust their crustacean-shaped bodies out of the faucet. Their long antennae join water users as they clean their teeth, or fill the kettle. Hilary's decided, after many near misses, to filter the water from her kitchen taps, otherwise she'll end up retrieving steamed prawns from everything she cooks or boils. Although friendly little fellows before death, cooked versions turning up in food and coffee cups at inopportune moments is embarrassing, and isn't ideal. It's generally agreed these cooked morsels are not the best accompaniment with one's first, or any, coffee of the day. She's not alone in this experience. Most villas along the low-lying coast experience this horror; we too can attest to this. How many times has someone at our villa choked on their beverage, coughed and spluttered up some nautical nasty because we forgot to filter the water?

As summer finally vanishes with generous tear drops conveyed from dark skies in late October and early November, her water woes improve, as do ours. The rain quenches the yearning earth, filling our deep thirsty wells once again. The prawns and other feisty, skittish little fishy fellas who'd made their home in the wells in summer, disappear like undesirable high season guests. Shimmering spherical raindrops have a way of driving them off. Where they go, I do not know.

While Hilary grizzles about her temperamental toilet, we have problems with our shower. At our villa it is what people remember most about our bathroom when staying with us. There you'd be, merrily frolicking around in the nuddy, expecting an invigorating, if somewhat quick, soak under the shower. Just as you've got lathered to a fabulous froth, you'll get one hell of an almighty spine-tingling electrical shock. The shocks shoot along your body and exits your toes. The irritating dilemma with these electric shocks is that it's like playing Russian roulette. The shock is not consistent, but occurs now and then when you least expect it. It could be as you fine-tune the water temperature or turn the shower on or off. Talk about touchy taps. If you want an electro cranium to colon job, this is the place to get it. This taste of what the electric chair must be like cuts short any malingering sopranos pumping out Figaro in the morning. With the seven of us using the shower daily, it proves to be an effective way of getting us in and out in quick succession.

I can't remember how many times Dad has pleaded with an electrician to check the taps to make sure we won't fry alive under a reign of water speckled with steamy prawns. But every sparky from Sidari to Spartilas and beyond insists the shock and awe we are experiencing isn't shocking or awe-inspiring enough to be too serious and a threat to life. "You just need to fine tune your taps," they say.

Have they tried it in the nuddy? – that's the question. Well, not on our watch, they haven't.

As electricians leave, they laugh and say things like, "Use rubber gloves, or wet suits, if you're still worried." They jump into their vans after payment and depart with a friendly *"yasoo", goodbye!*

'Bloody dodgy dunny diagnostics if you ask me,' grumbles Dad lighting a cigarette and pouring a consoling cognac. Did I happen mention these are his panaceas for all of life's perplexing problems? Yes, I think I did.

It was during those first few insightful summers on Corfu that we learnt a valuable lesson about Greek bathrooms. Whenever we moved villas, Dad would say, 'Come on, kids, let's do a lavatory inventory. A ten-point tap test and score sheet on the shower and toot's performance. We don't want any of Hilary's problems, now do we?'

Laughing with him we soon get down to business with our trusty pencil and check list. We're determined we won't rent a villa with a dodgy Greek dunny like Hilary's, or endure the excruciating agony of another electro-to-colon, super-charged shower ever again. Amen to that.

Chapter 7

Idols in the Market Place

The patron Saint of Corfu is Saint Spyridon. He's the wonder boy who, according to local legend, could do more than whip up a storm and change the course of history. A super-man of sorts, some say he could even leap tall ships' masts in a single bound, stopping the Turk's occupation of the island, so Corfu never experienced the tyranny of the Ottomans like much of the rest of Greece. Apparently, he was no basket case either, even though in much of his iconography he is represented as a wise, yet humble soul with a wicker basket on his head. Local sceptics smile and say, "He was hatched, dispatched into the life of a saint, then promptly thatched."

This saint was so famous after his death, the church hierarchy had him mummified, or "stuffed" as Dad says. I suppose back then "stuffing" someone had a different subtext to today. Apparently, it was quite an honour. After his mummification, his remains were taken to Constantinople for safe-keeping. Patriarchs, as well as the occasional Byzantine Emperor, all apparently partial to praying to preserved body parts, attended great festivals in his honour. He was the star attraction. This conserved saint didn't stay there, but was soon scooped up and sold to the highest bidder. Then it was going, going, and gone – gone to a man with a savvy eye for a bargain and a very sound business plan. Shipped to Corfu, a church was built in his honour. In 1524, the saint's relics were given to the Vulgaris family as part of a dowry. I'd heard people say with a smile, "Now if ever there was a deal sweetener, this was it. Marry my daughter and we'll throw in the saint."

Five times a year the family allows the Saint to go on public display. On these emotionally charged days, crowds pour onto the streets as he's paraded through Corfu town in a glass case to the rapturous applause of adoring and curious spectators.

Today I'm coaxed into celebrating the Saint's holy day with the ladies from my village. For this special trip to Corfu town, the *yiayias* dress head to toe in black. Three-quarter length skirts team with soft velvet boleros and head scarves. There's not a skerrick of makeup on any of them. I'm warned that wearing makeup of any kind on such a holy pilgrimage is a sin of the most, "*Po, po, po*" kind.

The women recommend dark sunglasses and I wear them for good measure. They don't say why; I just placidly follow instructions. After all, I'm the new kid on the block and have much to learn. Anyway, perhaps it's best to go incognito to these events? Especially when not wearing makeup. These rules might yet be a worthy tactic, distracting the divine powers that be in the hope they won't recognize us nor punish us for our transgressions; it's worth a try. Once I merge with the group of giggling grannies, I feel like I've been swallowed by a diffuse array of nimbostratus clouds; we resemble a stormy dress rehearsal for Onassis's funeral. Woe to anyone who stands between us and their man, their hero, the one and only Saint Spiro.

The Church of Saint Spyridon sits comfortably in the pulsating heart of Corfu town. It has a distinct red knob on top making it stand out from other churches. The church was built to provide a place for parishioners and visitors alike to meditate on the pleasure or pain of their passions. Who was it that said, "Suffer, baby, suffer," and was it always a pulpit practice in this church? I'm surrounded by serious faces in an airtight space of intense self-restraint, the kind that comes from a reverence that suggests souls have been stripped bare and examined – it's solemn stuff. Or is the atmosphere in response to something profound emanating from a good sermon? What about something light before mass, like an Ecumenical Council? I can see it all now. The tempo and pace of ecclesiastical debate peppered by a few serious blasts from bishops near the baptistry. But then, perhaps not. The intense incense is playing games with my mind …

However, I digress. With the edict of Milan, Emperor Constantine in 312/13 AD declared Christians could affirm themselves in full freedom within the expansive Roman Empire. They were suddenly no longer the target of pagan persecutors. No more throwing Christians to the lions and such. The end of human sacrifices which Dad told me had been part of the "Bread and Circuses Policy". The policy may have ended horrific deaths in the arenas for Christians, but history records some Christians spent their time throwing pagans into stadiums, or pulpits for the sheer pleasure of revenge. It was a case of conform or cop it. Following on, many pagan temples were mowed down and churches erected on numerous ancient sacred pagan sites. The early church, with this edict from the emperor himself, gave the Christians licence to formally set-up shop. Create a hierarchy which, in the beginning, was inclusive of women, but then it all changed. Very soon men put in place rules and guidelines limiting the role of women in the church hierarchy, cementing church theology, architecture, literature and art, these male ecclesiastical pioneers determining a patriarchal way forward for the church and its selected entourage. It was, and still is, disappointing for many women wanting to be ordained.

Saint Spyridon, a humble shepherd-come-monk on a mission, did his best a few years later supporting the "Orthodox" viewpoint regarding the doctrine of the Holy Trinity at the Council of Nicaea. After a few death-defying miracles with the heads of mules and other marvels, his sainthood was given the thumbs up by the ecclesiastical mega honchos. When he got to Corfu as a capsulised mummified corpse, locals say he stopped the Black Plague raging across the island. He's credited with a raft of other miracles too. No wonder this blessed Saint developed his own cult, the cult of Saint Spyridon.

And like other churches, Saint Spyridon's endeavours to recreate heaven on earth, in a way, I think this has been achieved. Many Christians feel they are being taken from the ordinary into the extraordinary simply by crossing its threshold. The churches history a miracle too because it has survived and the ladies beside me appear to agree as they nod and cross themselves seemingly in rhythm with my thoughts.

There to greet us as we wedge our way through the masses into the centre of the church, ethereal portraits of three-dimensional post-Byzantine images peer at us from above, those all-seeing and all-knowing eyes providing a snapshot of what will surely become of us if we don't capitulate to Christ. As I look around, some of the frescos scare the living daylights out of me. It's those protuberant eyes. Eyes that have the power to ensure conformity. How can it be otherwise with so many sets searing, casting forth lingering, judging expressions?

As I'm rocked by jostling bodies, I'm fully aware that this is no stage set. Before me there's elevation through salvation, transformation via the senses. Can I hear *Ave Maria* echoing from some far-off cave in Cappadocia? But then, perhaps not.

Yes, I'm wrong. There's only the sounds of male voices chanting, and art works telling yarns through depictions of scenes from the Old and New Testaments along crowded, shadowy walls. Such narratives. Witnesses to the wisdom of Moses. Others highlighting the hosts of angels mixed in with the tears of weeping women gathered at the foot of Christ. Images as instruments of passion, poignant and solemn. Their longevity made manifest through the construction of sacredness. Manmade actions reinforced and continued, ritual after ritual. Year after year. Century after century. These icons and frescos, eyewitnesses to centuries of passing parishioners, spectators to our sins as we parade before them while they flicker luminously in a mass of a candlelight show.

There are none of Goya's, Rubens', or Caravaggio's provoking veracity in these images. A glittery, dressed-up iconostasis stands laden with martyred Marys, triptychs of pious prophetic prophets and balding Byzantine bishops. These look refined, transcendent in long brightly coloured vestments, the whole scene punctuated by a few naphthalene and lavender smelling, napping nannas, backs up against the walls, sitting like they are donkey riding, only now on solid wood pull-down seats, getting in a bit of shut eye before the next service starts, or ends. Not just holy days, but every day. This is their whole world, this sacred space – services providing reassuring regularity, a comforting compass, a lifeline, a place to solve life's unresolvable riddles, or achieve salvation.

I had no idea the Church would be so packed. We are squashed in like canned sardines; the rule book on polite public proximity was abandoned hours ago. Indeed, there's no need for miraculous displays of bread and fishes. Just the need for a gush of fresh air. For, as day drags into night, can't someone open a window, please, I whisper.

With an ominous and unsettling feeling mounting in my gut, it slowly becomes clear: I'm stuck in the church till dawn. My fellow black-garbed village belles are literally bedding down for the night. No one mentioned this when we set out. I realise now there's no escape for me, or anyone else from my village, even if we wanted to. I contemplate the Last Supper as my tummy rumbles with hunger. Getting up close and personal with God, and the good Saint Spiro, must continue through the night. The last bus has long left town that could have transported me and any other arbitrary, but brave retreater, from this now mesmerised assembly, safely back to our snug little beds in the hamlet.

Through the haze of transcendent smoky incense and in a moving sea of what can only be described as a mourning mass of motion, I sway my way through this holy night. The do's and not to dos, that is the question, and I ponder them deeply because this is not the time nor place to commit any diabolical heretical taboo. I'd never get out alive! All night, as the worshiper's hands work in unison, crossing three times here, three times there; a tempo is worked up to a fever pitch of rhythmic fingers, all to the chant of chanters and chitter chatter of church bells.

There's a sense that everyone's transfixed in a spellbinding out-of-body experience. It leaves them dazed as if in a collective communion of consciences with all eyes focused on the prize. Yes, the prize. How can one forget? The sedan style, elevated glass-faced coffin placed in front of the altar. It contains the great saint himself. There he is leaning slightly, propped up by prayers in a stand-alone position; well and truly trapped like the rest of us, only more so. He's mummified, immortalised, impassive; an unmoving genuine Egyptian job. The real McCoy Pharaoh of Egypt style, patented by none other than the patriarchs. Impermanence made permanent by being gutted, then filled up again. A withered mass of wrinkles miraculously held together by a crumbling dusty diaphragm. Skin brown with an animal hide-like derma dimension to it, resembling thin sheets of covering, not dissimilar to tar-coloured cigarette paper. It sits parched over his distorted skeletal shape, framed in the robes of a golden monarch.

He's all teeth and bones, with sunken eyes the focus, an alien face only a mother could love, I would have thought. But here they are, the cult of Saint Spiro, adoration of the highest order. A coffin covered with kisses, germs, wishes and prayers of pious worshiping masses. For the captivated in the hot-pressing pushing crowd, they can queue and go past the body again, and again, in chaotic quick crunch pasts all night into the dawn if they desire.

The concentration of energy in the church is intense. Moving mouths in murmuring, indecipherable motions. The eyes of the dedicated congregation shot backwards, some with only the whites showing in quivering ecstasy. A kind of frenzied expectation hangs electrically in the air. If there's going to be a resurrection, will it happen here? Is Saint Spiro going to suddenly sit up and say, "Hi, I'm back!"

We wait for hours with the incense intense, making everyone giddy with God. But whatever anyone anticipates might happen doesn't happen. Well, for me anyway. As the night comes to an end with delicate flickers of welcome daylight making their way through the incense-shrouded windows from the east, another Saint Spyridon's day has passed. For me it can't end soon enough. I want to go home. Perhaps the miracle is exiting the ecclesia.

As our dark little group of tired village pilgrims make our way out of the crunch of the church into the shock of a cold Corfu morning, the reason for the sunglasses becomes clear.

The glare from the sun makes our sleepy eyes weep as if salt has been cruelly flung into them. On the slippery smooth marble path in front of the ecclesia, pushy sellers from markets around town have quickly set up pop-up shops. These are assembled in rows along the wide cobbled walkway leading to the Liston.

Idols in the marketplace sell salvation, available to all who have the money and are willing to pay. After all, what price peace of mind when, with a quick if uncomfortable confession, heaven is assured. God, after all, is out to get the sin, not the sinner. It's worth considering that even if you are the most wicked and nefarious of nasties, you'll be forgiven. It's very reassuring. In this way, who doesn't want a gong, a nod or guernsey from God? And for those who have faith, souls rot as I write warning us that we exist in a temporal state. We navigate our way precariously between heaven, earth and hell. We mere mortals are in a constant battle balancing good against evil. How, when Christ is the measure, can we ever be good enough?

So, these trinkets of crosses, incense burners, candles and prayer books ease the conscience of the sinner a tad. It gives probing pilgrims something to hold onto. I suppose it's to be expected that among the mountains of wares for sale, there are no encaustic or egg tempera icons in the mounds of merchandise. Or, great Giotto's, dark and gloomy El Greco's to add to the cheerlessness of the moment. A Donatello or two would be nice – a real treat among the mass produced, cheaply painted and carved reproductions, all assembled this morning on rickety tables. At best, tacky kitsch pictures pasted onto wood; an art critic's nightmare. Anyone for a game of tack tossing?

But with the delicious smoky aromatic scent of freshly roasted chestnuts wafting through the cold morning air, we sleepy pilgrims know it's all over for another year. Time to head for the bus-stop with our hands full of warm and oozy apple and cinnamon *milopitas, apple pies* to help stop the tummy rumbles on the bumpy bus ride home. Still armed with our dark sunnies, we agree we are all looking forward to a quiet day and a long siesta in the afternoon. Yes, even I will partake on this occasion. The ladies assure me there will be no olive picking for them today.

I reckon if the ladies ask me to join them next year, I'll decline. After all, I could set up my own exclusive petite domestic shrine at home. Use my new incense burner. Have it puffing away gently purifying my world as it sits on a ledge with that little triptych of Saint Spyridon, the one I purchased in the marketplace earlier today. I can do my own Saint Spyridon celebrations in the comfort of my villa. After all, travelling diptychs were designed for this very purpose. It wouldn't be rude or irreverent doing this. After all, if there is a God up there, or down here with me, I'm sure he'd prefer to see this little bug snug and safe cocooned in her home. Lighting an incense burner, or candle at our villa on this day means I am thinking of him.

On Corfu, faith and hope are not haphazardly plucked like fruit from trees, but exist all around me, even when prayers are not answered. The locals are relentless in their faith. They believe God and Saint Spyridon can change the world. They're convinced prayers and positive thoughts can change us too. The *yiayias* say, "Faith and hope are the threads, the conduits that give flight to all our anticipations and dreams. Never forget, God is in the detail."

I think that's the key, or crucial element to Saint Spyridon's Day. It's the detail in the transformative power of our thoughts and prayers. They have the impetus to change our world. Who knows, if I pray hard enough Dad might start writing his book, and much needed drachmae will drop from the heavens.

Chapter 8

Lentils and Beans Saved Greece

Katerina's my new friend and she lives in our humble hamlet. As it turns out, neither of us go to school because our parents can't afford to send us. As a result, we spend a great deal of time hanging out together. In a way, we are like the wild herbs and flowers in the surrounding mountains because we grow-up free from the excruciating stresses of examinations and tests.

In my case, it's because my brief encounter with Correspondence Courses from Australia during our first summer in Greece proved to be too expensive and a catastrophe. Firstly, my tiny inheritance – and it was tiny – was left with an aunt in Australia. The few items that made up my inheritance were swiftly sold by her to cover the costs of six months of courses and postage for two of my brothers and me. Then the comical thing was that my parents played truant more often than we did. They found teaching us exceedingly tedious, and bolted at the first opportunity, leaving us to self-monitor and muddle through on our own. With a few vague instructions and no supervision, it was bound to be a disaster. In fact, it was farcical because it was never going to work. Without strict discipline and supervision, only steps away the coast was beckoning seductively and away we'd flee, grabbing our flippers and lie-low in mid-flight, abandoning our studies to swim and fish. Other daily delights include picking olives or fruit, visiting friends or simply wandering the alluring hills of Spartilas or Saint Markos foraging for *xolta* and herbs.

After this home schooling, classroom and teacher missing in action catastrophe, our formal studies are given the flick. Well, except for my little brother who attends the local primary school, and later the high-school in town. At the age of twelve and a half, formal education becomes a very pleasant mere distant memory that would come back and bite me in later years, for who would have ever known that never being a school form captain, milk or ink monitor could have such a negative impact on my life? At this stage, my chances of success are looking grim. In the meantime, life becomes my instructor.

As for Katerina, primary level is as far as her parents will allow her to go. In this way we two are a pigeon pair. Perhaps her destiny will be to marry a handsome local farmer or fisherman and assist him in his business. God only knows what my future will be. There was, for one brief moment, a time when I quite fancied a good-looking goat boy from the hills. But that wasn't going to work. When he wasn't busy herding sheep and goats, he was preoccupied with rounding up tourist boys in summer. With Katerina and I having so much free time on our hands, we pass the long hours of our days also chatting about life. Our conversations cover all sorts of fascinating topics, including scandals in the hamlet and more broadly, local villages. It's riveting stuff! Sitting under the olive trees today, we are talking about food, and it's my turn to talk on the topic. I'm relishing the opportunity to have a good whinge about my experiences with beans and lentils.

In the Homeric epic, Odysseus may have dined on Corfu delights, but the vicissitudes of our financial situation deny us such culinary pleasures. And I let Katerina know this.

'I wonder, as Moses stood on Mt Sinai, did God in all his

wisdom ever say to him, people are either bean and lentil enthusiasts, or they're not. Let those who aren't learn to love and appreciate them. But Moses in his rush to get God's words onto his tablet, and go back down that treacherous mountain, gave the 11th Commandment the flick. It was too hard for poor Moses. As a result, he didn't include it with the other Commandments as he paused for a nice cup of tea with the Greek Orthodox monks on Mount Sinai before delivering God's commandments to his people.'

Scratching her chin, Katerina laughs and enquires, 'Are there Greek Orthodox monks at Saint Catherine's Monastery in Egypt?'

'Well, Katerina, yes there are, but perhaps not when Moses was alive. This is a reconstruction of the Biblical story, and it's all for your benefit.'

Katerina throws her head back, and laughs at me teasingly as I reignite my story. 'Well, as novice overseas travellers, we were experiencing how expensive food in Europe is. Out of desperation in France, my mother squeezes tins of lentils, baked beans and corn into the back of our two cars with the rest of our belongings. We children, not used to this type of tinned tucker, don't adapt well to what we call Mum's, "Frugal food rations."

'A few days later, and still on this unpalatable diet, Dad plucks up courage after a few too many French wines, and refers to them as, "Your mother's frigging frugal food rations." When my father realises his comment isn't lightening the severity of our diabolical food situation, or stopping the rumblings of rebellion in the ranks, he tries to make light of the situation by saying:

"Hip, hip hooray kids, let's hope these lentils and beans keep our nasty tape worms at bay."

'But you see, Katerina, no one laughs because the situation

is serious. Deadly serious! These diabolical food circumstances are caused by a reaction to the fall in an invisible contraption called currency exchange rates. These temperamental phenomena thrust us head-long into the most fundamental realities of living outside Australia. We must cope with the trials and tribulations of the ducking and diving Australian dollar. It's like trying to work out which way a grumpy kangaroo will jump when cornered. Fat chance of finding that out until the kangaroo has bolted.'

Katerina holds up her arm, signalling me to pause. 'I've never seen a kangaroo. What are they like?'

Waving a belligerent fly from my face, I remind her, 'Yes, you have, I showed you one in a picture book the other day.' Suddenly Katerina remembers, and nods her head.

'Well, that's exactly what they look like in real life. Now, stop interrupting me. The constraints of my father's le petite fixed Australian Army pension and the moods of the world's money markets, direct and to a large degree, determine our quality of life from then on. My mother loading her car up with high octane food on our way through Europe goes down like a lead balloon. I mean, who can blame us? We've gone from dining like King Louis so and so on Cordon bleu in Paris, to Cordon yuck at Mont Blanc.'

Katerina giggles and I smile as I continue to tell my story. 'With dodgy le toot apparatus across France, defecation needs explanation as my stomach turns from kryptonite, to dolomite. By the time we make it over the Alps into Italy, I have excrementa like sloppy cementa!'

Katerina stops me for a moment and touches my hand. 'Do you mean toilet problems?'

I laugh, 'Yes! Big toilet problems. The closed and confined spaces of crammed bodies in a car don't help either. My woes with lentils and beans don't desist once we've made our way across the stunning northern frontiers via Brindisi, into Greece. On Corfu, your Aunty Helen, our dearly beloved landlady, bubbling with excitement at our arrival, visits us with baskets full of yummy delights. This was her way of a special welcome to the island. I'm thrilled to see that among her gourmet treats there's not a bean or loo, loo lentil in sight. It's heaven. Hallelujah. A legume free zone for the first time in what seems like a lifetime.'

Katerina's face lights up. 'Yes, my aunty is a very good cook. Her *baklava* is out of this world, and she is a magician with *moussaka.*'

'Yes, I know. All our waistlines have expanded because of their deliciousness. But I have to tell you, I was over my mother divvying out lousy lentils, and cold canned beans with a malfunctioning can opener, and a bent teaspoon from the back of her car. Yes, and all the while as we shuffled from foot-to-foot, ankle deep in the snow on random side roads across Europe, it wasn't the grand tour of a lifetime we'd anticipated before leaving Australia. Even tinned chilli beans couldn't warm the cold cockles of this kid's heart.'

I pause as we watch Yannis, the mule cart man, returning from town with a load of planks and boxes on the back of his squeaky wagon. We wave and cry '*Yassoo*' then I continue to grumble. 'In fact, Katerina, I tell Helen I'd be happy never to spy or sigh over another lentil or bean again so long as I live, so help me God. But I'm in for a shock. Expecting a sympathetic ear from your aunty, especially after I told her exaggerated stories about the horrors of eating terrible tinned tucker on our long, winding, not to mention, windy trip through Europe. She looks at me oddly, the way she does when she's confused. I wondered about this, and then ask her, "What do you think about lentils and beans, Miss Helen? Do you like them?" This is a deep and probing philosophical question for two virtual strangers to be contemplating so early in the morning, but I think, no harm in asking. Such intimacies between virtual strangers are not unheard of. Your aunty turns to me and says:' "*Fakas, fakas, fakas* and *fasolia*?"

Katerina interrupts, saying, 'Yes, *fakas* and *fasolia*, that's what everyone calls them.'

'Ah, but, Katerina, you don't understand. I didn't know that. Then your Aunty Helen throws a pinch of icing sugar into the air as if to thank the Gods for their sweet bounty, and repeats herself saying,' "Yes, *fakas* and *fasolia*, I like them very much."

'I wonder if my hearing is playing up? *Fakas, fakas, fakas* and *fasolia*? And Helen likes them? Back then, Katerina, I had no idea what the English 'F…' word meant. I still don't, really. But I knew the 'F…' word was a doozy because back in Melbourne, my mother organised an extremely lucrative swear jar, and it was always the 'F…' word that derived the biggest profits. It was quite the money spinner. When Helen said: '*Fakas* and *fasolia*,' 'I was shocked because I thought she was swearing. I'm wondering … what does she mean? Where's the famous Delphic Oracle? As I reflect on her reply and consider Helen's radiant face, I think I must be wrong? It must be some kind of misunderstanding. Perhaps something's got lost in translation as can happen when dissecting, as best one can, a yet to be learnt language without an interpreter? But then I wonder, is there a chance that even after her kindness to us, she's being rude? I like your Aunty Helen, so I doubt she's deliberately being offensive. Then I say to Helen, "Are you telling me that '*fakas*' means lentils in Greek?" I hope to God that that's what it means and that I'm not offending her. Her smile expands, and she replies: "*Fakas* means lentils, what do you think it means?"

'Helen bursts into laughter. Then, I do too. Talk about bad

timing. We are still on the touchy subject when my mum strides into the kitchen, and this proves disastrous. Your aunty, as if invoking wisdom from her pantheon of gods, which I reckon she nonchalantly keeps on standby tucked up one of her sleeves, goes on about how important lentils and beans are in Greek cuisine saying: "Beans and lentils, we Greeks live on them most of the year, and always as part of fasting."

'Katerina, I think to myself, how silly of me. I should have guessed. Then your Aunty Helen continues: "But also, because meat is very expensive on Corfu, *po, po, po!* Legumes are protein packed; they make us strong."

'To illustrate this, your aunt makes a theatrical gymnastic flexing pose with the muscles on her arm. Holy Moly! Beans, glorious beans, and a labyrinth of legumes thrown in for good measure. Here we go again. I hoped she wouldn't have a pile of rotten old *'fakas'* recipes to share with my mum. But, oh, no! I'm wrong. The pair of them conspire and come up with many weird, new and exotic concoctions for *'fakas'* and *'fasolia'*, which results in collective exclamations of horror from us kids. My mother and your Aunty Helen are like two crazy alchemists at the hearth cooking up an enormous catastrophe. Then your aunt goes on ….:' "It's the lentils' powerful punch," she raves, "that makes them so healthy."

'Truly, Katerina, it's a disturbing sight for us kids to behold as the two of them carry on like doves cooing over their weird recipes. Then days later, we capture on gentle early morning breezes the alluring fragrances of lemon, gardenia blossoms, strong Greek coffee and ouzo as we make our way through the chaos of vendors in Corfu town's markets beneath the *Neo Citadel*. Well, you wouldn't credit it. It's ditto for disaster. Well, for me anyway. Before our eyes, a world of lentils spreads out before us in large hand-woven baskets. Time has literally split peas and legumes like the atom, and they've appeared in every imaginable colour, and size under the rainbow. Red lentils, black, pink, green, yellow and brown ones everywhere. It's as if I'm stuck in a legume horror movie, or a bean time warp that's unending, ah!

'My mother's even suggesting we grind dry lentils and make flour. It's getting worse by the minute. Are we being taken over by Greek lentils? Oh, did I mention then there are the falafel chick pea recipe suggestions she discusses over too many vinos at her friend Hilary's place. Recipe suggestions? More like indigestions. It's one hell of a bean, chick pea and lentil debacle.

'Fired up by all this, Mum's hooked, reckoning she's got her finger on the pulsating pulses pulse. From then on, our family sits down to beans, chick peas and lashings of lentils almost every other night, with leftovers lingering around for lunch the next day. Once again, against a barrage of complaints, Mum's response is: "Stop whining, kids, you don't know how bloody lucky you are. It's not like we live in France, so don't expect *foie gras* and *crème brulee* ... cos it's not happening!"

'Mum's right, we don't live in France, and given our precarious financial situation, at least we have food on the table.'

'Mum goes on, "Oh, for heaven sakes, kids, get a grip. Lentils and beans have been around since the Mesolithic, and the pulsating Palaeolithic periods dating back over 13,000 years. Even old Hippocrates was hip about eating lentils. You're lucky we're not tucking into snails and lizards. That's what the Greeks had to eat during the war years, and if things get much worse, God knows. So, stop with the wise cracks."

'Mum lets her words suspend between us like a menacing threat. Katerina, how does she know this, I mean about the

Mesolithic and Paleolithic periods? But then, mums know everything, don't they?'

Katerina smiles and nods wistfully in surrendered agreement. 'They think they know everything. But they don't.'

I smile in support of her validating reply. 'Then, Katerina, my mum goes on ..., "So, if you don't like it, lump it!" 'Katerina, she said "lump it". I couldn't have put it better myself! Often in the days that followed, I stood next to Mum helping her at the kitchen sink. She reminds me of what your aunt said about Greece during the war. Up to nearly half a million Greeks starved to death in Athens under the German occupation. God only knows how many more died in other parts of the mainland, or on the islands. I let her remarks meander, heartbreakingly unanswered between us. According to Helen, the reason some people survived and others didn't is because of "Lentil and bean soup."

'Then she trumpets with patriotic vigour, her fist flying in the air, "Lentils and beans saved Greece! Lentils and beans saved Greece!" You can picture her, can't you?'

Katerina nods and laughs as I continue. 'At home it's become a kind of mantra, with Mum determined to carve your aunt's words into my memory forever. I have to repeat her words in Greek, "*Fakas kai fasolia essose tin Ellatha!*" This is a kind of pulsating Greek language, and history hell for me. But it's a lesson I'll never forget. You know, Katerina, I may complain about our diet here in Greece but in truth I've learnt to weigh the merits of the humble, yet bountiful bean and realise it can make us healthy and lean. Also, the poor, if somewhat neglected lentil is its gentle comrade. Now I have to surrender to them both, asking them for forgiveness as I am grateful for their treasure trove of bright colours, versatility and flavour. And for the fashioning of their very existence as my thoughts of them are bound to this fragrant land of yours that thankfully yielded them. I have to admit that this simple, repetitious diet of ours with its harvests of lentils, beans, bread and tomatoes, keeps starvation from our door. These humble foods continue to save my family, and yours, as they did the Greeks during the war.'

Katerina, agrees and I pull a five drachmae coin from my pocket and challenge her to a race to Hoppy's *kafeneio* in the village.

'Come on, let's get some sesame and honey sticks or *halva*. It will take our minds off boring *fakia* and *fasolia* for a while.'

A huge smile spreads across her face showing rows of perfect teeth. 'What a great idea! But I can't go in – my mum won't let me. But you go in. I'll wait by the shrine near the curve in the road and pretend I'm praying until you return. You know what? I think we're going to be friends forever.'

I nod enthusiastically. 'I think so too.'

Chapter 9

I Have a Little Lamb, and My Name Isn't Mary

Glorious light, ambient from an Indian summer, emits golden rays that land on our neighbour Lefteri's shoulders as he approaches my father. Dad's sitting under the flickering, gently dappled light of the olive trees in our garden. He's enjoying his first cool *retsina, a white wine that is stored in pungent pine barrels*, of the day. Lefteri's approach is laborious as if he's wearing reinforced marble shoes. His tenuous steps test the waters.

He calls out, '*Yassoo, Kirios*, I have a gift for your daughter. Can I give her this lamb?'

He's hesitant to get too close, so slows his steps but he knows he must be brave and proceed if he's to fulfil his objective. Dad looks up irritated but is curious.

'Can I please give this to her?' he asks again, this time with greater urgency, lifting the lamb into the air, tilting it toward the sun like a snow-white trophy.

Dad's surprised to see the man, let alone watch him offering a lamb as a gift. Our encounters of late with Lefteri have not been pleasant. Dad eyes him with suspicion and a poorly suppressed dislike. None of us has forgiven him for shooting my dog Prince a few months earlier, and the mystery of who poisoned Athena, my other dog hasn't been solved. Rightly or wrongly, we suspect Lefteri. And as Athena had given birth to six pups the day before she died, all her pups followed suit dying within days. Their demise was a slow and painful one because we were unable to care for them. They effectively starved to death. Powerless and heartbroken by the pup's rejection of the tinned milk, the only milk available to nurture them, I'd turn away from Lefteri whenever I saw him around the hamlet or village. Yet, Dad is polite to the man. He breaks the iciness in the air by asking him a question, but hopes he'll continue on his way and take his lamb with him.

'Ah, Lefteri, how are you?'

'I'm good, good.'

'Why the gift?'

'*Kirios*, it's for your daughter. This is a better pet for her instead of dogs.'

Dad's not impressed. 'Where can she keep a lamb and how can we feed it? We don't have a large plot here, or even a proper shelter? As a neighbour, you know this more than anyone.'

Lefteri feeling courageous ventures a solution, saying enthusiastically, 'She can keep her lamb in our barn. It can go to the *livathi* with my sheep every day. But it will be her lamb to keep, if she wants it.' Lefteri needn't say much. His sad eyes express what his words perhaps could not.

After some reflection, Dad pauses and calls me. Seeing Lefteri in the garden, I keep Patch, our new dog inside. He's not getting his hands on her.

Lefteri stands with a small shivering lamb in his arms. He holds the tiny soft white parcel out to me. Is it a sacrificial lamb, I wonder? With Lefteri's killing record, I wouldn't be surprised.

Dad's eyes worryingly search mine, then he says, 'Lefteri has something he wants to say to you.'

I stand leaning on my father's shoulder, guarding myself from a man I do not trust, waiting for the farmer to speak.

'*Perdi mou*, this is a gift for you. I'm sorry for your loss, but we Greeks have known terrible wars and extreme poverty. For us, even simple village bread has the power to become a God when you are starving. Its humble, bland taste will linger forever on your lips more delicious and precious than anything in the world when starvation hovers unrelentingly at your door. When dogs kill our chickens, we must decide what is best for our family – hunger, or the life of a dog? You are a child and have never known the horrors of hunger, perhaps one day you will understand. Of course, I hope not, but who can tell what the future holds for any of us? It's all in the hands of the gods.'

As he looks to the heavens I must concede, Lefteri has a point. I haven't suffered the things he and his family have suffered. What do I know of these horrendous events? To him I must seem like a child living in a gilded gold cage. I mourn my precious dogs but what choices do we have when human lives are at risk? What would I do under the same confronting circumstances?

I smile a weak smile and think this tiny lamb probably has a better chance of survival with me. Even so, as he holds the lamb out to me, I'm reluctant to take the animal, remembering what Mum says about Greeks, or anyone bearing gifts. But I relent. I take the soft tiny lamb gently into my arms, putting one arm under its body, my other arm under its head to hold it steady. I look into Lefteri's eyes. He's right. Even though I'm not convinced it was my dog that killed his chickens, and I don't know who's poisoned my other dog. But my heart has softened, it's an incredibly generous gift, and I believe he genuinely wants to make amends. With a nod from Dad, some of the mistrust and dislike I have for the man evaporates in the morning sun. I have a little lamb and my name isn't Mary.

My lamb is a strange pet to have with his springbok prance

and bounce. But it's his pre-mature escalation into adulthood which contributes to his cuteness eventually fading in my eyes. As he's grown, he's lost his soft goat like cashmere cuddliness. Consequently, I need a long-term plan for my lamb now he's a sheep. After much thought, I decide to let Lefteri and his wife Frosso look after him. I make one condition with them. My condition is that they can have him back so long as he doesn't end up in Theo, the local butcher's shop as lamb chops or souvlaki. After all, Greek lamb is expensive per kilogram, and I don't want anyone profiting from his demise. They agree, promising to keep their word. This time I trust Lefteri.

My now not so little lamb makes his claim to fame as an absolute stud. He's become a prized ram instead of lamb chops. Well, we'd all been rooting for him. After all, the reality is I can hardly take my heavily fleece-laden sheep now he's matured for adventurous walks to town or out to restaurants for company. Or linger with him in the agora when the shadows have disappeared in the long, stretched out summer afternoons without people thinking me eccentric for, unlike Patch, he can't sit on my lap and have cuddles. He isn't even allowed in the house.

Dad, chuckling loudly, reckons, 'If he comes inside, he'll end up the laughingstock of the local Greek flock and his peers would 'baa' him.'

Magically, what my lamb does is mend the rift between Lefteri and myself, and as a result, helps heal my mourning heart. Lefteri hadn't been kind to my dearly departed and much-loved Corfu dogs, but my sheep, well he's well ahead of the local flock, and going to live a long and happy life. I'm extremely grateful for this.

Chapter 10

Serenading Chickens

In humble kitchen hearths, locals spark olive wood into ignition with tired but patient breath. As the fire returns its reward of crackling warmth, bodies begin to thaw and glow around the firelight. Rituals such as this herald the end of another calm cold autumn day. Smoke rises and merges as a pale veil sitting at head height. It lounges in the quiet dreamy air where the fragrant scent of orange and lemon blossoms erupt and interlock merging into the smoke's stretched white ethereal fingers. It makes my head heady as the lessening sun sets swiftly in the afternoon's early darkening. Glum but still stout skeletal frames of ancient grape wines have nodded off for winter. They cling to rickety supports now stripped bare of their drapes of summer's malachite leaves. These brown and yellow torn remnants endure on the ground decomposing slowly, stacked from a day-old storm like funeral pyres, yielding as they squish beneath damp leather soles.

It's here in the busy hamlet close to our villa where my insights into the animal kingdom beyond our rickety front gate are so richly flavoured. Most days in the late afternoons, I pass through the hamlet on my way home saying *'yassoo'*, to any dark but familiar bent figures as they move past me in the fading cool light, shapes stiff from the cold of working close to the damp earth all day; wood crushes others under kindling, weighing down hard on their forms as they dart to shelter their weary load from impending rain. They scramble with their precious cargo into barns, or pile them haphazardly beside ember-dusted hearths to dry before sacrificing them one by one into hungry crackling flames.

I pause in passing close by to check on my pet sheep. He's been elevated to honorary ram status for his amorous endeavours. Locals pat his rear and remark with relaxed laughter, "He's very strong … a real stud like all Greek men." I laugh at their boasting while they continue to brag assuredly and conceitedly in return.

There in my lamb's barn in his golden bed of hay, Lefteri leaves him secure, dry and well fed, my lamb's mouth still moving even after a long day of devouring plucky shoots that pop through the rich earth on the moist *livarthi, fields,* the place where the daffodils bloom in abundance and sway in the breeze in the springtime. In his barn his mouth draws in the dry yellow stalks of hay around him like a weaver pulling wool from a pile. Eventually these golden-brown strips disappear in compressed lines into his mouth. This chewing motion creates a calming rhythmic settling feeling in Lefteri's humble barn. Each day I see my sheep before I go to bed to make sure he's not been kidnapped, and made into souvlakis or stew, for it's the Greeks who often remind me that the earth lusts for the flesh and bones of all living things – especially the Corfiots with their humble diet. They have long considered the flesh of sheep to be particularly delicious, as do we. Still, while I may yearn for meat, I cannot sacrifice him.

At this time of the day in the hamlet, it's not only my lamb's bedtime, it's also bed time for the local chickens. There are three different families living in humble dwellings near one another, and they release their chickens during the day to run wild and free. Because of this practice, it lends itself to the need for an effective system ensuring the right chickens return to the right coop each night. No sleep overs or hens' nights for these local chicks or there'll be accusations and feathers flying.

To overcome misunderstandings about chicken ownership, the local women have come up with an ingenious singing system. Around 5 pm, give or take a few dramas around the village in the winter, or later in the summer, each female elder stand outside their stable poised to perform. In full voice they execute their own unique, rhythmic chicken song and sing home their chickens for the night.

Frosso flings a few tempting pellets for her pullets and performs a rhythmic Tango tune. Her passion for Latin music has never waned. On hot summer evenings as the fireflies' flirt and dart vigorously in the night air, she dances with her husband Lefteri, executing old Tango moves with unbridled wildness on their earthen porch. What she represses the rest of the time beneath the drudgery and hardship of stifling day-to-day village life is released like steam from a pressure cooker on those clammy nights. Tango music played from her old wind-up gramophone is reminiscent of the war days, when she fell in love with her Lefteri, and when they parted it was excruciating because she didn't know whether she'd see him again. Here in the hamlet at dusk, she clings to her idealised notions of love, and romance as one might preserve wilted roses pressed into a precious book for safe keeping; dried petals crumbled from being kept too long from a past love, splayed now and compacted, nearing a form of fine pink dust taken to the very edge of extinction. A Tango, an enduring appeal to the gods to relive the romance again, resurrect the petals of the roses – a chance to turn back time – her audience of chickens oblivious to her deep, cavernous yearning. She clears her voice and fires out, *"Chicha mou, chicha mou, chicha mou"* then adds a sad, *"Cha, cha, cha"* at the end. She sings her song until all her chickens return to their coop.

Then Maria from next door arrives. She varies her pitch from Frosso, crying out "*Kotta mou, kotta mou, kotta mou,*" elongating her words to their fullest extent like a piece of thick overstretched elastic. And in so doing, conducts herself like an Italian soprano aria prima donna. With her substantial breasts protruding, she stands as if expecting an encore, swinging her plump arms back and forth as she sprinkles day old crumbs on the damp earth. Red florals in her small bandana are a sharp contrast against her premature entry into the black garbed world of widowhood. The flaming red florals in her bandana are a hint at her Venetian heritage from centuries past. She boasts, "This song makes my blood run hot and steamy!" Releasing a white toothed giggle, her wild eyes blaze, imitating green embers hissing in a crackling fire. In years to come, I will recall what the *yiayias* told me about the gypsy boys, and wonder, is she one of their ancestors?

Elefteria arrives in the clearing and won't be outdone. Maria, upon seeing her, thrusts her chin dramatically in the air and departs in a huff as Elefteria defiantly sings, "*Ella mou, ella mou, ella mou, ne, ne, ne*" mimicking the Beatles, "She loves you yeah, yeah, yeah,". It's her jaunty chicken pop song. More laid-back, Elefteria is the grooviest of her performing peers, and while the local women tease her for not being more of a classical artist, not sticking to the old traditional favourites, Elefteria doesn't care. She's a rebel. But somehow, irrespective of their personal tastes in music, as if by magic, the chickens know which song is their call home for supper and roosting. Miraculously they always return to the right barn.

Who says Greek chickens are stupid? Not me. They might have sensitive dicky chicken tickers from time to time, are prone to heart attacks – well, according to my father – but they're not stupid. Tucking away their troubles for the day, they snuggle into cosy coops, closing their eyes as the day that was becomes a mere sweet memory.

Chapter 11

Bread and Tomatoes

I deliver my daily mantra. 'Mum, I'm starved. What's for lunch?'

Her automatic response, 'Bread and tomatoes.'

'Oh no! We had that yesterday and the day before. Isn't there something else?'

'Nope, now kiddo ... you don't know how bloody lucky you are!' comes her swift reply and she says it all the time. It's as if she is going back in time to some event that I know nothing of. And that look of hers ... is she riling me with her sarcastic expression and tone? But that's just like Mum, always reminding me of how lucky I am. But luck had little to do with being fortunate to get a meal out of bread and tomatoes. It turned out Mum had more secrets shoved inside her than there are fish roe on a SAYO bickie at a cocktail party. But I have jumped ahead of myself.

But she's got my point. Every day when this food is served, I make a point of rubbing it in. It's not all bad. The truth is I love bread and tomatoes but I'm not telling her. I want her to suffer, make her feel it's her fault that we eat this monotonous Greek peasant food. Yet, the bread from our local baker is lip-smacking good. I can't deny that. His modest shop sits on the sloped, white-washed narrow street in Pyrgi village. Wonderful smells emanate from his premises. That wide-mouthed oven of old Spiro's bakes bread six days a week, and on big days, the villagers' circular trays of roasts get shoved in. What emerges ... heaven on a plate. But our usual lunch, chunks of crusty white bread; soft in the centre served with slices of organic tomato and garlic, it's not so bad, drizzled like it is with thick green olive oil, served simply with a pinch of salt and a crack from that old brass pepper grinder Dad picked up in some artisans' shop down a noisy lane in town. This too is what heaven is, but why tell Mum?

With bread, garlic, olive oil and tomatoes eaten, I head to Katerina's place. Today we're invited to watch an execution. The pig we've been feeding for months is going to be slaughtered. After the execution, his remains will be shared among Katerina's extended family. The two of us loiter anxiously near the well waiting for the carnage to begin.

Soon others join us in the clearing near the well. We stand in an informal, semi-circle with Katerina and Fortis' family. They pull the heavy snorting pig into the centre of our ominous human horseshoe. I sense the poor creature knows what's about to happen. The pig's eyes widen; they appear human. I feel for the animal because there's no escape for him. The men don't have much of a plan, only a knife and a few vicious-looking sawing implements. They've arranged them on a tarpaulin which lies on the ground. Fortis volunteers to cut the pig's throat while George holds the pig steady with a rope. Fortis struggles to get his knife into the pig's throat. The animal is too strong and won't keep still.

Frustrated, Fortis screams, 'Come on, George, give me a hand, you idiot. You can see he's not staying still.'

George holds the rope fast around the pig's head to steady the beast but the pig is having none of it. Again, Fortis berates George, 'You idiot, what are you doing; can't you hold the animal? How can I cut its throat if you won't keep the animal still?'

Red-faced and puffing, George retaliates, 'If you'd hurry

and get the knife into its throat it would be over in no time. You're the idiot!'

The women laugh at the men. They think it's hilarious. Katerina and I laugh nervously too.

Without warning Katerina's mother steps forward into the centre of the group armed with a brick. Wearing wellington boots and a colourful house dress and apron, she brings the brick down on the pig's head with a thump. I'm stunned, but the pig isn't! It releases a cry that could raise the dead. It's a horrible sound; I tremble. Taken aback by the animal's reaction, the men cower away. Katerina's mother holds her nerve and steps forward again. Once again, the brick comes down on the animal's head. The pig repeats its cries of agony. Katerina and I look away in horror gripping each other's bodies. Still, even with our eyes closed, we can hear the thud of the brick on the animal's skull again and again.

Eventually, the beast stops screaming. Relief ripples through the gathering. Katerina and I open our eyes and venture to look at the animal. Its mutilated head stares unblinkingly through a pool of blood. It's arrested our eyes in a frozen clamped stare. We're shame-faced captives held in this uncomfortable holding pattern of dishonour until we find the courage to wrench our eyes away. We look down and shuffle our feet as if to bury our guilt in topsoil. Clouds shift the focus of the light's rays in the early afternoon. How many times had I told this pig when it was a piglet that I loved it? How many times?

I stand mortified while opportunistic chickens cluck and peck, looking for something upon which to feed. They scratch unapologetically around our feet, defecating in the pigs dribbling blood until they are shushed out of the way with a broom. A donkey brays in the background and long moments pass. A few thin clouds cast shadows over our deeds, allowing the muted sun to hit the pig's pinkish, eerily transparent flesh.

The men reassemble and take charge; the pig's glare doesn't deter these accomplices. The silent animal is picked up as each of the parents grabs a leg, dragging it in step onto the outstretched tarpaulin. Without pausing, they begin the task of hacking the animal's body to pieces. They divide the beast between families; squabble over its sweet meats and pulverised head. They store particular pieces to eat later while they salt the rest of the pig's flesh. This will be kept for the long winter ahead. Katerina's mother doesn't have a refrigerator. A square metal basket with a latch door hangs in their kitchen from the ceiling. It is here that nominated pieces of unsalted meat are stored to be eaten later in the day.

Returning home after the kill, I ask Mum, 'What's for dinner?'

She replies, 'Our cheque hasn't arrived from Australia. There's a mail strike in Melbourne. Looks like it will be bread and tomatoes.'

'Oh, no! Not again!' I reply intentionally, theatrically.

Around dinner time I visit Katerina. I want to make sure she's like me and recovered from the day's trauma. Her family has grouped enthusiastically in their kitchen and are about to relish the luxury of grilled pork. They invite me to join them. The smell of meat cooking over an open coal fire, flavoured with oregano and lemon juice is too much of a temptation for me. I can't refuse. Shooing a few chickens off a seat at the kitchen table, I join the family. I don't come to this feast empty-handed. I place my offering in Katerina's mother's tired brown hands. My gift: a bag of fat ripe tomatoes.

Chapter 12

A Wheel Within a Wheel, Within a Wheel

Of late, Dad's normally upbeat chirpy personality has taken a battering. These days he's writing under the olive trees in the garden, but not the intended type of typing he'd promised back in Melbourne. He's composing letters. Some letters end up on local administrators' desks and are, we believe, ignored. Administrators such as the management of Corfu's electrical company are a perfect example. The suffocating claws of island bureaucracy makes him feel as if he's being forcibly held down like the lid of a pressure cooker. Weeks go by and still his letters go unanswered.

'How can anyone attain peace of mind when one must deal with the perplexing contradictions of life,' he moans?

This is because one day he says he loves the Greeks with an undying passion, puts on his fisherman's hat and dances *hasapico* with gusto around the garden. The next, he's ready to exterminate any Greek that dares put a toe on our tiny portion of leased property.

Why? Some of our bills are outrageous, especially our electricity bills.

He acknowledges we pay more than the locals for many things but when it comes to the power bills, he's convinced we are paying more than our share of the account. Could the hamlet and half the village be connected to our meter box? The way the dice get thrown in Greece nothing is impossible. With this thought pounding in his head, he releases his frustrations over a few chilled *retsina's* with Roberta, an expat from England. Roberta tells him her electrifying story of how horrified she was upon discovering she was coughing up money for the running costs of a couple of villas, and a small factory located at the bottom of the hill near her property. Irritated by the snail pace of Greek bureaucracy, she was tempted to not pursue the issue, putting it down to the price one has to pay for the luxury of living on this alluring island, that is, until her fury eventually surpassed her frustration and generous disposition.

Determined to root out any whiff of corruption and ensure this isn't happening to us, Dad goes to the village and makes additional phone calls, comes home and writes another letter to the power company and our normally friendly Helen, the landlady. All are ignored.

'I know someone's pulled a swifty.' He rages and a dark mood settles over all of us as the family budget is squeezed of any residual drachmae.

Not one to hold back her feelings, Mum scoffs, 'Well, you fool, don't just sit there – grow some Greek *axethia, balls,* and do something about it!'

Unable to dodge her contempt for what she sees as his inaction indefinitely, he eventually rises to the challenge as a brave attempt to defend our consumer rights overwhelms him. With the threat of legal action, Helen confesses she may have made a slight error.

'Might have ... just might have made a slight error,' roars Dad, his cheeks turning a very unpleasant beetroot colour, not dissimilar to a baboon's bottom. 'The woman has all her villas electrical wiring connected to ours and we've been copping her bills ever since we moved in and she didn't know!'

In the wider scheme of things, it's also ill-advised to

challenge and get on the wrong side of one's landlady when one has no clear rights, well, at least in writing. Or, at the very least, arranged alternative accommodation just in case we are tossed out. We soon discover part of the problem is in the rush to construct villas for the rapidly evolving tourist industry, Papadopoulos's policies which provide generous loans for various tourist developments and projects has led to all sorts of dodgy electrical setups done on the run; and it seems often to the disadvantage of naive foreigners like us. But isn't it illegal to have one meter box for multiple rental properties? Didn't we know it was part of the rental deal to pay our landlady's share of the bill? Blah, blah, blah!

Any euphoria my father feels winning the case without having to go to court is short lived. It may have put him in the good books with Mum, and improved the household budget but it makes us suspicious of any further bills we receive, and Helen. Soon after, we discover her cousin works for the electrical company and has influence in the accounts department.

Roberta reckons, 'Might be worth your while in future checking any office workers wrists for Rolexes … and suss out if there's any Mercedes parked out the back of their office.'

She has a point.

As Dad hasn't decided on the focus of his novel, he daily throws ideas into the air, all of which seem to miss the mark and splatter on the ground. He suggests a book for expats offering them a gentle guide to the pitfalls and highlights of living in Greece. He wishes someone had written a handbook on the subject before we'd arrived; it would have saved us a lot of time, heartache and money. Then the next day he thinks why bother with this type of a book. After all, what's the point: not only is it too late for us, but he's constantly being disturbed because someone always wants something. Or Mum's in one of her anti-Greek-and-everything-else moods and so it's his turn to listen to her gripes which can go on for quite a while. If only she would shut up ... then perhaps he could settle on a plot and nestle in his nice shady place in the garden to compose in peace.

'Lock yourself in a bloody monastery then if you're not happy. I can see you perched up there on Mount Pantocrator producing prose with the priests,' yells Mum in legitimate frustration.

But each day brings new temptations on lower ground. A friend offers another enticing book for him to read; someone drops in to while away the hours under the olive trees until it's time to say goodnight and collapse corpse-like into bed. As an inexperienced writer, he wonders is it better to read a new book and chat with friends for inspiration for his book, or sit and stare at the typewriter in a monk's cell waiting to be divinely inspired? His mind needs order. Things need to be compartmentalised. Let women deal with multiple concepts, their minds are designed to be all over the place. And it works well for them too with their ability to think a million different thoughts at one time while simultaneously multitasking. A man's brain is like a fragile system that can easily be set off course with its need for balance and order. The problem according to Mum: 'Your father never worries about anything of significance ... he's off with the fairies, trying to find his inner child. His mind is a landscape of places in which he happily vanishes to escape us. I wish he'd hurry up and find himself. If he's got artist's block, I reckon a good mix of prunes or Falariki figs will fix him.'

From electricity bills to costs of living problems Dad's erased any ideas of being self-sufficient. Likely it was the screaming pig and brick incident that turned him off the idea of living off the land. He may not have seen the incident first hand, but it was the haunting sound of that screaming pig echoing through the olive groves that did it for him. Or perhaps it was the reality of our situation. We don't have enough land, like Mum said. But it's more likely to be the dwindling drachmae that's anchored him under the trees in the garden and increasing inflation. It's not cheap setting up a small holding and we no longer have much spare cash.

But life isn't all bad. Mum has moments of being happy for a while, luxuriating publicly anyway, in the hollow title of being a novelist's wife. And me, well, I'm finding my feet in this new land, beginning to learn the language and mix more with the locals than possibly my own family. But when I'm at home, it's reassuring hearing the tap of the old typewriter. I liken it to another heartbeat and the action needed to deliver a hard copy from the Gods of creation into our spheric world in the form of a successful book.

For companionship Dad has the usual suspects – his glass accompanied by a pottery carafe topped up with local wine, or whatever alcoholic brew is on special at Hoppy's taverna – a crumbled pack of Pallas cigarettes, and a neat pile of airmail writing paper sitting securely beneath the weight of a bleached fist-sized pebble. This pebble has been saved from the waves that lap the edges of the Ionian Sea lying just across the road. The pebble is placed there to stop the afternoon *Maestro* from sending his lightweight paper flying, flapping into the air, then all over the garden. Yes, the marvellous *Maestro*. That cool miraculous little jolly wonder with which the Greek gods have blessed the islanders with through June, July and August. As temperatures sky-rocket above one hundred, its relieving breath of coolness makes our lives worth living.

The heat bothers Dad and I'm not fond of the very hot days either. As a result, his place under the dancing dappled shade of the ancient olive trees is like a mini–*Maestro* Mecca for us. It captures the meandering breeze and is the perfect spot to jot. You will find him here almost every day since he's refocused his attention on writing.

Having recovered from the electrical company ordeal, today he's merrily typing letters home to Australia as a cigarette hangs diligently from his mouth, ash about to collapse off its end. His eyes squint as he sucks air through the sides of his mouth. His letters are filled with rave reviews to family and friends about Greek island life – nothing about our diabolical financial situation, or the ever-present threat of political reprisals with political informers everywhere. No one trusts anyone. Well, except Dad who, with a pal on holidays from Australia, grabs some fishing gear and the long wooden oars belonging to our boat Hercules, and at speed the pair row out deep into the lapping turquoise waters surrounding Pyrgi Bay. Then Dad lets fly vigorous discussions about our complex situation, all under the guise of an innocent fishing trip, Mum lifting her wooden spoon into the air as they leave.

'You'll get caught talking politics, mark my words.'

But the men just laugh.

We notice more and more American battle and nuclear submarines visit the island as anger rages beneath the surface about American leaders meddling in Greek politics, and as tensions increase in the Middle East and between Greece and Turkey. Nor in his letters home does he mention Mum's increasingly unsettling moods. His letters are inaccurately whisked with sunny salutations. Then, when he's done letter writing as a form of distraction, he might ponder various themes for his book again. But then, perhaps not. He's just as likely to be switched off with eyes half closed, detached from his life within his wheel, within a wheel; imbued in a mysterious labyrinth, especially when we kids have buzzed off for the day.

Some days Mum might make herself scarce too, out from her simmering control centre, giving the Elizabeth David, or Chrissi Paradissis's Greek cookery books a deep breather. These have become her constant cooking companions since we've moved here. At least once a week she will take a break from the torturous task of making meals out of very little. It's an opportunity to rest her housework weary hands and dress up a bit. Perhaps she's headed to Corfu town on a mission to find a mysterious ingredient, pulled by the wafting of alluring spices, and restock our humble shelves. She'll while away the morning trailing along narrow laneways and charm fruiterers, fishmongers or butchers, haggling while fluttering her eyelashes and laughing with delight then leisurely browse the upmarket clothes shops as if she has pockets of money. Reaching for the tempting fabrics, her fingers lovingly cascade over them as if travelling gently through dreamy recollections of calmer waters. Then she'll let them drop dismissively from her touch as if they are not good enough as reality takes hold while the shop assistants look on disappointedly. Or she'll visit her expat chums in the tiered olive groves of the hills around Saint Marcos, perhaps go further north to Nissaki for a bit of a local catch-up over a few rough reds while enjoying the view from the restaurant by the bay. She's a lady who sometimes lunches when the tide comes in even if only on a bowl of beans in tomato sauce or x*olta, greens* drizzled in olive oil and lemon juice.

On days like today, Dad can be a disengaging figure, off in his own inner world languishing in la-la-land, sitting on his bleached foldup canvas chair, occasionally pausing from tapping as if waiting for seeds of inspiration to arrive out of the ether to jolt him into writing again. Or, while they are around, he's enjoying the graceful darting of the swallows above his head. Speaking of swallows, we'd noticed shortly after we'd moved into our humble villa by the sea, and each year following in early spring, that a graceful pair of these beautiful birds had also taken the brave step of moving into our villa, compliments of the house, for the summer. They'd taken up a spot in the corner above our front door, under the ceiling, suspended in the air, creating a curved mantle of blistered mud on the veranda. Anna, our neighbour, noticed them too and said with a huge smile, "*Ta helidonia enai poli kali teehee, the swallows are very good luck*. Your summer will be a happy one."

Based on this auspicious omen, we'd never deliberately disturb them. But with the comings, goings and daily dramas of our noisy unconventional family, it's a wonder they hadn't given up, spat the dummy and flown away ages ago. As evening slowly creeps in at the end of the day, our new residents sit in anticipation for that light switch moment, that delicious magical time when the front light goes on and illuminates the porch. Primed and ready for action, our winged pilgrims gorge to their hearts' content on the insects that flutter in fascination, drawn into the mesmerising white glow. Soon they are even more restless, and our tenacious two-winged tenants disappear each night, off to Corfu town to fly in their immense mansion in the sky. They swirl the town like panopticon spectators circling crumbling Venetian town houses beneath their wings with ease, along with flocks of other chirping swallows, all enjoying their aerial advantage over our world. Then back they fly to their nest until the eggs arrive. Each morning we are handsomely rewarded with more than their flittering beauty and melodious songs.

Dad, doing a convincing job of being excessively dramatic, carries on crying out as if mortified, 'Throw those swallows into the gallows! They deserve to die or be cooked into a yummy pie.'

We kids shout in protest at the very idea even though we know he's only joking. He stands like a Hugh Heffner look-alike in his bedroom attire a safe distance from their moist calling cards. Ironically, he's as fond of those birds as we are.

'Stiff bloody bickies if the only reason you got out of bed in the morning is to see if your luck has changed and you find this sloppy green lot on your doorstep. If you don't watch your step, you'll end up arse over tit on their multi-coloured greeting cards of slippery shit,' and, pretending to look indignant, 'I don't know … such gratitude daily deposited on our doorstep. Geeze, you take your life into your hands living in this place.'

Hearing the commotion outside, Mum joins us on the pooh-spattered porch and grumbles, 'Come on, kids, clean it up!' Then a debate ensues about whose turn it is to throw a bucket of warm soapy water over the terrazzo porch. Who will have the unpleasant task of quickly pushing the old straw broom back and forth, lifting their messy blessings from above and scattered sand dragged in from the beach?

When the chicks arrive, there are more blessings. As the chicks grow, they pop their heads out of the sides of their nest. With shiny eyes and open beaks, they peer at us below. Then all too soon, they take flight, encouraged by their chirping parents sitting nearby in the protective olive trees. As the little ones gain confidence, they swoop cheekily overhead.

Spying the daily delivery on the ground I think, what a blessed mess. Now when we argue about who's going to clean up their droppings, we say 'Me, me, please, Mum, please let it be me! It's my turn!'

Then suddenly, without saying 'Goodbye', the swallows are gone until next spring.

Chapter 13

Judas at their Table

Our villa rattles and groans. Shutters break free from their latches, cracking like whips against grey walls. Roof tiles shift as the night storm weighs upon our home. Frightened by the intensity of the gale, I snuggle in bed beneath my blankets. A branch taps repeatedly at my window. Its eerie appearance resembles the long arthritic finger of a timeworn witch. From the light of crashing thunderbolts, sheltering on my windowsill sits a *koukouviya, owl*. I spring from under the blankets to retrieve it from the storm. Flinging wide the window, a mighty gust blows the bird fluttering onto my dressing table. There it sits blinking; trembling.

Closing the window, I realise what I have done. I have let in a *koukouviya*. According to the villagers on Corfu, someone dies when a *koukouviya* enters a home. Why, I curse, are the Greeks so superstitious? The bird continues to perch on my dressing table, blinking. As the storm rages, I gradually sink into a fitful sleep.

A long ray of sunshine falls across my face, warming my cheek like the touch of a gentle hushed kiss. I open my eyes and recall the shivering wide-eyed bird. I look across the room; there is the bird. It's still wide-eyed and shivering on my dressing table. Trying not to frighten it, I get out of bed and pick it up. Flinging open the window, I discharge it from its overnight shelter. It ascends into a clear blue-sky hooting as it departs.

At breakfast, the news breaks that a life has been stolen in the night. Our neighbour's *yiayia* died. Miraculously, her transparent soul winged its way through the stormy night to the mysterious sorting yard where all lifeless souls must wait.

'I knew it, I knew it,' I scold myself. 'It's my fault, I shouldn't have rescued the *koukouviya*.'

I resolve not to mention the owl. Later I join villagers and visit *yiayia's* family. At her villa I'm invited to join the mourners. We perch on assembled chairs set around the lifeless woman's body where she lies flat on her bed. Before I or others arrived, *yiayia's* body was prepared and laid out. Special *moirologia, mourners* had embarked on a sequence of bereavement rituals. The women washed her body with vinegar, then dressed her. They placed candles at the head and foot of the old woman's brass bed. The icon of her name saint, her treasure, rests on a now still heart. The women placed two gleaming gold sovereigns in her eye sockets. These will pay the ferryman. Even in this Christian community, her passage to Hades is considered. Still the locals wonder is it God, or do the Gods throw the dice; they concede it's always best to cover all bases? An evil eye on a white ribbon entwined with garlic hangs from a bed knob close to her head – more pagan measures against evil forces.

Now in the halo of the luminous wavering light of candles and lanterns, I experience the ancient phenomena of *moirologia*. I'd never seen this ritual. The tradition heralds back to the Iliad: The Odyssey, the 8th century BC. *Yiayia's* female friends embody the skills of adept mourners. The locals say it takes a lifetime of accumulated knowledge to become an expert in the art of mourning. When ready to proceed, the principal *moirologia* begins her lament then the other women, one by one follow suit and wail. Their voices flow into a continuous chorus of crying. The sound moves beyond our world to the mysterious secret, sacred places where mere mortals cannot go until their time is ripe. As *moirologia* voices ascend, the sounds enter a world beyond our own, the afterlife. During the lament and wearing no makeup, the women loosen their long hair, allowing it to fall. It hangs wild and at liberty like tatty dark shawls around their shoulders. Yanking at their tresses, they chant, and the pitch slowly increases. Rocking and swaying back and forth, the women move in tempo with each other. Grief moves outward and into the spectators.

Amid subdued trembling light, *yiayia* looks beautiful. Her braided hair frames her white face in a decorative bun. Threaded beneath her white headdress, white ribbons entwine her plaited hair in traditional Corfiot style. Her headdress falls in a short cascade over her shoulders. Only one ear, her right ear, boasts a large gold earring. Bursts of colour emanate from blooms that negotiate her head dress. Y*iayia's* white blouse sits beneath a black velvet bolero jacket. Hand stitched gold eagles mount its delicate front. An eagle perches on each breast symbolising Christian Byzantium. A gold Christian Orthodox cross hangs on a chain around her neck.

I recall how she wore this outfit on festival days; her black skirt ballooning from the many petticoats beneath. Now the outfit makes her shoulders and face appear tiny. An ethereal Mona Lisa smile traces her lips. The pale landscape of her skin is as wrinkleless as plump gardenia blossoms. Wearing tiny polished black shoes, it is as if she is a maiden resting peacefully before departing for a celebration in the village.

Friends bearing autumn flowers place them around her luminous body. A generous bouquet of perfumed basil and lemon blossoms garnishes her touching fingers. She's attended with unhurried love and care. Her hand embroidered linen is on show around the room. They are a fine barometer of her life's effort embodied in delicate stitches. Her daughter-in-law, hair hanging around her face, shows each masterpiece with pride. They are hers now.

Later the smell of ouzo and brandy served on a small tray mingles with the aroma of damp clothing and moth balls. These potent shots of spirits are served alongside Greek coffee in delicate demitasse cups. A sheet of incense rests at head height as frankincense wafts unencumbered from *yiayia's* crowded bedside shrine. Her much-loved icons send out a final tribute to her from the light of her grandmother's crackling oil lamp. From time-to-time friends and family, overcome with grief, fling themselves over her still body. They wail. It is as if they are endeavouring to call her back from where she has gone, but they fail. White starched handkerchiefs pass along the row of discombobulated chairs. Old bodies, once young, bend with effort, touching her face with rough tenderness – farmer's hands gnarled and purple from olive picking and wine making. Even in the milling, a melancholic final lingering caress from a once ardent lover; past passions left to yesterday. Tears drop warmth from above.

'The funeral, the funeral, we must speak of this,' comes the voice of the daughter-in-law. It's time I left them to their arrangements.

During the night I have a dream about an icon I'd seen in an old church in Corfu town. It depicts the terrified dead plucked off heaven's ladder. Devils push and pull at those ascending it by using every conceivable temptation. At the bottom of the icon, the dead scream in torment as the fires of hell engulf them. The Orthodox believe the soul of the deceased meanders floating around for forty days after death. *Yiayia's* soul is on a journey through what the locals call special 'aerial toll houses.' During this time, they say *yiayia* will reappear like a ghost in places she frequented before her soul departs evermore. If her soul fails its trials, demons will drag her to hell with tempting lures. I wonder if this will be my soul's destiny? A burrowing and unsettling malevolence hovers in the shadows of my dream and I awaken to wild pounding in my chest and a sick feeling in my gut.

A few days later, I join the solemn procession on its way from *yiayia's* house to the hillside church. We make our way with the coffin held aloft through the olive groves. Upon entering the church, the familiar smell of incense, the flickering of icons, tempered by the sound of chanting. Before me is a scene of gold and silver. Juxtaposed against dark, huddled bodies, sagging shoulders, the coffin sits unmoved, the mood echoing an image reminiscent of a gloomy El Greco painting. We pause before a now open coffin. It faces head to the east in front of the altar. The priest's voice rings in my head. 'She is only sleeping; she will rise again.'

I panic. Will she rise again and punish me for saving the *koukouviya* and killing her?

Later, walking behind the coffin, the solemn congregation makes its way to the graveyard. I walk with her family and I am cloaked in guilt. Golden autumn leaves rustle and swirl around our feet, their colour contrasting with the Greek flag blue sky. It is a serious scene as the sun emits rays warming us from the bite of the wind. Next to *yiayia's* prepared grave, I see the remains of the former occupant – not mere morsels of mortal remains – these discarded body parts are recognisable. Legs, spine and skull. They attend by protruding through clumps of sodden soil and they send shivers down my spine. I avert my eyes and whisper to Maria, my neighbour, 'Whose bones are by the grave side?'

Shuddering, she wraps her black shawl closer to her body. She explains, suddenly releasing an unexpected smile, 'I don't know. I can't recognise the bones but it must be someone from the village. I forget these things as I'm getting older. This one's bones, that one's bones. After a while they all look the same to me. The family to whom the bones belong must eventually collect them. Then they'll wash the mortal remains and place them in an ossuary. This seemingly unholy act of desecration allows *yiayia* a grave to rest until she's lifted out of the earth; placed into an ossuary.'

Keeping her voice low, Maria continues, 'In Greece, cremation is illegal. It is not a Greek Orthodox tradition. We believe we will ascend again when Jesus returns. As most of the population in Greece is Greek Orthodox, it's hard to find a space to bury the dead. Plots are leased for three years. When this period ends, the authorities notify the relatives to witness the removal of the skeleton from the ground. If they want to keep the remains in the grave, they need to continue paying rent.'

Pausing to cross herself, Maria reflects, 'If no one pays the rent on the grave or removes the bones, what remains, the authorities move. They'll dissolve the leftovers in chemicals. Any remnants get placed in a common burial plot. The clergy believe incineration violates the mortal body. But what of the chemicals … do they not destroy and dissolve the remains? Ah, priests, sometimes I think to hell with the lot of them, and their dubious logic.'

I bow my head low at this disclosure. My spine continues to crawl as I turn the collar of my coat to the cold wind. Here in Greece, it's a tortuous road to salvation that awaits those who oscillate between loving and despising the dictates of the church.

Hesitating at *yiayia's* grave site, the priest shakes his head as he sizes up the coffin. He decides the grave is much too small. After much animated conversation among the men, they exchange bitter words. The women discover what will occur next. They release primal howls. Appearing feeble and helpless, their horror and rage sits in the icy air. Informed, the grave diggers cannot dig a longer hole. If they do, her coffin will encroach into the sacred lot of another's grave. More debate and the priest insist the end of the coffin be shortened so it can fit into the ground. We stand waiting as one of the altar boys races back to the priest's house. He returns with a saw.

Pulled from the ranks of pallbearers, the priest commandeers a strapping young male. With shaking head, the recruit reluctantly takes up his unfortunate assignment. He must saw off the end of the coffin without damaging *yiayia's* body. He fumbles for his gold crucifix. Finding it beneath his coat and jumper, he raises it to his lips, looks to heaven and kisses it. He prays out loud, seeking absolution for what he is about to do. The lid of the coffin opens so the executioner may see where to aim his saw. Howling begins. Black arms haul women back in horror from the graveside. Edges of the saw shine in the sunlight. It saws and cuts with shark-like razor teeth at the end of the coffin. This desecration continues until the length of the coffin is the correct size. The priest, after assessing the scene, remains strong. Yet, his steadfast face cannot hide the secreted tears that pool and quiver in the cavernous grey sacks beneath his eyes. He must follow church rules even if it distresses his parishioners and his own heavy heart.

When the task is completed, the priest signals the coffin to be lowered into the ground. With prayers, the priest pours olive oil and wine in the sign of the cross over the coffin lid. Soil lands with a thud on the coffin. *Yiayia* lies beneath the cold earth. The scene before me is heartbreaking and I am to blame, yet I stand stoic in a deceptively fixed stance. I don't go to the *makari, mercy* meal that follows. They wouldn't want Judas at their table.

Chapter 14

Shorelines of the Nile

In summer, my body resembles the red shore-lines of the Nile River. I'm a stark reminder of Moses' curse on the Egyptians. The red represents the tell-tale signs that again I'm severely sunburned. The daily reality of living on the beach with my extremely fair skin has on many occasions left me in tears from the sun's damage. These burns are my shameful marks of mortification on flesh, creating blinding contrasts that annoy my mother. 'Hurry up and tan, will you?' Ah, the jolly joys of summer.

Thongs, or flip flops as the English call them, are an absolute no-no in our villa. Mum refuses to let us wear them. At the very suggestion she fires, 'Disgusting! Who ever heard of such a thing! They are footwear for the poor, and I won't have my children wear them.'

I wonder who she thinks we are? In summer I go around with bare feet or wear my old worn-out Aussie Clarks lace-up, brown leather school shoes. These have seen better days now, and are often accompanied by sad looking, mismatched socks of varying lengths. I have nothing else. Perhaps it's me, but I don't think they are a good look with bikinis. If I protest, she says, 'Well, you have shoes, don't you?'

'Yes, I do, but …'

'Well, no buts about it! If you only knew how bloody lucky you are, kiddo! Now stop snivelling … I'm busy, so scoot and take a long dive off a short pier.'

As she goes back to chatting with her friends, we kids don't do the thongs thing, or me even the sandal thing. I can't help but think in terms of shoes – I've left an extremely low carbon footprint on this planet. The issue of shoes raises other concerns as well. When you retire, as my mother has done, should one aspire to brand new attire? Or, more precisely, when you move to the Greek islands? These questions need to be asked. On this Dorian doorstep, are our Aussie duds, doable? Or, like Dad, do we need to readdress our dress code and get into some newfangled Corfu dress style? Indeed, how does one begin to revamp when funds are scant? The question is, in the heat of a Corfu summer, can we do Corfu cool on a budget and not fudge it?

Considering she's under huge financial constraints, Mum does better at Corfu summer casual than we do, partly because she looks great and thrives in the heat. To her credit, she's the only person I've known who can melt like a wax voodoo doll into a pool of pearly sweat and moments later emerge refreshed, energised and ready to take on the world. To her advantage, she's attractive, slim and has great legs, or 'pins' as Dad affectionately refers to them. Caftans are 'in like Flynn', as Mum says and are 'so in Vogue', so much so she's fallen head long into the Corfu Caftan craze. I hold Demis Roussos personally responsible for this fashion flurry. The main contributing factor to her wearing caftans, apart from the 'in mode thing', is that in her humble wardrobe of a few bibs and bobs, she has three of them, two for day wear and one for evenings. One of her caftans, her regal favourite, belonged to Hollywood legs legend Ginger Rogers. Ms Rogers had in turn given it to Innes, the wife of costume and stage set designer Roger Furse from their Hollywood days. They are now living on the island or have done since the early 60s. She passes it to Mum, saying, 'Here, hun, try this on.'

Mum loves this caftan and tells its history to everyone she meets – that is if she happens to be wearing the 'thing', as I call it – its Hollywood connections. I hate its stripes of orange and brown. I can see why Ginger gave it away. It must have been too ginger for even Ginger!

As foreign residents we move in and out of the expat circles on Corfu. The numbers in this varied group of some random short-term walk-ins and long-term elites fluctuate season to season, year to year – eccentric, arty friends, some with genuine Picassos hanging nonchalantly on the walls of their understated minimalist, white-washed villas with their stunning views – others with awards and Oscars to show off – others showing them discretely, rightfully earned from their glitzy, show biz days, their star-spangled labours under the flood lights.

Roger was one such friend who did well in the prize pool stakes, having two Oscars. In his home, he used them purely for functional reasons. I liked him for this. None of the show-off for optimum effect on a stage-sized mantelpiece for all the world to see for this man of the movies and stage. But rather he kept his awards on the terrazzo floor of their lounge. Why, you may well ask. I did. They were placed there to stop the door length creamy white shutters to the veranda from rattling and banging in the mid-morning when the *Maestro* arrives. Is this a show biz sin? After Roger's death, his wife Innes kept them where they had always been saying, 'What else can I use them for?'

'Good question!' I reply, and we laugh.

While I'm staying at the villa for a few weeks, Richard Harris strides vigorously up through the steep rise of the Furse's undisciplined garden. He has a script under his arm. The actor joins us on the veranda where a statue of Nelson sits shaded beneath a pergola draped with grape-vine leaves.

That night in the company of my friend Innes, we dine at a bayside restaurant at Benitsis where she and Richard talk show biz gossip. This meeting of old friends is a much-needed chance for her to catch up on the latest news from London and Hollywood.

I sit dreamily enjoying the lilt of his Irish accent, his wit and their banter about the theatre and film industry. Oh, what lives they've led. I think my life, a little life. Of course, over the years they'd mixed with the best of them – Agatha Christie, Vivienne Leigh and Sir Lawrence Olivier, to name a few. The Oliviers had dined in Benitsis at this very spot when they came to visit her and Roger. They wanted to ensure their dear friends had settled happily into their new life on the island. On the Benitsis hillside, behind the unimposing facade of their white-washed minimalist villa, friends could stay, cloistered from the flash of cameras and curious reporters. It had been Vivienne Leigh's dream, after her divorce from Olivier, to retire to Corfu but tragedy struck. Her declining health destroyed her plans. She'd struggled with tuberculosis for years and died in 1967. A signed photograph of her sits on the dressing table in Innes' guest room, and I'm reminded of the actress and their close relationship whenever I stay.

Innes once said, 'We are born with an invisible rope around our necks; it's called the passion noose. If we don't honour that noose, and live our passion, we will slowly die of strangulation. I have often wondered about this, people unhappily lugging unlived lives behind them. What a miserable burden to bear!'

Innes has a point. Leigh and Olivier were luckier than most; they fulfilled so many of their passions, and not necessarily with one another.

Roger was an extraordinarily rare breed of artist. In one night, he'd won two Oscar awards in 1949. One for the costume design in the black-and-white film of Lawrence Olivier's *Hamlet*, the other for its art direction. Images of the original sets and costume designs adorn the walls of his study. He also designed the stage set for the famous *Mouse Trap*, the world's longest running play. Agatha Christie asked him at the time if he preferred to be paid a lump sum for his work or be paid a share from each performance. He was not sure how long the play would run and so opted for a one-off payment. He once said it was the biggest regret of his life. After his death, Innes left his work room as he had left it, his art pens, brushes and paper resting in still silence on his desk as if waiting for him to return any moment.

Socialising among the mixed backgrounds of the expat circle, and living on the hardy but not so gentle lentil, bread and tomatoes diet isn't easy when others have champagne and caviar budgets to spend on clothes and luxury items. But somehow, we get by. No one more so than Mum. I put it down to the fact that she's got good taste. That in itself puts her in a position of advantage over others because many of her friends are into labels and the who's who among the designers' stables, rather than simple, timeless and understated chic. So, no one can ever accuse us kids of spilling Fanta on Mum's Oscar de le Renta. She can't afford one! But no matter where we are, Mum looks the part, whether carrying on in a caftan or shushing around sashed in sarongs, flashing her tan. It's how she puts things together that makes her shine.

On Corfu, tans make the man as much as the woman and are a must-have fashion accessory keenly sought by the rich as well as the poor. Skin cancer never comes up in conversation. Well hardly. Mum keeps her tan up by regularly applying a concoction of well shaken and never stirred, olive oil and vinegar. This is her home-made fun-in-the-sun tanning oil solution that smells like a fermenting Greek island salad without the feta and onions. She encourages everyone to use it no matter their skin type. It's a one size fits all oil. If I complain about the sharp acidic smell, her logic kicks in. She says, 'Well, if everyone uses it, soon you won't notice it. It's like garlic – when everyone eats it no one can smell it. After all, look at the Greeks. They cope very well applying this philosophy to their lives so, so can you!'

Not only does her concoction catch the ultraviolet rays and violate my skin, penetrating deeply, burning into the delicate layers of my fair flesh, it's a wonder I haven't evaporated into a nuclear mushroom from the magnetised heat waves it generates. Throw a match at me and I'll ignite – vaporised in vinegar from Volos. Whoosh! As if that isn't bad enough, her potion attracts insects. When I complain, her dagger eyes sear through me. 'Stop being a pain. Wade in the waves. That will keep the creepy crawlies at bay.'

She's right. It does. Mum also assures me, 'One day you'll tan, kiddo, just keep trying.'

Still, as hard as I try, fry and cry from severe sunburn, I never, ever, tan.

Mum's social elite mates love the idea of pure organic ingredients sourced from local farmers. As a result, her simple shake-it-to-me-baby suntan product of oil and vinegar goes down a treat. Their skin drinks it in as they dunk in and out of their palatial pools keeping the bugs at bay, just like us only with a lot more style. It's reassuring to know that even the Guggenheims smell like salads, cook and shake as they partake in a kind of ritualistic tribal insect stomp and uncomfortable romp like me.

Inspired by her friend's positive responses to her potions, Mum dabbles in other concoctions as well. Laughing and mucking about in our primitive bathroom she says, as if casting spells, 'Abracadabra, now stay away everyone because the place might blow!' That's reassuring. Mum's set out to create a beauty care range of potions, products like her olive oil and peach daily facial moisturiser. She thinks this is a sure winner because hard financial times demand affordable solutions. All this fuss to delay signs of aging in the very competitive world of her face-lift friendly friends and their regular visits to the expensive beauty parlours in Corfu town. In this way too she can't compete with them. Gone are the days of Lancôme and Elizabeth Arden for her. It's sad because she goes without even the most basic skin and hair care products, products she'd taken for granted in Australia. Who'd have thought dishwashing liquid would become a rescue remedy when we run out of shampoo? For a while our hair looked and felt like Brillo soap pads. Her solution for a conditioner, a mix of olive oil and egg yolk. Note to self, apply dishwashing liquid to rinse the said conditioner out. So, we're back to square one! But what's the point of saying anything? She just keeps fiddling with her potions in the hope that one day she'll stumble upon an amazing ingredient, a winning amalgamation that will make us a grand fortune. In the meantime, we, her reluctant lab specimens at the end of each day, reassemble like scapings on a petri dish in the kitchen for a head count. Will her experiments never end?

Dad has a no-frills and purely practical attitude to basic beauty and skin care. As a result, he doesn't bother much. Like me, his fair skin burns 'to buggery', as he so delicately puts it. He stays in the shade refusing Mum's pungent sun solutions or skin moisturisers. Wise man. Up until now he's simply made sure he was shaved and showered and that's pretty much it. But he eventually decides to grow a beard and thus gives his shaving gear a shove. Apart from the appeal of not having to shave every day, it's his rebel response to the inflated price of razors and scissors increasing exponentially just as Papadopoulos tightens his grip and threatens more punitive actions against long-haired students and hippies.

As Mum's invested in new vestments for him to wear, i.e.: a safari suit for every occasion, perhaps now he'll look more like a writer? – especially after his bold decision to grow a beard. However, the question remains … if beards and clothes make writers of a man, does this mean Dad's going to turn into a hunter in his safari suits? I think about this. Well, maybe not in the new duck egg blue one. Still, the question must be asked. Can writers also be hunters and fighters? Can he be a hunter with a pop-up pen, instead of a pop gun? Be chic with a Bic? Get quick with his quill. Is he equipped? He needs to click quick with his Bic or he's in big trouble. He is after all, formally a writer. He must be – everywhere we go Mum introduces him as such. It's the main motivation for our move half way across the world, isn't it?

Chapter 15

Bouboulina

I sit hot and frustrated beneath the sagging leaves of the olive trees in our garden. Dad sits beside me commiserating. 'Talk about a Greek tragedy. Where's the *Maestro* wind the Greeks always rave about? It must have died somewhere off the tippy toes of Italy. Ah, and this bloody heat just keeps rising!'

Dad's right. This warmth is a rehearsal to hell. After midday now and the inextinguishable humidity refuses to shift. It's holding on with an iron fist. The *Maestro* should be in by now. Where is it? Even a surrender to the sea is no reprieve. The Ionian, only a step away lies flat, warm and uninviting. Marietta's old donkey Ajax shadows against the trunk of the mulberry tree with as much enthusiasm as a goat about to face the point of old Thanasi's sharp blade. He's waiting for Marietta to finish our washing so she can ride him home. Only then can he relax in the shade of his crumbling but cool stone stable.

Hot and bothered I consider my options. Our villa has no cooling. Not even a fan. I'm a great fan of fans in summer. With food always on her mind, Mum has revved up the wood stove in the kitchen. I wonder if she's a screw loose lighting the stove in this heat. It's a death sentence inside but I brave the heat and stick my nose into the kitchen. She stands close to her arsenal of recipes, feeding driftwood into the fire. Mum is like a spotlight in the hot hissing firelight. I'm sure she loves to crackle like pork when she cooks. In fact, she wallows with delight in the suffocating fireball atmosphere, likening it to shushing around in a sauna only with more flour than steam. When anyone complains, she fires defensively, 'Well, as soon as the electric frypan arrives from Australia, we won't have to light the wood stove, will we?'

She has a point.

So, the heat's on for an electric frypan to arrive with my grandmother to take the pressure off the heat in our villa. Good plan. Hurry up, Gran. I retreat from the coalface of the villa but where can I turn? Even in Dad's top spot to jot under the olive trees in the garden, the air hangs stagnant, gluggy and thick. There's no sound of him typing because in this heat even he isn't subscribing to his own scribe. Angry at the unquenchable spiralling temperatures, he wobbles, 'My scribble is a pile of rotten old dribble.'

He rips a typed sheet out of Grandpa's old typewriter; scrunches it into a ball. Tossing his written efforts angrily in the bin, it looks like his Hippocratic Oath to write is in melt down again. It's too much for him. He opts to sit out the heat drinking chilled *retsina*. He justifies its rapid consumption by saying, 'Before it evaporates!' This I might add, is an adult practice that should only be attempted with constraint in the hot months of June, July and August in a shaded area.

As the liquid disappears down his throat, his eyelids close as the wine's mellowing after-effects hit their target. He mumbles, 'I'm reserving my energy for later in the day when the gods will hopefully bless us with a bit of wind. Yes, a good dose of wind. You can't beat it. Who'd have thought wind would be so vital, hey, kiddo? We usually complain about too much of it: bloody beans.'

He has a point.

I smile knowingly as he shuts his eyes and, with no further conversation from my usual sources; my siblings slink wilting around the table under the trees looking glum, so I head down the side of the villa. I'm following the sound of a lively radio and the laughing voices of Marietta, our well-appointed OMO Laboratory Olympic washing champion, and Anna, our neighbour. At least they have life in them! Everyone except these two women is pooped or cooked. I refuse to sit this heat out without conversation or entertainment to while away the gravity of a long hot afternoon. This is one of those times when conversation is a much-needed heat-breaker.

Down the side under the shade of the grape vines, my bottom finds its centre of gravity, snuggling between Marietta and Anna. With my posterior now fused onto the well, I deposit a hot sigh of frustration into their conversation. In the heat, each of us shuffles aside so our bodies don't touch. The women continue to chat, laugh and eat lunch. A snappy Nana Mouskouri song plays in the background. Anna, always the clown, laughs and says, '*Aukous, listen, then eanai Nana Mouskouri, einai Banana Mouskouri, it's not Nana Mouskouri, it's Banana Mouskouri!*' We laugh.

I love how these women pull legs and stretch the truth like moistened chewing gum. The games they play pull at me and I'm like an insect propelled by the wind into the captive power of their web. Yet, it's in their exaggerations and mirth where they keep something of themselves hidden – past wars, and the crushing Junta have taught them survivors' tricks: never reveal who you really are. It's the key to protection and self-preservation.

Anna, bursting with excitement, says, '*Aukou se me, listen to me*. I want to tell you a story. It's a very serious story about a famous Greek heroine.'

I raise my eyebrows doubting I'm going to hear the whole truth. Still, I smile encouragingly. I'll listen to anything to while away this hot afternoon.

Anna begins. 'Once upon a time there was a beautiful

Greek girl called Bouboulina. She was born in a prison in Constantinople, today's Istanbul, while her mother visited her father. He had been imprisoned there by the Turks. They'd charged Bouboulina's Greek father with collaborating against the Ottoman Turks. At the time, much of Greece was under Turkish occupation. When her father perished in that prison, eventually the family moved to the Greek island of Spetses where Bouboulina grew up. Bouboulina married and when her second husband died, she offered her substantial inheritance to support Greece's uprising against the Turks. She joined with many others including the famous Lord Byron. You see, she'd not forgotten, nor forgiven that her father died at the hands of the Turks. This courageous young widow instigated ships to be built using them to repel the Ottoman forces. She organised shiploads of supplies, even funded her own Greek army consisting of followers from Spetses. She called the most eminent of her eight ships *Agamemnon*. It was the largest war ship used in the 1821 battle against the Turks. She was famous for her strategic blockades and, without her support, it's doubtful that Greece would have gained its independence when it did.'

Taking a deep breath, Anna continues. 'After Greece achieved its independence, a civil war broke out. Bitter factions grew out of what Bouboulina thought would be a time of peace. Brother turned against brother. Bouboulina became disillusioned and heartbroken because she'd given all her wealth assisting Greece to gain its independence. But out of the ashes, bitter rivalries in the Greek Civil War brought only more heartache. Bouboulina found herself up on charges and arrested, then exiled to Spetses with her fortune exhausted.'

Anna pauses to sip some water from the shiny metal bucket beside the well and, after wiping her face with a wide sweeping hand, continues. 'Bouboulina died – some idiot shot her through the head in a family row. Can you imagine such a thing? Apparently, the incident occurred when she was protecting her new daughter in-law. Well, that's what mothers do! There were suspects but no one was charged. Of course, there were many rumours at the time about a cover up. Need I say more, *po, po, po*!'

Anna pauses again and the two women bow their heads in silence out of respectful reverence for this noble Bouboulina. Suddenly Anna lets fly an outlandish accelerated laugh. 'Do you know how she beat the Turks out there on the high seas on her ships without using a gun or sword at the start of a battle?'

I shrug my shoulders and say, 'No, tell me.'

She laughs again, slapping her wide hands, still purple from wine-making, against her simple black skirt. She bursts out brazenly, 'Bouboulina stood on the bow of her ship. When the Turkish ships got close enough the beautiful Bouboulina, her long hair flying in the wind, opened the front of her blouse surprising the Turks. She stood brazenly, flashed her magnificent breasts while her soldiers took aim and fired at the stupid, preoccupied Turks.'

With that Anna and Marietta look around. Once sure the coast is clear, in an instant they open their blouses and boldly flash their breasts at me in unison. Suddenly I have a minefield of bosoms bouncing back and forth in front of me. As they flash their breasts, they cry out teasingly, '*Bouboulina, kita, kita, look, look, Bouboulina, kita, kita!*'

The fact is, unlike the Turkish soldiers, I don't know where to look! And I wonder what's going to happen next. Are these hilarious grannies going to do cartwheels and streak around the garden? Laissez faire, they act as if nothing's happened, button their blouses up before anyone else can see them.

After my initial shock, I roll around in laughter. Bouboulina, this cache of a power woman with a fetish for a fight against the Ottomans becomes our secret joke. We only have to say '*Bouboulina, kita, kita,*' and the three of us giggle knowingly and end up in fits of laughter, making jokes about bosoms. After Marietta and Anna leave for the day, I endeavour to find out more about this famous heroine. I want to know if she really existed. I wasn't sure if Anna was making up stories for the fun of it. But after searching through a few books, it turns out Bouboulina really existed. She's the only woman awarded the rank of Admiral by the Russian navy for her efforts during the Greek War of Independence. Her face even adorns the fifty drachmae note, and one drachma coin.

As time goes on, I discover more about this famous woman. Madam Hortense in Nikos Kazantzakis' book *Zorba the Greek* is supposed to be a parody of Bouboulina. It's not a particularly flattering one. Indeed, she's portrayed as a character to look on with pity, and tragic amusement, not a woman to take seriously. In the film, Anthony Quinn as Zorba the Greek gives Hortense, an elderly hotel owner on Crete, the pet-name Bouboulina, referring to Hortense as, "A woman who has known many admirals," suggesting a promiscuous past. It's interesting to note that, after the real Bouboulina's death, she gained a reputation as a woman prepared to use her secret weapons of 'mass distraction,' to get what she wanted from men.

By keeping this story alive perhaps I'm perpetuating the myth too. But separating fact from fiction, the real Bouboulina did what she felt she had to do to save her country in true patriotic style. She gave everything to do this. Such sacrifice! Whether she was a female flasher or not, I think it's the Turkish sailor's, post-battle, who were the ones left feeling like boobs. They lost the battles and eventually the war; not Bouboulina. Her heroism will continue to live on in Greek history. *Zita Hellas. Zita Bouboulina*!

Chapter 16

Sweet As

My gran is on her way to Greece. I'm excited because I can't wait to see her. Dad's not so cheery and reckons her reason for visiting from Melbourne is: 'To not only save the day, but to deliver a much-needed electric frypan, thus rescuing your mother from the kitchen before she melts, disappearing forever into the terrazzo floor. Oh, and to make sure we haven't been rounded up, lined up, locked up, then shot by Papadopoulos and his marauding band of military generals.' Dad, like Mum, can be a tad melodramatic.

Mum, also unable to muster a smile over her mother's arrival, is cranky and can't sleep. She thinks Gran's coming to spy on us, report back like some deviant infiltrator to the rest of the family in Melbourne about our perilous situation. After all, Mum estimates, 'It's one thing to live under the shadow of a military coup, but quite another to slum it on the Greek islands in this poky villa.'

'*Sosta, mama,*' *right, Mum*, we agree obediently in Greek to which she replies dubiously,

'No Greek in the house!'

'*Sosta, mama,*' and we run like the clappers for the hills.

A few days later, Gran, seeing us alive and living as locals on lentils, is relieved. And just as quick as you can flick a pork souvlaki on a barbie, she's made herself at home. It turns out Gran likes Greeks and souvlakis. Not so much the mandatory shovel loads of onion and garlic flavoured lentils and beans swimming in slicks and slathers of thick rich olive oil. But yay, as she tucks into bread, tomatoes and feta, she's practically one of us. She even learns the not so gracious art of wiping her plate clean with a crust of crunchy village bread too. I love Gran's common touch. Now recovered from jet lag, or hag lag as she dramatically calls it, days later she's scaling our mulberry tree collecting fruit with her new buddies, Marietta and Anna.

After their 'Me Jane' reincarnations up the mulberry tree, Gran rolls up her sleeves ready to tackle anything. Laughing and powdering my tiny freckled nose with flour, she whips together three enormous sugar-sprinkled, golden pastry pies filled with glistening ruby-coloured mulberries. Because Marietta invariably leaves Ajax tethered beneath the shade of our mulberry tree on washing day, upon seeing the pies Dad reckons, 'Ah, nothing enhances the taste of something as knowing from where the quality produce has heralded, and that goes for the manure too.'

Gran isn't fond of Dad, so she ignores him for the rest of the day – well, pretty much the rest of her stay. There's been conflict between them since he sanctioned Mum's decision to move to Greece. There was also the car incident. What a disaster that turned out to be. He was pressured by Mum to teach Gran to drive. Valiantly taking one for the team, he very generously gave her five lessons. However, it was disastrous from the beginning because they didn't hit it off. When she failed to get her licence, she gave up and blamed him. From then on, the battle lines were drawn. I don't think she ever has any intention of forgiving him.

When the pies cool, Gran gives one to Anna and one to Marietta. They're thrilled. With help from me, Marietta gets herself and her mulberry pie up onto old Ajax's back ready to go home along the stony backtrack to her village. I know where she stashes her precious drachma but can't fathom for the life of me where she's put her wages of a bottle of ouzo and loaf of bread. But I suspect they are somewhere under her many layers of petticoats in cavernous pockets. Then with a click, click of her tongue they're off and away with her balancing the pie in one hand and pulling reins in the other. With her white headdress flapping in the wind, she's gone.

As a gift the following week, Marietta gives Gran a bottle of Cumquat Liqueur. It's the traditional, real McCoy aperitif, a sweet and gooey brew made and famed on the island. Rumours flourish about this florescent, orange-coloured beverage. Locals reckon you can lose teeth simply by taking a tiny sip of the sickly-sweet drink so, only serve in thimble sized glasses. Others joke, 'The manufacturers guarantee that diabetic comas will follow, so beware. Drink at your own risk.'

While an exaggeration, this sweet nauseous nectar is like drinking thick and gluggy orange Fanta on steroids only without the fizz. It gets the thumbs down from everyone, except our Gran. In fact, she becomes partial to what Dad's christened, 'The old galah's gooey, orange glug.'

Marietta gets her supply of Cumquat Liqueur from a local friend. He's an amiable little farmer who claims he blends his special concoction in a run-down shed at the back of his plot behind the village. We've nicknamed him 'The Kolonos Kid' because he has dodgy teeth, and Kolonos is the only brand of toothpaste we can afford. There are other brands of course, but only if you step through the hallowed doors of the expensive chemist shop Mum has christened 'Boots.' This shop sits on the main walkway near Saint Spyridon's Church in Corfu town. And we seldom visit 'Boots.' As children we merely peer through its windows daydreaming about the wonderful luxury toiletries that are beyond our means.

This taboo on tasty toothpaste means we've developed quite a craving for Colgate. We even salivate with collective delight at the sight of tubes of Macleans. Well, anything's better than nasty old Kolonos. As a result, year in and year out we brush our teeth with the not-so-nice tasting, cheap and cheerless Kolonos toothpaste. However, as terrible as Kolonos toothpaste is, it would do the Kolonos Kid's piano keys a lot of good. In fact, it's just what they need as part of a twice daily dental hygiene regime. His fangs resemble rickety, mushy avocado-coloured defiled gravestones that are grave. I suspect they're hanging in there by their rancid, rotting, rocky roots. His shock of fangs coordinates well with the green military fatigues he wears everywhere. It's a kind of uniform for him. Perhaps he never got over the civil war? Or worse still, he's never cottoned on to the fact that the war ended years ago.

He gets around the island on a motorbike with a rifle flung over his shoulder and this also coordinates well with his military look. Lots of male islanders are laid-back about guns and take them everywhere, especially in winter. He also wears strips of bullets in a leather case either as an extra belt or thrown over his other shoulder. I think he looks a lot like the Looney Tunes character, Elmer Fudd, if Elmer had a moustache.

Once he'd spied Gran, well, that was it. I imagine him saying, "It's thunting season and I'm thunting for your gorgeous Aussie Gwanny," only in Greek, of course. Like my Gran, he must be pushing seventy. This gentle green-fanged man is pleasant enough so long as you don't stand too close to his breath. His other two annoying traits, from my parent's perspective, is his loud motorbike and his grand passion for my gran.

The sound of his motorbike is akin to an amplified

indestructible mosquito on the rebound after a drunken night on the ouzo bottle. He zips up and down our road, hovering, waiting for Gran to materialize. He's spied her and fallen for her. She's the one for him. Whenever he sees her, he slows his motorbike to a noisy crawl. For some unknown reason, this only heightens the loud annoying tone of its motor. Dad, sitting under the olive trees still artfully masquerading as a novelist in front of Gran, tapping on his typewriter, upon hearing the Kid's noisy approach, raises his eyes above his spectacles, spies his ghastly green gear and curses under his breath. He's irritated by the annoying one-way courtship he's having with his mother-in-law.

He grumbles, 'That ridiculous little man! Disturbing the neighbourhood for a chance at a quick granny grope with a disinterested granny. I wish he'd go back to cooking his cumquats, or whatever he does with them on his farm, and leave us all in peace.'

Life, however, is never that simple. He's overlooking the fact that Granny is quite a catch in these parts, not only because she has a comfortable house in Australia, can leap tall mulberry trees in a single bound but, miracle of miracles, she can also whip up a pie or two in no time. I'm told these are highly commendable qualities on our side of the island. And even though Gran isn't looking for a grand passion, the Kolonos Kid reckons he has a mandate for a date hoping to find his long-term mate.

He prides himself on being a great catch, or as good as any of the other widowed characters in our village's limited supply of eligible males. In the meantime, Gran's getting a reputation around the village with the elderly gentlemen – well, anyone with teeth and functioning limbs, that is. Marietta must have been bragging about Granny up the mulberry tree. Or Anna's raving about her pies that's creating Gran's score of male Nan fans. Who knows? But here's the Kolonos Kid reckoning he can use a gal like her on his farm to help him crunch his cumquats. And when you think about it, Gran has many commendable merits. In the Greek village marriage stakes, I'd suggest she'd make a great catch. But him? He isn't Granny's valentine variety.

On top of this, she thinks Greek marriages are far too complicated as they involve *brika's, dowries*. Every Greek woman must have one. Behind the scenes, even at the farcical whiff of an engagement, local men are at it. They flock to negotiate deals in smoky, dark tavern corners as women huddle over cups of tea and strong coffee getting down to the nitty gritty of gauging the value of their stashed gold sovereigns. But first, they have to remember where they have been hidden. Villas are tallied, plots of land measured to the centimetre, and a serious head count of fruit and olive trees undertaken. This along with a stock take on wells, grape vines, goats, chickens, wine barrels and anything that doesn't ferment, or move. In Greek *brika* terms, who knows how much Granny's 1960s AV Jennings house in Watsonia, Victoria might fetch in the local *brika* stakes? But no matter how you package it, this liaison will never work. Our widowed Gran is a no-go granny zone.

But the Kolonos Kid can't take a hint. Whenever he sees Granny sunning herself at the front of our villa, he stops and parks his motorbike in the bay area under the mulberry tree. This spot is exclusively reserved for our regular brayer, Ajax. It's our top little galloper's parking spot, not the Kolonos Kid's. How dare he park his bike there?

Flouting our unspoken garden rules, there he is leaning what he thinks is a flash, hotted up motorbike as if it were a fine chariot waiting to whisk his queen away. The reality is, his bike is something more akin to a rusty heap of nasty old tack.

Well, that's what Dad thinks. He warns, 'Careful, kids. Head for cover. Here he comes; we're about to go under bad breath and tacky motor bike attack.' And away we scatter.

But because Gran's a bit slow getting to her feet, she's hopeless at quick get-a-ways. So, dressed in his army fatigues, the Kid pounces, coming up close, sticking to her like industrial strength glue. But it doesn't matter what language you speak; bad breath is a turn-off in anyone's tongue.

As he pants like an enthusiastic puppy at her side, he tries his bastardised version of jumbled bits of multiple languages all pieced together in a disastrous attempt to make one communicable and comprehendible sentence. But it doesn't work. In fact, the harder he tries the more impossible they are for anyone to decipher. Then when Gran's had a few too many cumquat liqueurs, the situation becomes more complicated. She adds her sketchy high school Latin and oh, boy, communication just gets that bit harder! It's all hocus pocus and mumbo jumbo. After a while, the Kolonos Kid leaves, sad and frustrated because he isn't getting through. Somehow the language of love is lost in translation.

Not long after, and I would suggest out of desperation because his cumquat liqueur seduction moves hadn't got Granny grinning, he ditches his multilingual dialogue. He then tries a new approach to courtship. His solution is to rock up ready to grab Granny with his one-man singing act.

Today Granny sits frozen like an ice block in her chair. She's heard his bike approach but there's no escape. He's spotted her under the olive trees. She sits as if impaled in her chair, her huge sun hat casting shadows across her agonised expression of doom. None of us can believe our eyes. The Kolonos Kid, still in army fatigues, his rifle in its usual position nonchalantly thrown over one shoulder, now has a Bouzouki flung over the other.

Dad groans, 'Well I'll be. That's an impressive show of primordial dexterity if ever I saw one.' And he's right.

The Kid gets off his bike and comes up close to Gran. He gets down on one knee, strums, and sings, 'Dippy dop, dippy dop, dippy, dippy, dippy dop!'

Trying to be groovy, twanging to a fast-paced Paso doble beat, he sings as if he's a sped-up Gerry Lewis. We haven't heard this song before. No wonder, it's a shocker. Dad, looking peeved, murmurs under his breath, 'I don't care how rude this sounds but you can't put a daisy up a person's behind and call it a vase. This is one very shitty ditty.'

Time moves on and Gran desperately whispers, 'You're right, I can't take any more of this mad, shrieking sonnet. This nonsensical polyglot with his diabolical dictum and ghastly bouzouki. That beautiful instrument is being plucked like a duck. Kids, your gran's dying here! Please someone, anyone, save me!'

It doesn't matter how you package it. His phonetics are terrible. With a repeated chorus, the entire song is an illogical dual lexicon monologue. It's a brain-draining experience. Dad agrees with Gran, 'This hip hop of a flop in army fatigues needs to take a trot. The Kid's downright indigestible.'

Is there perhaps a subtext we Aussie newcomers to the island are missing? As a painful ten minutes of the Kid's long, boring song transpires, Dad's itching to wring the Kid's neck.

Now, my gran's been around a few gun-slinging males in her time so keeps one eye on the Kid's gun and her other on his crying bouzouki. Even though there's no doubting Gran's quandary, she is, after all, stuck between a rock and a hard place. Could the mulberry tree be an escape option? She's climbed it before.

Gran prepares to leave all options open, understanding desperate times demand desperate measures. What about the

Kid's motorbike? As a bit of a bushy from way back, she'd learnt years ago on the farm how to ride one. In fact, she's less rusty than his bike with her biking skills. Should she run? Crikey, he might use his gun!

A flash of headlines hurtles through her mind. 'Corfu's Singing Killer the 'Kid', cuts down Gorgeous Aussie Granny from Watsonia!' What about that for a top leading story in all the international papers tomorrow morning? It's terrifying stuff. Gran's visualising Reuters' stampeding with cameras and joyfully snapping the gory particulars of the crime scene. In the meantime, Dad's growing increasingly disturbed by the Kolonos Kid's obsession with his mother-in-law. Dad may have, on the odd occasion wanted to 'wring the old duck's neck,' but he reckons that doesn't mean he wants her to die at the hands of this village nut. So, Dad, in a valiant move, and it is a heroic step because he has a dodgy knee and is regrettably downwind from the Kid's breath, kneels next to the still crouching crooner. He positions himself ready to fling his body in front of a bullet to save our beloved Granny. Or, the other option, stretch, grab and tussle the mad, music man to the ground, all in the call of son-in-law duty.

With our entire family watching the scene unfold, Anna and Helen join forces over the fences between our properties. Mum, on the porch, floured up to the elbows, considers the outside hose as an option to get him off the property but changes her mind. The water pressure is too low to have any significant effect. It would be just our luck for the well to run dry as she takes aim. But someone must gag this guy.

Interrupting his cocked attempts at crooning, Dad gently breaks the news to the Kid, telling him to stop. But the Kid won't give up that easily. Suddenly changing lyrics, he sings in pleasing stanzas aimed at Gran, 'I love you; you are my rising Venus. My Aphrodite, my Aphrodite, I love you, I need you.'

'Grab his bouzouki, Mum. I'll distract him with one of Jo's lamingtons,' suggests Dad.

'Crikey, I'm not touching his bouzouki!' cries Gran, throwing him a horrified look.

As the Kid keeps declaring his love for Gran, Dad encourages him to stand. 'Your song is too long. And, mate, sorry ... but Gran's just not into you. Have a yummy lamington, instead. The wife just made them.'

Like a wolf howling at the moon, the Kid is unrelenting. 'But I love her, I need her.'

'No, mate ... save yourself a lot of trouble; lamingtons are much nicer.'

Re-baptised by us kids, the Kolonos Kid re-emerges as 'Dippy Dop the Singing Flop.' Poor old Dippy Dop never visits us again. From then on, we hear his mozzie-sounding motorbike take the back chook and mule route to the village instead of passing our villa on the main stretch by the bay.

'Good bloody riddance' grumbles Dad, pleased he's achieved something in retirement. 'He and his bloody bike have finally got the hint and taken a long overdue hike.'

Ever preoccupied with what's on the menu, Mum reckons, 'In hindsight, perhaps we should have offered him a couple of Gran's Ginger Nuts or Arnott's Milk Arrowroot biscuits instead of lamingtons?'

'Geez, love, are you serious? That's just what the old boy wanted. A bloody good granny root!'

As soon as Gran's supply of Arrowroots and Ginger Nuts were consumed by us, she left for Melbourne. She went back to packing the seats at the local church with her organ-playing performances every Sunday. I guess she must have missed Greece and her string of eccentric Romeos because she had a few other interested parties. Years later she returned to the island, but only for a short while. She'd hitched her heart to a star but not one with aspirations of becoming a bouzouki strumming singing star. But shortly after she returned to Melbourne. She was disappointed because, as Mum tactlessly put it, 'The man's not into pussy cats, he's into tom cats instead, Mum.'

After seeing her off at the airport, Dad mumbled under his breath, 'Thank God for that. Like the Kid, she's finally got the hint. Well ... there goes her plane ... Hallelujah, we finally have lift off.'

Chapter 17

Let's Talk About Sex, Baby

Sex is practically a hot pagan practice on the golden Greek islands, especially Corfu. Consequently, I need to learn more about the subject. I widen my consultation processes beyond my parents because they're staying 'mum' on the topic. Katerina also shakes her head, giving me blank looks. At this rate, I'm in for an incredibly naïve life, especially living on an island surrounded by 'hunks of burning love', as Elvis so eloquently put it.

My solution: turn to nature. This is a constructive move as my dog has an impressive day off the leash. She has an eye watering orgy with all the male dogs in the village. Now, you'd think I'd be able to work out the carnal secret as I battled pulling propagating pooches off her as they performed the doggy Karma Sutra on her. Yet, later, as panting Patch the pooch flops cross-eyed on my bed recovering from her orgasmic experiences, I screw this up because I'm still not sure. My solution ... check out the goings on in the local farmyards.

But as time goes on, this is not enough. I need a human perspective on the subject. I then consult the local *yiayia's*. They laugh and slap their black-skirted thighs, crossing themselves saying, '*Po, po, po!*' about anything to do with sex. Then one giggling *yiayia* confides, 'My child, you must be careful of the good-looking green-eyed gypsy boys with white flashing teeth.'

It's in one of those light bulb moments that it dawns on me that half the villagers have green eyes and flashing white teeth. When I ask them about this, they're short on detail until one lets it slip, 'We Greeks always say, everything goes better with Greek feta, except sex! We also say, clench a pomegranate between your knees, it's the best precaution. If you have strong knees, not even the barbarians can invade.' This is followed by fits of laughter.

Another *yiayia* says, 'Near the sacred temple of the triangle you will find the map of Aegina. Let me tell you, some foolish women even shave their sacred welcome mats. Of course, these are foreign women, never Greek women. This is because a real man wants to sleep with a real woman, and let me tell you, Greek women are real women. We are Olympian gymnasts in the bedroom; after all, we invented the Olympic Games!' She looks to heaven and quickly crosses herself again.

The *yiayias* laugh hysterically, but I scratch my head because I'm still confused. Clearly these women accept that lust and laughter go hand in hand with a good dose of religious caution. I suppose I should say 'Amen to that,' but what exactly? Even so, that doesn't stop them gossiping about who's 'doing' whom. Or, for that matter, who's up who and who's paying the rent?

I turn to Soula from the village bread shop for advice. She tells me it's all about the 'Hankies-pankies and tight Levi tzeans.' This trendy new 'tzeans' phenomenon accentuates the need for 'hankies-pankies' and makes men crazy for sex. The tighter the 'tzeans', the hungrier they are for 'hankies-pankies and nookie, nookie'. All the men want a pair and now the local women are clamouring for them too. Her friend's podiatrist wears tight tzeans and he always wants to massage and play with her feet. Jokingly, she reckons that's why her friend has nicknamed him Play-toe. But this talk of "tight tzeans," "hankies-pankies," "nookie, nookie" and "Play-toe's" is not helping me. I'm still totally baffled.

There is a local hunk, whom the women and girls refer to as "eye candy" cos he has a body that's a cross between Achilles and Adonis, and is reputed across the island for being an absolute stud of a Greek god. They say he's ripped and ready, because of this the local girls call him the Rock ... Rock Candy. Captivated, they think when God created man, he created him. He has shoulders and thighs the width of mantlepieces. They say he'd make a great centre-fold for a woman's raunchy magazine. This guy comes from a different angle on sex ... the male angle. Because of this, I consider him a good avenue for discourse on intercourse.

Plucking up courage, I quiz him on the topic. In his deep lusty Greek accent, he confides, "Sex is like being intoxicated with sweet, luscious nectar gathered from the nests of wild honeybees. It's so wonderful, I want to die making love...!"

Talk about melodramatic. If he wants to go out with a bang, short circuit his system for sex, then it must be fabulous. This aficionado of amore reckons, "The more amore, the merrier!"

Yet, he mentions nothing about love. Well, except that "Master-bashion is supreme because you are making love to someone you really love ... yourself." He, like my brothers, and the rest of the local Casanovas in the village think it's all about conquest. Even the quiet guys agree.

A local Greek girl tells me, "The quiet ones, they're the ones to watch. They go from mild mannered Clark Kent characters to Jet Jackson super studs in seconds. You see why Greek girls always have chaperones and the boys during courtship must keep their hands on the table or behind their backs at all times?"

Still confused, I agreed as if I knew what she was talking about.

I have heard the local lads laugh at the tourist girls who come to the island on "Sojourns for sex!" These guys wear belts with notches in them representing their conquests. The more holes, notches or studs in their belts, the bigger the stud. Or, so they brag. My brothers call these notches, "*Nooki, nooki* notches." All these guys insist on marrying virgins. Women are to be conquered, and once conquered, cast aside. Everyone I consult agrees on one important point about sex ... always be careful. But careful about what? I'm about to find out.

As Dad admires his slice of the Greek dream at first light, he hears George, our neighbour, fire shots from his rifle. A billy goat's cry fills the air. Then a low whisper can be heard from rustling bushes beckoning Dad down the side of our villa. 'Psst, psst, David, help, help me, mate!'

Curious Dad follows the sound. Late night Aussie party reveller Mullet Clitus squats, completely naked under the bush, except for strings of flashy gold fertility symbols dangling from his sunburnt neck. Unshaven and with hair in disarray, he's been hanging around the village for days, but never like this.

Looking up at Dad, Mullet whispers, 'Geez, please, mate, I'm in a right old Pericles pickle ... I'm as dry as the Pope's nasty under here. That Anna's as mad as a cut snake. I have to get out of here fast.'

Surprised by his discovery, Dad whispers, 'Mullet, for a second I didn't recognise you without your clothes! What the hell are you doing under there ... You look like something the cat's dragged in. Mate, where's your clobber?'

'Please, I'm in the shit, big time ... I beg you, get me some shorts, a towel, anything. I'll explain later. The ants are climbing up my legs; they bite like bloody blazers. Not only that, I've got cramp from squatting here for hours. And I'm dying of thirst ....'

'Stay here, mate, I'll be right back. I can't have you doing a Flash Gordon across my garden with your wiggly jiggly bits and fertility whatnots. I've got two daughters and a wife to think of!'

With Olympic sprint speed, Dad races to the villa to get Mullet a pair of shorts and a bottle of water.

In the meantime, Anna from next door arrives on our doorstep with a broom. Wielding it like an axe, she's poised ready for battle.

'Mrs Jo? Mr David? Hello, hello? Please, are you home? Have you seen that Australian tourist, Mullet Clitus anywhere?'

Dad swiftly steps to the door before Mum can get there. 'Good morning, Anna, ... no, I haven't seen anyone this morning. What seems to be the problem?'

'That tourist girl, Ursula, staying in my villa next door, she knows she can't have men in her room. But I am like a bloodhound with these girls; I watch their every move. I can smell a man in hiding a kilometre away!'

Bragging, she taps the side of her nose. 'And I saw her early this morning with that Mullet Clitus in my villa. They both ran naked into her bedroom. I chased that idiot out of her bedroom window with my broom. He must be hiding here somewhere?'

Dad, playing the part of a sympathetic neighbour, encourages her to continue. 'I'm angry because the two of them have not respected me. And his clothes are in her room. Where can that *"skilos," dog* be without his clothes?'

'Of course, you're angry. After all, tenants should respect the rules you set down in your villas. If I see him, I'll let you know. Why don't you go home; put your feet up? You must be exhausted; after all, you've been up all night. I heard gunshots earlier. Byron's days must be numbered?'

As she nods, Dad slowly and strategically leads her out our front gate. She remembers her husband George hasn't fixed the gate where a week earlier her randy billy goat Byron, had dented it.

'Sorry about your gate, Mr David. Byron won't do that again! George is gutting the goat now. I keep nagging him to fix your gate but ...' Her voice fades.

'Maybe that's why he won't fix it. Men don't respond well to nagging.'

They smile.

It's well known around the village that Byron had dodgy eyesight. His eyesight was so bad he'd go for anything that moves in a skirt, or rustles. He even mounted Father George dressed in his long robes, thinking he was a female. As a result, the priest limps around the village on crutches, stubbornly refusing to forgive the billy goat, and reckons, with his excellent contacts in heaven, he'll guarantee the vile beast will rot in hell for the rest of eternity.

As Dad stands near the gate waving goodbye to Anna, he smells olive-wood smoke drifting from George's BBQ next door. 'Now you go home, Anna. I'm sure Mullet and Ursula will be too scared to do anything risky again. You and George enjoy your billy goat for lunch.'

Trying to look assured, she heads to her villas, ready to whack Mullet should he reappear. Sniffing the smoky morning air, she wishes the same fate for Mullet. She's imagining him with a metal rod entering through his mouth, and exiting his rear as he sizzles over hot coals. This makes her feel much better.

When the coast is clear, Dad heads for the front door. He

ducks inside and grabs a pair of shorts, and a bottle of water. He's about to race down the side of our villa when Mum pounces. 'Where do you think you're going? And why was Anna here? What are you doing with your shorts and that bottle?'

'Now, now calm down, dear; you need to stay here. Mullet Clitus is naked under the oleander bushes hiding from Anna. She'd caught him naked with Ursula!'

Keeping his voice low, Mum catches on whispering back, 'Oh, my God, not that sexual termite? Is Ursula completely insane? Was she on the ouzo last night …? That drop has been the downfall of many a good woman. Did I ever tell you the story about the Irish woman who drank so much ouzo, the next morning when she woke, she was convinced she was Greek?'

'No time for jokes … Anna's on the rampage. Keep your eyes peeled in case she doubles back. If she does, distract her, will you? I'll get Mullet dressed, and out of here before she spies him.'

Moments later, 'Aww, fantastic, mate, you're a bloody legend! I heard gunshots … What's happened? Geez, Anna's not after me, is she?'

Dad hands him the shorts. Mullet struggles from his uncomfortable squatting position under the ant-infested bush to stand up, and slips them on while Dad keeps watch. 'It's okay, Mullet. George shot Byron, his randy billy goat for too much philandering around the village. Mate, you could be next. Listen, you don't have to explain. Anna's already given me the lowdown on your late-night shenanigans. Seriously, take advice from an old boy like me: if you booze, then snooze, you lose around here. The Greeks are a pretty religious lot. They take a dim view of men visiting tourist girls in their rentals. So, for Christ's sakes, man, keep your hands off, and your strides up from now on!'

As Mullet emerges from the oleander bush, he looks like a transformed man. His skinny sunburnt frame looks ridiculous in Dad's oversized shorts. Using one hand to keep the shorts up and the other to shake Dad's hand, he quickly retracts it and goes back to scratching that unfortunate part of his anatomy where the ants have laid siege on his crotch. 'Got to go, mate.'

'You won't forget to return my shorts now, will you?'

'Oh sure, sure … I'll get Spartacus to drop them off at Leonidas's.' Mullet pauses to greedily swig the bottled water. 'If you get a chance, can you try and get my clobber back?'

'Mullet, I don't think you realise the gravity of the situation. There's not a chance in hell of that, mate. Anna's on the war path. She wants your scalp. I've even heard rumours of her lopping off and storing in pickle jars the testicles of previous male tenants who'd flouted her rooming rules! And I've seen firsthand how her Biblical curses have a nasty sting in their tail too. I doubt Ursula's going to risk her neck trying to smuggle your kit back to you. In fact, I wouldn't be surprised if Anna doesn't chuck her out. Take my advice and scoot while everything's still intact. Truly, buddy, I don't want to see your bits in a pickle jar on Anna's kitchen bench the next time the wife sends me to her place for half a tub of Greek yoghurt. And don't think for one minute I wouldn't recognise your sunburned, waxed or cryonic offerings in a glass jar either.'

Looking terrified, Mullet disappears down the road as fast as his skinny legs can carry him. Returning to his spot in the garden, Dad hums his favourite Maurice Chevalier song. It's from the film, *Gigi*. He smiles as he thinks about the lesson's life teaches about passion and sex. He sings, 'I'm glad I'm not young anymore.'

That night with the distant throb of bouzouki music drifting across the bay from a nearby restaurant, it is as if we are fated by the winds of time. Our family sits down to dinner lit by a huge smiling moon, fireflies dance their merry dance in the fragrant air as we talk on that rarefied topic of sex. As we do, we all laugh about Mullet's amorous endeavours as I pat our now pregnant dog.

There in the flickering darkness, I learn the importance of not confusing the passion of a one-night stand with that of genuine, enduring love. The island's Casanovas with *'Nookie, nookie'* on their minds are disappointed about this.

As for Patch, she's been well and truly dumped. All those amorous male dogs are panting after some other female in the village. I reckon life for the female sex can be a bitch. But, on a brighter note, Patch has yummy billy goat bones for dinner, donated by a very generous Anna.

Mullet gets off the island with his tackle intact. Ursula persuades Anna to let her stay on for the summer, promising she'll never entertain men in her room again. Even so, that doesn't stop Anna sniffing the hot summer's night air looking for tenants flouting her rooming rules.

Spartacus, Leonidas' friend, returned Dad's shorts on his bread run to the village.

And we all know what happened to bad boy Byron the billy goat. Poor fellow, he didn't stand a chance. He's one of the few males in the village that didn't get away with his amorous escapades. His *'nooki's,'* now knackered. Indeed, as the village scapegoat, poor Byron had slipped too far into the 'tzatziki dip' to ever be saved.

Earlier in the day as Father George ate lunch with his wife, Anna and George; he licked with delight the heavenly tasting goat fat from his fingertips. Reaching across the table for one of Byron's grilled testicles *kokoretsi, sweet meats*, a delicacy on the Greek islands, the priest reckoned he'd squeeze Byron through those pearly gates and into heaven after all!

Chapter 18

Troubles in the *Kafeneon*

The warm sweet smell of fermenting wine emanating from Hoppy's cellar hits your nose the second you set foot in our local *kafeneo*. Men mingle with the waft of sweat, tobacco and Greek coffee competing for room in this quintessentially male domain. The only other semblance of female existence, besides me, are two faded calendars located in the middle of a crowded spirits shelf behind Hoppy's counter. One calendar depicts Greek movie star *Aliki Vougiouklaki* in a very brief, crocheted bikini. The other, an image of Brigitte Bardot alluringly draped in a white see-through silk sarong and looks as if she's vying for center stage on the dusty shelf in an attempt to usurp her attractive Greek rival.

There's a hush, an intake of a lungful as I enter. It's a male thing. They probably don't notice it, but I do. Once they see me, they resume their conversations. As a young *xeni, foreign* female, I'm tolerated in this space, just. God knows, I'm not here by choice. I'm on an errand again. It seems to be the story of my life these days, especially asking for credit. Dad has left us in Greece and returned to Australia because my grandfather is dying. We don't know when he's coming back, and the money he sends us from Australia falls well short of what we need to survive.

Time has moved on, and another one of my siblings has made the difficult decision and left for greener pastures beyond Corfu's fair shores to Northern Europe where he can work under the radar, unlike here in Greece. I don't know when I'll see him again, or my other siblings. Perhaps by next year they will have saved enough money enabling them to return. For now, I remain with my mother and my younger brother in the cheapest accommodation we can find. The good thing is our new villa clings close to the coast that we have come to love so much. The villa is even smaller than our previous one but at least it's a comfortable place and a secure roof over our heads as long as Dad keeps remembering to send us money.

One of the pleasing benefits of this move is that I get on well with our new landlady, Athena. I'm teaching her English, and she's kindly rewarding us with fresh eggs and fruit from her orange and mandarin groves. She even gives us bottles of dense, rich, green olive oil from her trees. On cold days, it's so thick it becomes cloudy and solidifies. On winter mornings, I happily spread it like glistening melted avocado butter on my bread.

Every day my poor mother torments herself. She wonders out loud, between breathing in the toxic fumes of cigarettes washed down with generous glugs of black coffee or wine, if Dad's coming back. He's been gone for nearly a year. I wish she'd keep her thoughts to herself. I'm worried enough as it is. I don't want to believe we've been abandoned on the other side of the world. I know in my heart he would never do that. But she keeps jabbing at the topic like she's vengefully attacking the unpalatable remains of a charred chicken carcass. Her voice trembles between fits of anger and sporadic laughter. Sometimes she makes my skin crawl.

There's a strange madness in the air. With raised white knuckles she tells me, 'Your coward of a father is showing his true colors. I ask you; how long does it take someone to die? No one lingers on the verge of death for a year! It's a ploy, a deliberate ploy by your grandparents to keep your father in Australia. We'll never see him again. You know that, don't you? I wouldn't be surprised if your father is having an affair while we slowly starve to death in Greece.'

As she tries to lay my hopes to waste of ever seeing him again, I know we must hang on.

To counter the possible onset of starvation, we've amended our pleading skills, just like the island's Scale and Weight Inspectors who regularly check that all the businesses and shops' weights and scales are correct. It's a fine balancing act borrowing from George to pay Yannis, then borrowing from Dimitri to pay George. And so, it revolves around and around. This is not something new for me, but now it's an unpleasant and frequent occurrence.

In these volatile political times, my socialist friend Dimitri says, 'Nature doesn't say who is, or isn't worthy to receive. Nature just gives; therefore, so should humans. It's as simple or complex as that. Is this not true?'

I nod appreciatively because I know we owe more than the locals say we owe. But sensing our situation, they're not inclined to impose a yoke-like bondage around our necks. In fact, they often brush aside the meagre money we offer them. They do this by making the 'tut' sound, lifting their heads in the sharp traditional Greek sign language way of saying *oxi*, *no* and then smile.

Yes money, the few precious dollars that come courtesy of Dad and Par Avion from Australia. I suppose if anyone knows what it's like to go without, it's the Greeks. Thankfully they don't judge and I'm grateful to them for this. They've made it easier for us than if we lived in a place where people haven't suffered and starved to death on and off for hundreds of years. But inflation in Greece has made things even harder for us. Petrol has skyrocketed and so has everything else. It looks as if the good economic times for Greece are beginning to tumble.

There are days when I wonder why my mother can't become a writer? The act of writing might take her mind off things – after all, my grandfather's typewriter sits waiting to be tapped on the desk. She loves to cook. Perhaps she could become another Mediterranean food writer like legendary Elizabeth David? Focus on recipes from the Ionian Islands. Especially the lesser-known Greek islands that are bundled together under the regional unit of Corfu, Paxos, Othonoi, Ereikoussa and Mathraki. Traditional recipes beyond our staples of bread, tomatoes and the dreaded beans and lentils, of course. Yes, those regulars that form the basis of our mundane diet. But she confides in me that she thinks she's going blind. I'm shocked. I wonder how long she's known this. Did she know this before we left Australia? She's also developed asthma. Some days her asthma attacks are so grave I think she's going to die. It's terrifying to watch.

It has to be stress and cigarettes doing this to her. She says Dad knows. I press her to tell our other family members in Australia, the Australian ambassador in Athens, the British Consul here on the island. Anyone that can assist us; help us get back to Australia and proper health care; remove us from the escalating troubles brewing all around us, but she refuses. I feel helpless. It's a terrible feeling. She has medication for her asthma, but the chances of her seeing an eye specialist in Greece are remote: so, my worries keep multiplying daily.

I'm going to turn fifteen soon. I have resigned myself to the fact that it's only a matter of time before I'll have to leave Greece and seek employment somewhere in Europe. I don't know where, but my immediate focus is to try and stay positive, yet the thought of leaving the only bit of security I have terrifies me. I feel very frightened and alone.

I stand at the front of the counter looking at the small range of goods in Hoppy's glass refrigerated cabinet. Today it doesn't matter how limited his array of stock is as I hungrily eye the fat fleshy, black and green Kalamata olives, their weight tugging them beneath a sea of brine like bulging oversized rounds of glossy caviar. Pink roe preserved in pliable wax lies close by as do thick logs of *mortadella* from Brindisi, and blocks of *kefalograviera* cheese from Macedonia and Epirus. If I ask, the meat and cheese I select will be fashioned by Hoppy into thick slices by his razor-sharp knife and arranged like a geisha's fan on grease proof paper. Then he'll wrap them neatly, only to have his fancy paper work torn open with frenzied delight when I get home to what remains of my family. Sometimes he might even slip some slices of *tahini halva* in the bag for my brother and me.

Muffled conversations continue around me; chairs scrape the pitted terrazzo floor; the old radio continues to thump *Hasapiko, butchers* dance music in the background. The shiny new black phone Hoppy has recently installed in his shop rings. Everyone pauses to hear its sound as if they can't believe it works, let alone someone, somewhere, would contact this small provincial *kafeneo*.

Hoppy limps to the phone and speaks to the person on the other end. He pauses to look around, then he calls my friend Yannis, the fisherman, to come to him. It's his brother. He's ringing from Athens. A religious hush falls into place as we all look at Yannis nervously positioning himself behind the counter. He clutches the side of the bench as if to take the weight off his long spindly legs. With a fumbled exchange of hands, Yannis, looking perplexed, awkwardly holds the phone to his ear under Hoppy's kind guidance. The radio has been flicked off while everyone glues their eyes on a very anxious Yannis.

'*Ella,* Spiros, it's me, Yannis, your brother. Can you hear me? Are you okay?' he bellows into the phone as we, the entire assembled hub, tune into the one-sided conversation because we have no choice – his voice booms piercingly around the *kafeneo* as if he's shouting to his brother in the next building.

At the conclusion of the conversation, Yannis gives the phone to Hoppy who has been on standby next to the phone in case Yannis needs further assistance. Then Yannis proceeds to tell us all about the conversation he's had with his brother.

George, the sandal maker, stops him in his tracks, crying out. 'Why are you telling us this? We heard the entire conversation. In fact, the dead who've been lying in the graveyard for thousands of years heard your conversation. For God sakes, man, you've cured the deaf with your noise but made everyone else deaf. You don't have to shout, you fool!'

'What? Of course, I have to shout. It's Athens, it's Athens – it's very far away! There are big problems in Athens, tanks on the streets, soldiers, police are everywhere. Am I not right to worry about my brother?' replies Yannis, genuinely conveying in simple terms a humble village man's perspective.

Moving his hands as if chopping and clicking through kilometres in the air, he endeavors to show us the distance between him and his brother in Greek sign language. All the men burst into laughter, leaving old Yannis standing in his thread-bare jacket looking like an impoverished jester, with a baffled expression on his face. Seeing me by the counter, he's suddenly embarrassed by his comment and simple demonstration. He pushes his familiar, faded blue fisherman's hat firmly down on his head with both hands as if to hide his dejected, shame-filled eyes.

I feel like reaching out, protectively shielding him from their ridicule for he is my friend. Of course, he's right to worry. His brother could be part of the student rebellions and a possible target. It's a shocking situation for this humble and kind man to be in. He wants a better life for his brother; that's why he's in Athens, but it could all end in tragedy. How many times has he, out of the goodness of his heart, given me fresh fish plucked from his sturdy hand-woven basket as he has passed our villa? He'd have been out all night in his fragile row boat with its little lantern bopping up and down in the bay. With no sail or outboard engine to guide his way in a storm, he lays all his faith in the fragility of his oars, and small anchor. He'd ask for nothing more than a smile, while politely enquiring about my mother's health.

A clock ticks loudly in the background then, in an act motivated by the need to affirm his masculinity, he forcibly turns to Hoppy and orders an ouzo. Taking a single slug of his drink, he brings the now empty glass down hard on the chipped counter, then rotates his neck around to face George. He fires back bitterly, 'Hah, you call me an idiot? As if you can talk. My father told me when the first car came to this village your stupid father put bales of hay in front of the car when it stopped in front of this *kafeneo*. Your father even set before the car a bucket of water. He thought the car was a strange animal. So, you tell me who's the idiot! Idiots are in *your* blood, not mine. My brother works in a big office in Athens. Does this not tell you how important and smart he is, and by extension, me? My brother gets his brains from my family!'

Like tennis balls at a tennis championship, comments fly back and forth as our heads move from man to man as each let's his anger fly at the other. In a strange way, I'm pleased about this live Greek theatre because it takes my mind away from the hard reality of *our* lives back at the villa. Yannis, determined to be the victor of this debate, now drives his knife into Hoppy's heart as the hard-working proprietor leans his tired body against a chair, looking on anxiously. He's worried at any moment his *kafeneo* will erupt into a scene of unbridled violence.

'And you, Hoppy … your wife Elefteria still follows her mother's distinct pie recipe which she says demands the pie be made small because tradition dictates this. Of course, it was because of the size of your mother-in-law's oven. That's why it was made that size. It has nothing to do with any long-standing Corfiot tradition dictated by the bishops. Everyone laughs about it, but no one says anything because your wife, she's a good woman. And you're our friend.'

'Okay, that's enough; enough now, *palikaria, lads,*' responds Hoppy, raising his hands, signaling like a school master for George and Yannis to resume their seats. He pauses momentarily to wipe his hands on his stiffly starched apron, then offers us his wisdom with the words, and easy-to-read hands of a hardworking man who has experienced much in life. He stands before his counter and begins with reason, 'Advances in technology should not drive us apart, *comrades*. Technology should bring people together. Does the phone not let us speak to our loved ones far away? Is this not a good thing whether we holler down the phone or not? Does a car not bring people together whether we feed it hay or petrol? And is a bigger or smaller pie really important when you can still share the pie with friends? Come on, *fillia, friends* let's not let these new technologies divide our community. Let's acquire knowledge together for there can be no shame in learning new things.'

The tension in the room fades as measured smiles and eventually laughter reverberates around the room. Sensing he's on a roll, Hoppy philosophically continues, 'Of course not. The celebrated Mahatma Gandhi once said, 'Freedom is not worth having if it does not include the freedom to make mistakes.' Now is this not true, Yannis? We are all human, none of us perfect. Keep this in mind, my friends, and when I get home, I will tell my wife she can make a bigger pie if she likes. I won't embarrass her but simply gently say she won't be breaking with tradition if she increases the size of the pie. In this way she will only be making more of her delicious pie to share with others. *Ella, come* comrades, the drinks are on me.'

Peace returns to the *kafeneon* saved by our local hero Hoppy.

Now settled in their seats, the men return to slurping loudly, out of rhythm with one another, their demitasse coffees. They do this wantonly and without shame. I wonder how often Hoppy has had to be the peace-maker since the men continue unabated to drape, string or hook their hunting rifles and guns haphazardly on the backs of creaky chairs, or across the *kafeneo's* marble topped tables. Probably more often than I care to think for their firearms are like ominous ghosts having followed these men into many battles in the past – battles that still haunt these men, and now in these tense, corrosive times; their patriotic sons. There's a hovering itch for fingers to touch mustaches, triggers and alcohol. Sometimes all three. Indeed, we're all vulnerable under this potentially explosive cloud of a military regime. But I, unlike these men, remain unarmed.

In recent days the horrors of the polytechnic incident where students were shot in cold blood in Athens had turned many supporters of the coup into opponents overnight. The youth wanted democracy and called for "Bread, education and liberty." But their cries were quickly crushed by the brutal force of the regime. Papadopoulos may have tried in a desperate attempt to recover the situation, but he was ousted by the even tougher, hardliner Dimitrios Ioannidis, who was and still is determined to never give in. The nation went into shock. This was followed by even more hardline curfews. God only knows this is not a good time for Dad to have left us alone and broke in Greece.

By now, like swallows in spring, some men are stirred into action by the sun shining through the thick windowed alcoves of the *kafeneon*. Long shards of precious light streak across the terrazzo floor, inviting an exodus from the stuffy building. In response, the men loudly scrape the floor, dragging their chairs across the pitted surface in search of the prized rays emitted from a fleeting winter's sun at the front of the shop. Once outside, they prop their chairs next to marble topped tables that are weathered and stoic by necessity. A run of turkeys makes their way along the road in front of the men who by now are occupied playing *tavli, backgammon* and cards. Now preoccupied, these men absorb the sun's rays through their shabby winter clothing.

Running frightened as they gobble past, the turkeys are being herded by a couple of local women. These noisy birds unsettle tethered donkeys. The donkeys bray and buck, frustrated at being tied to wooden posts beside the *kafeneon* waiting for their masters to hasten and end their mingling. The women, festooned with traditional white head scarves, disappear, erased from sight as their upper bodies slowly dissolve like ghosts into the white-washed shops that form the backdrop of the pot-holed village road. They jiggle long sticks at their noisy rafters, eyeing the men with contempt. They think them *tempelis, lay-abouts* who should get off their arses and help their exhausted wives, mothers and daughters, not sit, drink and play *tavli* all day.

Demonstrating who's in charge of the animals at least, the women continue past, whacking their sticks at their terrified stock as they run, squawk and skid to avoid oncoming traffic and donkeys' hooves. These women will pause at the turn in the road where baskets have been supplied for their use near the old roadside shrine. This hallowed site is softly illuminated with candles and votive offerings for the festive season. Soon these turkeys will be stuffed. They will flutter with terror as they are propelled into large baskets sealed with hessian tops. With haste, these will be sewn with wide stitches into the basket's reeds, prohibiting their escape. In their enclosed dark world, they will be heaved onto old Yannis' mule cart and transported to the noisy markets below the *Neo Citadel* in Corfu town. They'll be sold to tough bargaining butchers, their chopping blocks already stained with the blood from previously sacrificed animals in readiness for the island's Christmas festivities.

Yes, Christmas. I wonder what ours will be like? I take my bag of appropriated supplies home to my depleted family. Generously, Hoppy has thrown a few extra things in the bag. *Tahini halva*, sunny orbs of large lemons with bright green scented leaves still attached, cloves of garlic enclosed in crinkly white and purple flaky skins, and a large green cabbage. There are also three pomegranates with shiny cheeks that seem to blush with crimson beauty beneath my touch. My little brother will hang these above our front door over Christmas. Come the new year, we'll smash them against our entryway, splitting them in the hope for good luck. I can't help but think Hoppy's not merely a local hero, he's my hero too.

Hoppy's kindness will endure through Christmas. I'm convinced of this because every now and then he gently pats my hand whispering knowingly, 'Everything is going to be okay; *paidi mou, my child*, you'll see. Don't be frightened of the future. Your father will return. I know this because he is a good man.'

I'm fortified by his words and believe him. I have to for the snow is already falling on the mountain tops of Albania and mainland Greece. The locals tell me that this year's winter is the coldest in years as they wrap their jackets close to their bodies and lug wood home on bent backs. As the Corfiots secure their homes against the encroaching cold onslaught, my mother huddles with her arms around my young brother in our small but warm kitchen. It's here, always here, in this small boy's curve that she clings to life these days. It's as if she holds onto him because at any moment he's going to be pulled from her clutching, clinging arms by some dark looming force.

Why do I see in these fleeting moments the terrified eyes of the 12th century holy icon of the Virgin *Pelagonitissa* of Macedonia, so beloved by Eastern Orthodox Christians? I see her face often now, in my mother's eyes. Yes, those doleful, terrified eyes never speaking of a darker more painful secret; the subsequent loss of a cherished son.

Still, under my mother's far away gaze I sit vanquished by the absence of her touch, as mine for her is repelled, set aside by her angry, dismissive hands, remote moods. It's as if I'm contagious to touch, contagious to love. Are all daughters repugnant or just me …? My young brother sleeps in her room now while I sleep alone in mine waiting for a *koukouviya, owl* to signal the passing of my grandfather in the night and herald the return of my father. Oh, how my heart longs for his homecoming.

I wonder if this year the snow will fall on Mount Pantocrator. I don't mean meagre sprinklings like the fine white icing sugar the town bakers sift onto warm *milopites, filo pastry apple pies*. I mean real snow. Snow that will silently fall then build up enough volume to tumble and roll with audacious boldness like cumulus clouds through the cold olive groves and reach our tiny village below the mountain by the sea. I sigh because the wise almighty God *Pantocrator* already knows the answer to my question, as do the ancient gods. Truly I am like a Greek now as, unlike my mother, I hope for the best. Can there be any other way?

Chapter 19

Villa Kapodistria

I watch as Christmas comes and goes with little feasting or fanfare. There are no decorations, no surprise Santas – not even the Greek version of a Saint Vasilis to put a local slant on things. Along with languishing nativity lights, it's a Christmas light on laughter. Around Corfu town it's as if we are in an unnerving lockdown. For fun we see a few shadow puppets of naughty *Karagiozis* dressed in Santa costumes, and that's about it. And, as it turns out, Christmas is light on snow too, just the gentlest of sprinklings on Mount Pantocrator. A few precious Christmas cards come through the post including one from my father. In the card, he jokes that my grandfather still hasn't fallen off the perch, but my mother doesn't find this news particularly amusing. I imagine my grandparents wouldn't either. Adversity has made Mum frugal with everything. Poor Mum, her smiles these days have the shop shelf life of a single, lit, Redhead match.

I suppose the only consolation is most Greeks are low key about Christmas. The very devout Orthodox fast like fanatics and deny themselves the wicked pleasures of meat, eggs and dairy products. We join in the fast, but not for religious reasons: economic reality dictates. After New Year, like clockwork, the Orthodox Christmas arrives on or around the seventh of January. I imagine people would envy our having two Christmases, but what is the point if both feel hollow. This 'second Christmas' is set by the Julian calendar. It's the date nominated in the Bible and predates the Gregorian calendar. Most Western Christians tend to follow the Gregorian calendar and, as Easter is traditionally the highlight on the Eastern Orthodox calendar, we hang out for Easter hoping our circumstances will improve. Other non-Orthodox families that have long fled the island for the winter are probably merrily tucking into truffles, turkey and tangoing under mistletoe.

Around us, winter has set in with gusto as lightning and clouds gather in the skies with unbridled fury. Rain falls in torrents. I wonder if the tourists who flock to Corfu in summer have any inkling about how much rain buckets down in winter. Corfu is not considered the lushest of the Greek islands for nothing. It's called the Green Island for this very reason. These moody storms release their rage along the island's postcard coasts thrashing our world the way village women take their revenge for their philandering husbands out on their *flokatis, sheep wool rugs*. They bash the hell out of them. Strong women, poor rugs! These storms wail and howl through the olive groves, shaking our home. I feel like crawling into the wide, crumbling cracks in our villa's walls and staying there until the storms pass. But it's my mother's turbulent moods that destroy any chance of inner peace or enduring feelings of safety even when the pelting rain and crashing storms have moved on.

Some nights, compelled by the gloomy atmosphere generated by her moods and augmented by a bad dose of cabin fever, I feel the urge to remove myself from our villa for a while. I dare risk my life and challenge the rage of winter weather and informers, venturing, stumbling like a drunkard into the dark through the olive and orange groves to visit my neighbours. Always welcome, I'm drawn with haste through thin slits of doors held briefly ajar into the low light from their open kitchen fires; barn-like doors slam, sealing me into their smoky inner sanctums. Wrapped securely in *philoxenia, love of foreigners*, truly these are my holy grails of hope, these warm inviting people and their humble sacred spaces. Immersing myself into this coalface of kindness, these villagers are becoming my adopted tribe as I desperately cling to their philosophical wisdom, kindness and light-hearted verve.

Nestled by the fireside at my friend Katerina's home, or the hearths of other friends, the smell of olive wood permeates the air. A fine mist of flat smoke makes our eyes sting, all the while chestnuts or, now after Christmas fasting, *souvla, grilled* sparrows no bigger than a child's fist are cooked over red coals. These tiny fragile birds are local hunters' trophies. A bullet shot through its centre or close enough to kill is practically bigger than the bird itself. I can't bring myself to eat them and the locals laugh at my rejection of their winter delicacy.

It's here in these intimate spaces that stories and poetry are shared about adventures in the mysterious Albanian mountains or along the vast remote borders of the mainland of Greece. The wise old sages in the village, part of our cosy communal collection of all sorts, tell of a time before World War II, before Albania became one of the most hardline communist countries in the world. They confide that many of their Greek friends and relatives are still trapped there desperately trying to get out. These time-swept elders speak of vast clear lakes full of fantastic fish longer than the length of a tall man's arm, and ancient Roman archaeological ruins that even the Greeks and Italians would envy.

They tell me how after big storms along Corfu's shorelines they find the smashed remains of primitive wooden rafts pitifully held together with handmade rope, or beaten nails that have been fused together with scant scraps of retrieved metal by desperate Greek and Albanian escapees. Their craft lie smashed, spat from the ocean and washed up along the coastline– sad relics of the brave who've fled the punitive practices of the communist regime just across our beautiful bay – our stunning bay of straits. Set between opposing lands which, for those trying to escape, are dire straits indeed. If spotted, the escapees will become machine gun fodder, fired upon by Greek or Albanian border forces. But stray too far north and Italy might join in the shooting.

The villagers are right about these vessels. I have seen them from time to time, splayed carcasses of abandoned wooden rafts and wondered at their origins. Where do these marooned souls go when they're dumped by the Ionian, lucky to be alive, flung onto the pebbled coast of Pyrgi and Ipsos beach under the veil of darkness? How often have I spied these ruins and seeing it merely as fortuitous pickings from the sea, salvaged them? Yes, ripped the torn wood apart with my young hands then lugged the mutilated remains home to dry. Once dry, I feed the wood into our kitchen stove in an attempt to satisfy its insatiable appetite. But, as to the mystery of where the refugees go, everyone shakes their head. They deposit blank looks of unconvincing ignorance into the smoky spaces between us. Surely, they know – they who are intimately connected to this land and know it so well. Even when its heartbeat is out of rhythm, or gives a tiny tremble, they know. They who see gods, or other ghostly silhouettes floating in the misty olive groves and around our sleepy hamlet; they know. Why can't these shadows speak to me too?

Alongside these modest firesides radios play *Rembetiko* music, and it inundates my being where it endures even today, a music with deep roots in the Ottoman Empire, especially

Smyrna where it was roughly cradled to life in coffee shops and dim hashish dens. Songs filled with epic tales of betrayal, oppression, poverty, the underclasses, political prisoners, lost love, addiction and war, it's a style of music that filtered into Greece via the fragmented sentiments of the displaced masses of over two million Greeks who fled Asia Minor when Turkey forced the Greeks out in 1923. The harbour cities of Greece became a fertile ground for this music to morph with traditional folk songs and expand into its current style with the bouzouki at the centre of its beating heart. It aided social outcasts, the partisans against the Nazis and anti-capitalists in the civil war that followed to birth their deeply held beliefs into substance through lyrical form.

In Greece, time pushes these songs into the present imbued with secret messages in cryptic stanzas, messages of warning about ELSA, the Greek military police, warning insiders – those who oppose the military junta from the left, clandestine supporters of the soon-to-be formed PASOK – understand. Moved by emotion, some nights my older friends, men and women alike, suddenly stand and lift the crumbs off kitchen floors with the worn soles of their leather shoes and dance. They dance as if in a daze, sometimes with eyes closed. They dance when they are happy and they dance when they are torn, ripped apart by grief. In this space, they are free to be moved to move. All the while I too am moved.

Before we'd arrived in Greece, greats like Nikos Kazanzakis, Melina Moukouri, Mikis Theodorakis and Manos Hadzidakis to name a few, had already made their mark as influential leaders in the arts, and the world craved more. But most of all, these legends created a new popularism permeating into the very hearts and souls of the Greek people, a sense of national pride redeemed through them irrespective of the Junta's repression and censorship. These writers, actors and performers have become as mythically important to the Greeks as their ancient gods, only these artists are real – some tortured and exiled for their political beliefs, others not. So, in secret, locals play their banned music, read and recite their literary heroes' poems and sing their songs, clinging to them, risking interrogation and reprisals. Locals tell me they are still numbed by the devastation of two World Wars and the civil war that followed, and for the Junta to have ripped their icons of the arts from them, is indefensible. What is forgivable for many, however, is the money that has flowed into the economy. Money has been central to Greece's recovery irrespective of its source, especially from America. Up until recently, it has kept Papadopoulos and his generals in favour with western governments, stopped the spread of communism and activated much needed development throughout the country so Greece can recover and thrive.

For many avant-garde, nonconforming artists, poets, musicians, writers and thespians, however, it is an unpalatable choice between a deep love of country, a penchant for civil liberty, crucial free will in artistic expression no matter a person's politics, and the vital drachmae with its price tragically thrusting the country into a sterile time warp. The young say they need both in order to become unified, democratic and whole again.

Some nights my friends teach me local songs, amusing songs about the lengths of men's penises and other comical refrains. One of my favourite songs is about the Italian soldiers during the war, and how whenever they heard cannons being fired at them by the 'courageous' Greeks, 'they shat pasta into their pants' and ran away ('*Ta Italiano mangiere macaroni, otan akouoe to kanoni, kanoon skata to pantaloni!*') It rhymes beautifully in Greek, while at the same time showcasing Corfu's unique local Italian inflection. Each time Katerina and I sing this, we laugh hysterically even though we've sung it hundreds of times. We adore its wicked bawdiness. We also sing another lewd song about Mussolini, the despised Italian tyrant. This silly little ditty we croon to the tune of Bill Haley's *See You Later, Alligator*. It goes like this:

> *'Mussolini has a teeny weenie peani,*
> *chop it off signor Mancini*
> *and feed it to his puppy Fellini.*
> *If he won't eat it,*
> *offer it back to Mussolini*
> *baked in a crunchy Italian panini,'*

and so on. How proud are these people that during the war, while the Albanian's let their country fall to the Italians in twenty-four hours, it was the brave Greeks who drove the Italians back into Italy from Albania, temporarily stalling the Italians' penetration into Greece. Even Churchill remarked on their outstanding courage.

On a cold night a few months later, a *kookouviya, owl* signals the death of my grandfather in Australia. Like a doomsday clock with a silent tick the bird sits looking inquisitively, blinking at me on our kitchen window sill as a flickering glow emitted from our crackling wood stove lights its furtive appearance. I tell Mum but she only laughs at my advanced warning of my grandfather's death, and my father's return.

'Don't be ridiculous! You mustn't believe those old Greek wives' tales. They're pure, unadulterated crap. Your stupid father may never come back. The sooner you accept it, the better.'

I say no more on the subject for no matter what my melancholic mother may say, she cannot entirely direct my thoughts, especially about something like this. Greece is a secretive land; and one must be open and willing to penetrate events, merge with and embrace fully its beliefs, perhaps not its politics, but certainly its customs and practices to ever have any chance of understanding it and its people. The land, animals, gods and myths have always had ways of revealing insights that are beyond human reason; beyond our simple capacity to comprehend. Even before telephones ring, or mail is delivered, these things are already known by powers beyond our inadequate imaginings.

My wise friend Hoppy was right, as I knew he would be. Within a few weeks of my grandfather's death, my father returns. He's been gone a full year and receives a distinctly chilly welcome from my mother, lingering hugs from my little brother and me. Dad's presence has a way of lighting the road ahead and distilling Mum's moods.

So, upon his reappearance there's a wonderful new sense of hope. My little brother leaves my mother's side and once again shares my bedroom. Over the next few weeks, there's an element of optimism in her voice – it's a much-needed sound.

It's amazing what a bit of extra money in the pot and Dad's presence can do to lift our situation out of the doldrums. Soon after, she announces she's made a decision and it's not about returning to Australia because of her health. Now her voice happily rings in the morning air, 'Okay, listen up everybody! It's time to pack um up and move um out! Let's un-circle the wagons. We're moving to the Villa of the Late Count Kapodistria.'

Chapter 20

Book Him

I reply to Mum's proposed move to Villa Kapodistria with a bland 'Who and when?'

Baffled by our lack of enthusiasm and ignorance, she continues. 'Geez, you lot need a history lesson. Okay, family gather round. Corfu's airport and one or two streets on the island are named after this famous Greek Count. He was the governor of the Hellenic State, established the first Greek bank, forged the new state and even introduced the cultivation of potatoes of all things. Now one of his family's magnificent villas is available for lease. I was speaking to Anna, and she says an academic by the name of Lord Alexei Alexandrovich leases the villa. Fascinating man, he's been writing his thesis about Greek saints. He needs tenants to take over the lease on the magnificent property and mind his rare book collection until he returns.'

What a turn-around.

She goes on, volleying a smile, 'Imagine the parties we can have?'

Off in her own world where exciting things can happen from time to time, Dad's trying to catch up and grasp the implications of this move from a practical point of view. He shakes his head like a sad clown. He's heard it all before.

'I don't want to be the one to throw the cat among the pigeons, dear, but it sounds very expensive. I don't know if this is a good idea. It might be hard keeping our fragile flock afloat financially with this move.'

'Rubbish! I won't hear another word about it. Your pension will more than cover it. I've already discussed the matter with Anna. Oh, my God, David, catch up and stop looking like something Frosso's goat regurgitated! We could be living in a fabulous mansion leased by a Lord! I can see it all now. Yes, bikinis and Martinis.'

She continues in flurried ecstasy, 'He's a Romanoff. His mother was related to Tsar Nicholas of Russia himself. Even you must agree that it's time to move into something more up-market ... more us. God knows I've roughed it enough. Anyway, you promised.'

Now Mum's dropped her Australian accent and pulled out her regal English one. 'According to Anna, when Lord Alexanrovich's mother fled from Russia to Britain during the Russian Revolution, she was given a title because she was related to the Tsar. That's how Alexei inherited the title of Lord.'

Mum falls silent for a moment and then fells us with one of her disarming expressions. 'And he's invited us to the villa for drinks tomorrow night, so everyone has to be on their best behaviour. We'd better scrub up alright!'

I too wonder if our dishevelled lot can pass this so-called Lord Alexei's white glove test. But she reckons if we try hard, we can, so the next day we arrive at Villa Kapodistria.

The villa is vastly bigger than our tiny Pyrgi home. In fact, the villa takes my breath away as the sun sets on its shabby, chic pastel, pale apricot walls, silhouetting white window frames and burgundy shutters. Crowned with faded terracotta tiles, it looks like an ice-cream cake dolloped with plum jam. The villa is so large it's been divided in half with relatives of Kapodistrias living in the top and bottom levels on the other side of the villa. The town side of the villa, which we hope to lease, scoops us up into its wide welcoming arms. I, for one, am hooked.

The interior's patchy, crumbling walls are a deep ochre colour and contrast beautifully with wide tiles down the central hall and its high white ceilings. Climbing the expansive elegant wooden staircase, we pass a number of mysterious rooms before entering an upstairs loungeroom. There's a vast fireplace, a piano in one corner, a round dining room table in the another. Elegant but dog-eared lounges and armchairs are set formally around the grand marble fireplace. I reckon those couches could tell a few tales. French doors lead to a balcony; windows on two sides of the room showcase vast views. The villa's wooden floors creak contentedly beneath our feet.

The evening begins with lots of 'How do you dos' and yes, Mum had given us the pre-function preamble to mind our P's and Q's – all the taboos and to dos. Especially never say, 'G'day, pig's arse, bonzer or tar, love!' But say 'How do you do?' and never, ever 'Pleased to meet you' because you may not be pleased to meet them.'

Anything else is a dead give-away that we are from, dare I say it, the colonies. Seeing through Mum's accent façade, one of Lord Alexei's English friends remark, 'Oh, I say, you're not from the Antipodes, are you? The old penal colonies, hey what?' Poor Mum ... it was bound to happen sooner or later. Normally people just let her go on. But tonight, it's as if we're on trial for doing a bunk from Port Arthur for crimes we'd committed in previous centuries. But as we've fallen in love with the old mansion, we'll do anything to secure a foot in the door so, Mum bites her tongue. Lord Alexandrovich makes his way across the sitting room to greet us. Pale, in need of a good feed, he keeps flicking his Hitler-style hair to one side. Is he androgynous, I wonder? Taken aback, he surveys me as one does a pesky insect. I'm waiting for him to swat me. Fortunately, he's restrained himself and I survive the terrifying encounter. He is, however, friendly to my parents, leading them back downstairs and along the wide hallway to a dark door. He stops and opens the door. Looking inside the dusty room, they see a large expanse crammed floor-to-ceiling with shelves of books. They stand and chat at the door for a while before returning to the gathered group upstairs. Then, as if by magic, by the end of the evening we have managed to get the lease on the villa on the proviso that his library is out of bounds. How can we refuse; the villa is fabulous, dripping with antiques and way beyond anything we have seen within our scant budget. And for such reasonable rent.

As soon as Alexei leaves for England, and much to Athena's annoyance, we depart Pyrgi and our beloved coast and move in. The mansion is located at the top of a hill generously sprinkled with olive trees and rows of tall cypresses stretching along a long winding gravel drive pitted with pot-holes. Very quickly we discover the decadent joy that can be derived from sitting in our upstairs bath, or using the toilet. Why? We have the most glorious views all the way down the island; almost to the tippy toes of Italy. To the right, across the bay we are spoiled with vistas of the protracted mountains where the borders of Albania and Greece nudge. We tease first-time guests to the villa inviting them upon arrival upstairs to our bathroom. With this odd invitation, we imitate Mum and put on English accents and say, 'Oh, do come and view the vista from our rather spectacular loo. Welcome to the throne room.' We think this is hilarious.

Not long after settling into the mansion, locals tell us stories about the strange and elusive Lord Alexei. They say, 'He's crazy. Last winter the *trelos xenox, crazy foreigner* smashed pieces of the villa's beautiful French and Russian antique furniture. He'd flung these objects into the fire to keep himself warm. He has no respect for other people's property. *Po, po, po.*' If villagers from Mandooki endeavoured to be kind, bring generous gifts of eggs and olives because he reminded them of an emaciated stick figure, he'd answer the door naked. Shocking the local women, in their anguish they'd fling gifts of olives and freshly laid eggs up into the air as they scurried and slipped down the embankment through the shady olive groves vowing never to return. It wasn't long after that one of our guests dropped their cigarette lighter down the side of a lounge cushion and, after rummaging around for a while, discovered a diary. Having had a few too many drinks, they shared with us the intimate details from the diary including the sexual exploits of one of Alexei's acquaintances. Compared to the stores of hallowed books downstairs, this was pretty hot stuff.

But the locals' dramas with Alexei don't stop us enjoying the villa. Keeping our promise, we don't enter his library, ever. Indeed, the days go by pleasantly enough as we luxuriate in the vastness of this charming villa. Well, that is until one day when the calm of our new home is abruptly disrupted just as we sit on the balcony eating breakfast and drinking in the spectacular views. A roar of police sirens, a stream of law enforcement cars followed by a large truck rumble at speed up the long gravel drive and halt at the front of the villa. Before we know it, the place is surrounded.

This is serious. Horrible scenarios detonate in our minds. Greece is an even tenser political hotspot now that Ioannidis and his co-conspirators have grabbed power. Because of this, the island is going through more police and state-imposed curfews with restrictions on people's movements. More than ever riots break out and everyone's contacts are once again scrutinised. Talking politics is always dangerous, that's been a given for years but more so now, and even though we've always felt reasonably safe in Greece, perhaps now we'll be thrown in jail. Has our family been deemed political liabilities? Are we going to be exiled, considered unwelcome aliens? Or will we be lined up against a white-washed wall, blind-folded and shot?

There's a loud thumping of fists on our front door. A tall suited man hands my trembling father a search warrant. The warrant is written in Greek, and he can't read it. It soon becomes clear that this man's team of armed policemen want to search the villa. We're shocked. What are they looking for, and what can Dad do? What can any of us do?

We're completely surrounded and still in our PJ's. This is not only terrifying, its undignified. Incredibly, the man in the smart suit turns out to be an Englishman; an inspector from Scotland Yard. The only thing he doesn't say to us and his trusty troop of uniformed Greek policemen as a joke is, 'Book 'em, boys!' But it's not funny and with nothing to hide, Dad flings open the front door and in pour the police with guns at the ready.

I pinch myself. Is this really happening?

The next minute the police are foraging through our belongings. I stand shell-shocked; they're even going through my underwear. I blush with embarrassment. But whatever they're looking for isn't among my uninspiring array of smalls, or our other humble belongings. Very quickly the police focus their attention on Alexei's library.

Lowering the temperature on the situation, and because the Greeks are renowned for their hospitality, Dad decides to extend the inspector an invitation to join us on the balcony for breakfast while the police continue their search. We are, after all, unarmed and unlikely to make a hasty getaway any time soon – especially not in our pj's or even over the side of our bougainvillea-covered balcony. Dad later laughs. 'Socrates may have had his anomalies, but I reckon not even he would try scaling our balcony – the spikes on that vicious bougainvillea would do more damage than all their bullets put together.' He has a point.

Scratching his smooth chin, the inspector considers Dad's invitation. He decides we're a benign lot and joins us. Sipping strong Greek coffee, he tells us why he's on this secret mission from London.

It seems Lord Alexei Alexandrovich is not a lord at all. Who'd have thought? He's not even a remote relative of the Romanoff family. He's an eccentric by the name of Joe Smith. Driven by his passion for Greek Orthodox hagiography, he'd taken leave of absence from university to write a thesis on Greek saints. Soon after, Joe moved to Corfu to do his research. Joe/Alexei is a book thief. He smuggles books he's stolen, many first editions, and sacred illuminated manuscripts out of Britain and then drives across Europe with them to Greece. At international borders, he tells curious customs officials that his books are insignificant secondhand, worthless copies. Apparently, he casually says in his superior voice, "I'm taking them to my villa on Corfu. These are my research books. I study Greek hagiography."

Who'd question a man with a pile of old religious texts? It all seemed so innocent.

Whenever he needed money, he'd sell a book on the black market. According to the detective, Joe had been under suspicion for some time. However, this time he was caught red-handed stealing from a prestigious library in England. Arrested and interrogated by the authorities, Joe eventually told the police about his secret stash of books on Corfu. Once notified, Scotland Yard linked up with Interpol and together set up a clandestine operation to zoom in on our villa. All the while the authorities were checking to see if we were part of this book stealing racket.

With surprising efficiency, the rescued books are carefully placed in secure boxes and loaded into the large truck bound for England. The complex task of working out where the books came from will be a nightmare for some poor administrator as pages with library identification information had been either very carefully glued to another page, or shrewdly removed by Joe. Apparently, he's quite the professional.

Dad strikes up a rapport with the inspector and in the evening, he joins us for dinner. Over a few bottles of local wine, the now off-duty inspector entertains us with stories about some of the weird and wonderful characters he's encountered investigating crime and corruption around Europe while working with Interpol. As the evening draws to an end, the now relaxed detective says, 'It's people like you that make my job worthwhile. It's unfortunate you were the meat in the sandwich of this undercover operation.'

The world didn't seem a bad place to be after this confession. Feeling comfortable enough to confide in the inspector, Dad lets go his relief by twisting, then pulling the cork on another bottle of good wine. He confides in him that the Australian Ambassador, only a week earlier, had made the journey from Athens, especially to see us. He expressed concern about the increasing political tensions in Greece, and wondered if we'd made plans to get out of the country if the need arose. There was much animated talk of the collapse of the seven-year Junta. But Dad still hadn't figured out his exit plan. Jokingly, he reckons he'd grab our passports and stick all four of us in our tiny patriotic blue and white rowboat. Crossing his fingers, he'd paddle like the clappers all the way to Italy in the hope of escaping Ioannides and his secret police. Or, on the other side of the straits, avoid being shot by the Albanian water authorities. Albania, being distinctly antiwestern, if we were captured it's unlikely we'd ever leave.

'I will deal with all that if the need ever arises,' says Dad taking a large sip of wine. 'But I have to admit, I thought all our days were numbered when I heard those cars with sirens racing up the hill!'

As for Joe, the book thief, he won't be returning to the island any time soon. He'll experience the inside of Her Majesty's prison for quite some time. Dad laughed when he heard this because the first time we met him at the villa, he'd overheard him skiting to one of his English friends: 'Oh yes, Gordon, I've found tenants to take over the lease of the villa. Bloody ex-colonial convicts from the Antipodes, I believe. Should have kept the lot of them locked up but just the same, they will come in handy minding the villa for me.'

Mum is appalled. 'Why didn't you tell me this before?'

'Ah, why say anything when we're living in this fabulous villa? This is what you always wanted, isn't it? A stunning, crumbling old mansion with amazing views and anyway, he got his Karma!'

Indeed, he did. I wonder if they put him in charge of the prison library?

Chapter 21

Mullet Returns

Is it a moving curse cast by a demonic Delphic oracle, or should Mum rub her eyes?

Through a sea of jumbled faces, she sees what looks like Mullet Clitus. Yes, it's his head bopping up and down in the crowded marketplace. Who'd have thought he'd have the courage to return to the island after Anna chased him naked out of Ursula's bedroom into our garden last summer? But it is him. It *must* be him. No one in the world looks quite like Mullet Clitus.

Following close behind is Ursula. It looks like she wasn't a one-night stand. As they're smiling, Mum assumes Anna hadn't pickled his testicles in an olive jar and stuck them on her kitchen bench either, as was rumoured around the village. Mum laughs to herself – after all, Dad may have said Mullet made it off the island, but how would he know? What a relief for Mullet. Moreover, what a relief for Ursula. No wonder they're smiling.

Waving one of her regal waves, Mum beckons them. Seeing her, they wave and head over to the café where she sits nestled between a group of local fishermen, their now empty baskets and her jumbled bags overflowing with green groceries. She is rewarding herself with a cognac for getting the shopping done by 9.30 am. It's her first tipple for the day.

As they draw closer, she notices Mullet has put on weight

during the northern winter months. It suits him. She smiles to herself. He's no longer the skinny, naked and sunburnt runt Dad described that fateful morning. In fact, he looks respectable. His hair's cut; he's showered and shaved. Even his clothes look expensive, you could say even elegant – a cut above the tight-fitting budgie smugglers he wore every day last summer.

She wonders if he'd gone back to his Greek mamma in Sydney and she'd forced him to smarten himself up over the Australian summer? Fed him lots of pasta and rice like the good local Greek women feed their children in the village at lunchtime through the schoolyard fence? Particularly their precious little Adonises. Perhaps Momma managed to keep him off the grog and away from women? But looking at Ursula, she thought not. Perhaps he'd managed to get a well-paid job in London? Lots of Aussie backpackers stay in Europe, especially during the UK winter. They work saving to return to their travels around Europe the following summer.

Carefully avoiding trampling on lambs being led through the market for Easter, Mullet and Ursula head to the café. As they reach her, Mum stands stiffly, pausing to tolerate a kiss on both cheeks from Mullet. She then reaches forward, giving Ursula a generous hug.

'Well, well, well! This is a surprise. What are you two doing back on Corfu? Are you here for the Easter celebrations or just passing through? I'm having a cognac. It's cheap at this café, and as such I'm ignoring the rather unfortunate waft of sardines and squid ink. Would you care to join me?'

Mullet's smile expands. He's like Mum and is fond of a tipple. 'Geez, Mrs Jo, g'day. How's your old man and the family going? Yeah, that would be real beaut. Nah, let me get this.' Mullet waves signalling a waiter, orders a couple of ouzos and another cognac for Mum.

'Me and Ursula are back not just for Greek Easter, Mrs Jo, but to get married. Yep, I'm finally tying the knot and Ursula's the lucky girl. Aren't you, love?'

Ursula jokingly elbows him in the ribs; he laughs and rephrases his comment. 'Nah, I'm the lucky bloke. And you wouldn't believe it ... I got lucky with the lotteries in London too. Who'd a thought?'

Who indeed, winces Mum giving him the lean end of a smile?

'Now I've finally got a few coins to jingle in me pockets, I caught up with Ursula in Sweden. We reckoned Corfu would be the place to get married. After all, it's where we met. Now we want to buy a villa and settle down here. Mum and her sister have a villa in Saint Markos. They own half each and well, you wouldn't believe it, it's for sale.'

'You don't say,' replies Mum, raising her eyebrows.

'Yep. We are heading out your way this arvo to give the place the once over. We were just off to hire a car for a few days ... give the rest of the island a gander too!'

They beam at Mum as Mullet tethers Ursula closer to him with his long lanky arms. 'My brother Stick and his chick Took from Thailand are coming out from England later this week with our new car. I bought a real beaut bright yellow Lotus in London. It's got bucket seats. One bucket for me behind and the other for me ice-bucket. Get it? Only joking. Nah, the other seats for Ursula, isn't it, love?'

Tempted to slug the vile man, Mum flinches as he laughs at his own joke. At the same time, she can't help herself; she's also impressed. Dollar signs tango temptingly before her eyes.

He stops laughing. 'That should get a few tongues wagging around the village. But, in the meantime, if you know of any other villas with sea views and a bit of land close to your place, would you keep us in the loop? Just not too close to

Anna's place, if you know what I mean.' He taps his generous nose.

Mum knows exactly what he means. She feels sick. How can this absolute flea of a human specimen be so auspicious and win the lottery? What a travesty. She smiles, irrespective of her deep desire to thump the man, grab his wallet and break the land speed record for the airport.

Mullet continues, 'I don't want her contemplating nailing me backside to any white-washed walls again and suffer poor old Byron the billy goat's fate!' A sheepish look sweeps across his face. But just as quickly it's wiped clean by a huge smile.

'Oh, by the way, Mullet, I should tell you we have moved. We no longer live in that small place in Pyrgi. We have taken a lease on Villa Kapadistria just outside of town. It's the Count's old villa, you know? It's a vast property up on a hill overlooking the New Port, not far from Corfu's main hospital, along the road and up the hill. It's not far.'

Smiling a superior smile, she's hoping a few one-upmanship points can be salvaged from this mortifying encounter. We might be financially strapped but she's determined to recover some self-dignity. Her British accent emerges as she recoils beneath his strong, grating accent. It's in moments like this that she derives enormous superior pleasure from playing down her Australian origins and usually avoiding Aussies with distinctive accents altogether unless absolutely desperate for company. Or, in this case, could turn out to be a primary source of much-needed gossip and a possible cash cow.

'It's a mansion, you know, split into two it's so vast. Part of the Kapodistrious family lives on one side, she's a doctor, having studied in America. The hubby is from Crete, I think. We rent the other side. It works very well. Tell me about your forthcoming nuptials? With your Greek Australian background, Mullet, are you getting married in the Greek Orthodox Church? Or, Ursula, are you thinking of some other type of service? You know you could hire a *kaiki, fishing boat* and get married in any number of the fabulous bays around the island. What about Nissaki, Paliokastritsa or Gouvia? Lots of tourists are doing that. It's quite the trend.'

Looking perplexed, Mullet turns to consult a distracted Ursula. 'Yeah, we talked about this and Ursula's decided to get dunked.'

Mum's confused by the term. 'Sorry, you have got me there. What do you mean, dunked?'

Distracted by voices and movement across the path, suddenly Ursula's gone. She's headed to where lambs are secured to the rear of a three-wheeled truck and she lunges into an animated conversation with a shepherd and butcher.

'Geez, there she goes,' laughs Mullet, unflustered by her rapid departure. 'Ursula's got a thing for those lambs. She's been on about them all morning. We flew in this morning and we've seen them around town tied to front doors, motorbikes and bumpers of cars. Poor little buggers. Yep, dunked in the Greek church when she's baptised, of course. We must get a priest to agree to baptise her and then, all going well, she'll be dunked in water and blessed with oil. Only then can she get married in the Orthodox Church because she's never been baptised.'

Chuckling he continues, 'I can see her now in a bikini in front of the altar! But me mum's got to come over from Sydney for the wedding. She'll have a few things to say, mark me words. Likely she'll rip us to pieces. She can get pretty cranky, me old mum!'

Looking across at Ursula he continues. 'Yeah, Ursula's become a vegetarian and doesn't like seeing animals treated cruelly ... ever since the morning old Byron got the bullet. I think she was looking out the window when the shots were fired. Looks like she's giving that butcher a run for his money. Not going to like those poor lambs being sold off for Easter roast.'

He pauses to raise his hand for another round of drinks and a plate of *mezze*. 'I mean, the way the Greeks treat them before they die ... Crikey! it's criminal, just bloody criminal, don't you reckon? She does have a point. Not much better when they die either ... sticking a nasty-looking, pointed metal rod up their backsides and out through their mouths. Geez, you wouldn't want to be born a lamb for quids!'

Mum cringes, but Mullet doesn't notice. He's busy watching Ursula, her hands still raised with passion talking to the butcher. Anguish has spread like soft butter across her pale face. 'The way they get them home from market's no picnic either, tying them upside down on the back of motorbikes or chucking them uncomfortably over a donkey's back isn't the kindest way to transport the poor little buggers back to the village to be slaughtered. Have you seen the way they sometimes throw them into the boots of cars, lying them down then slamming the hoods on their little white bleating heads. Bloody disgusting, if you ask me. Makes me ashamed to be a Greek. But there you are, what can you do? Things are certainly different here in Greece compared to Sweden or back home.'

'Yes, well, Mullet, I have to agree with you. My father was a hotelier and butcher by trade and he'd have a heart attack if he saw the way they chop up meat in this country. Indistinguishable chunks of grisly flesh hanging on hooks that dangle from ceilings dotted with the remnants of smudged fly excrement. Wasps hovering about gorging on the dripping blood of limp carcasses; no method to the butchers' hacking and sawing. The floors of their shops slippery like bloody skating rinks. Truthfully, Mullet, I cope very nicely in Greece turning the other way. It's the only way. Greeks can be incredibly cruel and it upsets me to even contemplate delving too deeply into the minds of local butchers. David and I have to peek, quickly point and pay for some semblance of sanity.'

She surveys the table as the newly arrived cognac sits seductively near the ashtray, waiting to be drunk. Glancing through smoke emanating from other tobacco adoring patrons, she lights a cigarette and inhales deeply. 'And speaking of cruelty, we had a drama with our neighbours when they killed a pig a while back. The hamlet turned out to view the poor creature's demise. Can you believe it? I'm sure it was the highlight of their winter. A local woman armed with a brick kept hitting the unfortunate beast about the head. It squealed and squealed. It was so loud, nothing like we'd ever heard before. Its cries of agony rang out through the whole hamlet. I'm sure my daughter's still in shock. Even now it sends shivers down my spine, and I didn't see it first-hand. But, by God, we all heard it.'

Again, she pauses before slipping into the newly arrived cognac and inhale the acrid smoke from her cigarette before continuing. 'It was a slow and agonising death for the poor thing. You're right, I suspect it won't be much better for all the lambs you see around the town and villages this week. But you already know this being an Aussie Greek.'

As she speaks, her mind conjures an image of Dad telling her the story about Mullet naked under the oleander bushes down the side of our villa last summer. The image isn't shaking free from her mind. Reaching for her cognac, she slugs the remains. The thought of him coming back to Corfu to marry Ursula, then living happily ever after and close by seems too far-fetched for words. But then this is Greece – anything can happen. It's the nature of the place. The Gods keep tinkering away.

Keen to extract more information from him, she changes the subject. 'Oh goodness, Mullet, your arrival is exciting. It's been a long depressing year since I last saw you. David went back to Australia because his father was dying. He fled shortly after you disappeared and left us with little money. And while away, he didn't send much to us, and of course, we can't legally work here. It was a nightmare. We were practically financially destitute. I became very down about things; I wasn't even sure he'd come back, so you can imagine my distress.'

'Geez, I'm sorry to hear that,' consoles Mullet.

'You getting married and settling on the island ... well this will give the locals something to talk about besides the last few olive harvests and why the chooks aren't laying. When did you say you're getting married? I suppose, but I can't say for sure, it won't be before Easter if Ursula needs a Greek Orthodox baptism, and organising a wedding, good luck with that! The paperwork will take ages. And with all this fasting. I mean how does one approach a Greek priest during Lent? Or any Greek? With great caution, of course!'

'You are right about that, Mrs J.'

'Personally speaking, I wouldn't go near an abstaining priest for quids,' continues Jo. 'Cranky as rattle snakes. In fact, the entire island is running around like chooks without heads preparing for it. You, as a G.O. would know this fasting caper tends to bring out either the best or the worst in people. It's intriguing how forty days without meat, eggs and dairy can turn the nicest people into absolute frazzled and frayed fiends. This one's accusing that one of sneaking in an egg here, or that one spied someone covertly buying slices of mortadella at the local deli there. It would be hilarious if it wasn't so ridiculous. There's black-market meat and cheese sales going on as if we're living through a nation-wide perpetual prohibition. Truly, without sounding biased, I think the Anglicans are the only ones who know how to do Easter properly. I hate to sound controversial, Mullet, but it needs to be said!'

'Nah, Mrs J, that's okay. I'm a G.O. alright. Just the same, fasting gives me the willies too. Nope, I don't go in for it personally. I'll probably rot in hell for it too. And now Ursula's a vego, the not eating meat bit doesn't bother me as much. But I'm not giving up dairy and eggs. Over me dead body. Mind you, I'm not averse to a chicken leg every now and then. And don't tempt me with a souvlaki whatever you do. But I suppose it's hard for youse non-Greeks to understand our traditions. Perhaps youse need to live here longer. Then youse will soon get into the swing of things.'

Pausing, Mullet thanks the waiter for producing another *mezze* of olives, sliced tomato and cucumber. 'Yep, I have to get Ursula dunked as soon as possible, preferably before Mum gets here. Not sure how she's going to take it if we don't get that sorted. She wants to book her flight soon.'

He continues uncomfortably, his smile no longer illuminating his cleanly shaven face. 'You see, Mum's got a bit of a nervous disorder – gets snippy about the tiniest of things. So, coming all this way for a wedding, back to her roots is bound to be emotional for her; her first trip since leaving the island thirty years ago. It's only now she's patched it up with her sister, otherwise I would have stayed with Aunty last summer. And I hope they like Ursula – they haven't met. Just breaking the news that I was marrying a Swede brought on one of Mum's dodgy spells. She was bed-ridden for a couple of days. Stick and Took wanted me to come home because they thought she was dying. But, like a trooper, she mustered all her strength and rose from what could have been her death bed. She told Stick she'd make sure she was here for the wedding even if it killed her.'

'Gee, Mullet, that sounds dramatic. I suggest your mother thinks no girl is good enough for her boy.'

'Yeah, well, me Mum's always reckoned I was a bit of a legend. I don't want to brag of course. She is blind-sided when it comes to her boys. But still I'm not going to be taken in by her fancy compliments. She's just going to have to cop the fact I'm marrying Ursula and that's that.'

The thought of his mother makes him raise his hand for the waiter to bring another round of drinks.

'Oh, Mullet, I shouldn't. But, okay. Only if you insist. You could make it a double to celebrate this exciting news though. Your big win! And a christening and a wedding. It's a lot to take in! Don't forget I'm a dab hand at catering – if you need someone to organise your receptions, I'm available.'

'I'll keep that in mind. Thanks for that real kind offer.'

Waving a pesky wasp from her face, Ursula returns to the café distressed. Flopping into the flimsy wooden chair, she takes a slug of one of the many ouzos lined in a row for her on the small crowded tabletop. Keeping her eyes on the lambs being bartered over, she looks visually shaken.

'What's wrong, love?' enquires Mullet, taking her hand and squeezing it.

In her strong cosmopolitan accent, she replies, 'Horrible butchers, selling those tiny innocent lambs. All of them to be killed for Easter. It's so cruel, barbaric. I wish we could save them from their inevitable fate!'

As Mum indiscreetly rolls her eyes at the very suggestion, Mullet soothes Ursula with calming words, drawing her close to him and whispering soft words in her ear. Feeling like a spare at a wedding and realising she must get a wriggle on; Mum bids the couple farewell while swigging the last of her drink. Before departing, she invites them to our new villa, if they're ever in the neighbourhood.

With a regal wave of her hand and an air of deference, she departs with an aristocratic *'Yassus,'* then disappears down a crowded laneway juggling her groceries between motorbikes, heavily laden wheelbarrows and bargain hunting shoppers. She can't wait to get home and tell us about this brief, yet intriguing encounter.

Chapter 22

Catching-up

Mullet and Ursula waste no time coming to visit. No sooner had Mum got home, told us the news of their arrival, and sat down to lunch than she's abruptly woken from her afternoon siesta. She's heard me rummaging around in the kitchen and she's not amused. Mum and Dad's afternoon snoozes are sacrosanct. I reckon I take my life into my hands if I so much as sneak the skin off a creamy custard when they are resting. But I've been sprung. It's impossible to suspend the inevitable any longer and I curse myself for not taking up Katerina's invitation. She'd invited me to spend the day in Pyrgi sharing in the simple delights of being close up and personal with the earth, picking early crops of tomatoes and cucumbers with her. Silly me.

'G'day, g'day! How you been?'

From behind me comes the distinct sound of Mullet's voice. He's spied me reading underneath a cluster of olive trees in the garden of our new villa. I do a lot of reading, especially since we have no television, I don't go to school, can't legally work and my mother has recently set up an English library, humble though it is, at the Anglican Church presbytery. Local expats meet there weekly and swap or donate books. Rising reluctantly from my top reading spot, I greet him with caution. There's something about the man that makes me slightly uneasy. Perhaps it's his poorly suppressed 'bogan-ness'. Yet, at the same time, I like his informality as it reminds me of home. After all, Australia is where I'm from. I'm not there now and may never return, but it still defines me, probably more than anything, in a mythical sense. I know as young as I am I will never fully assimilate back into Australian society either because of living in Corfu. There's a part of Greece that will always be a part of me. The bitter and sweet turmoil of this land has made its way into my blood and, I suppose, I'm forever bound to feel unsettled while all these parts and places that have morphed into me are far from the places where I am not. There will always be something missing, an element of absence from the physically complicated puzzle that is now me.

Glancing at Mullet, I'm flabbergasted by this new man standing before me. He's presenting a hell of a lot better than he did last summer. And there's Ursula, my dear friend. I've missed her and her pep talks. She'd proved to be a good sort. How my days were made so much more pleasant by her wise words, kindly offering simple but much needed insights into just about everything from kissing boys to beauty tips, all encapsulated in a loyal friendship.

After Mullet's shameful departure last summer, the two of us would disappear in Hercules, our family's small fishing boat, dipping the oars into the crystal-clear waters until we rounded the lush curves of Ipsos Bay. We'd anchor a safe distance from the shore in front of the exclusive French resort, *Club Mediterranee*. In between dips into the deliciously welcoming turquoise water and knowing all the while it was a restricted area, we'd sit and giggle at the nudists sunning on the beach. It's here we'd dive for discarded old and new pottery wine jugs the French tourists had tossed dismissively into the ocean after consuming the contents. We'd started quite a unique collection of beautiful coral-encrusted pieces.

None of historical value. It's in this tiny bopping row-boat where she'd listen to my gripes about life, especially about my mother whom I was still struggling to get close to. There exists an undeniable, irreparable unspoken barrier between us and it mystifies me, but it is there just the same. Why does my mother shame me for things that are out of my control? – for being a female – for menstruating and growing into an attractive young woman. My life should be bursting with exciting moments filled with joy as I move through my teens, blossoming and maturing. But if a male looks at me, I'm at fault for drawing attention to myself, and under her breath she'd call me a slut or a whore, and upon seeing my pained expression, 'Oh, stop snivelling, will you!'

Being a fair-skinned blonde has its disadvantages. She'd warn me, 'Don't let me find you under a bush, knickers around your neck,' or 'If you fall pregnant, you're on your own. You will be abandoned in Europe.'

I already felt as if I had been and, in the scheme of things, could I have a more effective contraceptive than my mother?

I confide all my worries to Ursula, especially how incredibly flawed and worthless I feel. Even though she couldn't explain how she knows, my guru Ursula assured me that I was lovable and that my mother isn't dealing with her life. She said she'd noticed that my mother didn't particularly like females, much preferring the company of males irrespective of their age, and of course, overtly favoured her sons, her little darlings.

'Your mother isn't very nice to you. Last summer when your other brothers were here, I'd worry about what she was teaching your brothers about how males should treat females. It seems obvious to me she's put you at the bottom of your family's food chain like some docile uneducated village girl. Boys absorb information from all around them, the other boys in the village and their sexist attitudes ... many have been socialised to treat females with disrespect, especially foreign women. Because of that, they are likely to impose their misplaced negative attitudes onto you, getting away with it because your mother usually backs them. Yours is not a normal family and your father is a lovely man but he's detached; his head buried in a book. I think it's his form of escapism. He's frighted to challenge her.'

I consider Ursula's words and she's right. My family isn't your conventional family, but then whose is? In my mother's eyes, my brothers and males generally, apart from my father that is, can do no wrong. Because I live in fear of my mother, too frightened to challenge her, as a result I will probably feel flawed and second-rate for a long time to come, and despise myself for being gutless. But why? Why is she like this?

'If you want my opinion, I think you have to deal with more than you realise. I get the impression your mother is projecting a lot of her bitterness at life onto you for some reason. It might be your destiny to determine why that is. Try and discover the root of her inner conflict because something's not right. Think about why she acts this way towards you and the choices your parents make. Their lifestyle is self-indulgent. Why does your mother berate you for being the problem? You can't tell me that theirs is not an irresponsible and selfish lifestyle. It doesn't take into account your need for an education, security, stability, and respectful and sober parents. Have you thought that their lives need dissecting, not yours?'

I have to admit it's a challenge being sober around parents who are drinking most of the time. At the best of times, they are unpredictable. My guts churn trying to anticipate what they will say or do next as their moods rise and fall throughout the day. Then there's the added burdensome woes about our finances on top of that; being blamed for the situation. Compounding this, they have for years pitted one child against the other and, in so doing, decimated our trust in one another. These only add to my feelings of isolation within the family.

Ursula tells me, 'And something else you need to know, drinkers make really damaging mirrors.'

But in this too Ursula had her own problems. She was longing for Mullet, the man she'd only briefly met but loved just the same.

Our woes seemed more pressing than the tensions between Papadopoulos and one of his co-conspirators, hardliner Dimitrios Ioannidis. Their fallout resulted in a desperate move by Papadopoulos to release the 'General's' control on power in order to quell outrage over the slaughter of the polytechnical students last November in Athens. It was an event that shocked the world. The eventual democratisation of Greece, which Ioannidis was against, became the inevitable end of Papadopoulos's career as he tried to distract local and international pressure away from the incident. Ioannidis had successfully mounted a coup against his co-conspirator, which led to increasing tensions about Cyprus. The influence of the Turks in the UN amplified the situation because it served foreign powers to create friction between the two countries in order to control and manipulate them. It was all turning into a nightmare for the Cypriots; daily people were literally being slaughtered on the streets.

Over the years I'd seen hatred for the Greek Monarchy escalate at different times, resulting in the end with the eventual complete abolition of the monarchy in 1974. Every so often villages and town folk lit bonfires that released spirals of smoke into the air as flames gobbled up portraits in public displays of rebellion and hatred for the Greek royal family and, in more recent times, Papadopoulos. It's hard to believe that this same man had given himself the title of Regent in the King's absence, was now himself in jail and facing the death sentence. Still, some Greeks hung on and put their regal images into storage, securing them in safe places because this land has seen many a victor come and go. The portraits may need to be resurrected later, perhaps even those of Papadopoulos.

It's difficult to imagine that over the past months Papadopoulos had fallen and an even more repressive Ioannides had taken power. He was steadily driving Greece into further conflict with Turkey by making the liberation of Cyprus a matter of urgency; victory against the Turks jumbled in with a revived sense of nationalist pride. He hoped by stirring up heated patriotism that he'd distract the Greek people's attention away from problems closer to home: the sporadic student demonstrations that would continue over the next months. But in the meantime, driving had been restricted once again with only certain number plates permitted on the road. Limitations on gatherings were imposed yet, for the most part, tourists and expats seem to be excluded from many of these rules ... unless of course they are long-haired hippies, recalcitrant civilians, druggies or riff-raff sleeping on beaches.

Mullet's face bursts with childlike eagerness as he asks excitedly, 'Where's your folks? I've got some good old Aussie contraband from Kangaroo Valley in London and a few Duty-Frees for them. There's a ripper store in Earl's Court where you can buy every Australian product under the sun. It's not cheap, but, when you are miles from home, at some stage you gotta give the Pommy nosh a break; get stuck into some dinkum Aussie tucker or you'd go bloody bonkers.' He has a point. I know exactly how he feels on our back-to-basics diet. I can only dream of Vegemite, Four and Twenty meat pies, pavlovas and Western Star butter. I could go on ....!

'I'd give the full loo tour but my parents are asleep. They don't like being disturbed during siesta time.'

'Loo tour? Nah, nah. I don't know what that is but she'll be right, love.' He dismissively punctures and releases the air out of my afternoon by walking past me and sitting on one of the creaky canvas chairs at the table. Crossing his arms, he's determined not to budge. Ursula shrugs her shoulders helplessly because he's not listening to her attempts to convince him to walk for a while and stretch their legs. Turning a mousy pale, she looks on apologetically.

This is awkward. I feel trapped. What can I do? – that is, until they reach into their shopping bags. Like a couple of magicians, the pair place jumbo blocks of Cadbury's chocolate, slabs of British Cheddar cheese, a couple of jars of Vegemite and Peanut Butter on the table. It's like Christmas day, only better! But I'm stuck. Under these circumstances I'm compelled to offer them something in return for their generosity. It's only polite. I suggest coffee, tea or wine? But Mullet stops me and produces four bottles of Foster's Lager and a bottle of Jameson, my mother's favourite tipple.

Pointing to the beer, Mullet says, 'You better put these in the fridge, love, for your old man before they get warm. I tried warm beer in England. Disgusting stuff. I'll be buggered if I know how the Poms can stomach the tepid liquid. I'm sure your old man wouldn't want these to get hot now, would he? Come to think of it, I wouldn't mind one me-self. What about it, love?'

Ursula shakes her head, signalling she'll only sit. She can see the concern in my eyes. 'Mullet it's rude to barge in like this. We should pop back later.'

'Nonsense,' he laughs, throwing back his head. 'Nah, love, the very idea Jo and David wouldn't enjoy this kind of disturbance!'

What can I say? I have little choice but to leave the table with their bounty and put it in the kitchen. Yet, as soon as I open the refrigerator door, I hear the voice of gloom and doom from Mum and Dad's bedroom upstairs.

'Who's in the kitchen? Get out of there! I know you are in there, you nasty little termite.'

I knew this would happen. Mum's happy bank account has just hit deficit. I'm in trouble and I want to stick my head in a dumpster and die. Instead, I frantically gather enough courage to climb the stairs and poke my head into their oversized bedroom. It's like facing an execution. I lower my voice to reduce any collateral damage and tell them about the goodies in the fridge. Upon hearing this, their ears prick up and the mood swiftly shifts.

'How many bottles of Fosters did you say? Are they large ones?' enquires Dad, now surprisingly fully awake.

'Did you say a bottle of Jameson and English Cheddar?' echoes Mum.

Now it's as if we are under nuclear attack and the immediate evacuation of their bedroom is crucial to their survival. Yet, I know they are angry with me, it's in the tone of their voices, their exaggerated, aggravated movements. I shake my head wearily knowing I'm being covertly blamed for the intrusion. Yet, in all fairness, I can't see why these visitors are my fault. I leave them to dress.

Chapter 23

The Pillars of Greek Society - you like-e-fakelake?

Shortly after, they emerge from the villa like bouncing, smiling celebrities. It's the hypnotic power of duty-free goodies that will do it every time. While my parents greet with sweeping welcoming gestures, I've been immobilised by their searing looks. It's enough for me to pull back. I fade into the background where I sit and watch the scene from a slight distance and allow the afternoon to unfold.

It's true: long winters tend to bring on a sudden arousal of unexpected sentiment at the sight of English-speaking compatriots laden with goodies. My parents enthuse around their guests. Dad's hand fires from his side like a bullet from a gun to greet Mullet.

'Oh, you bloody beauty, mate. Good to see you and yes, you will be pleased to know Spartacus returned my safari suit shorts. Yeah, and good old Marietta gave them the once over with that miraculous olive oil soap of hers and well now, as you can see, they look as good as new!'

To illustrate this, he stands and does an exaggerated yet surprisingly light-footed ballerina or Greek equivalent *Avazona fustanella* twirl in his pale blue shorts while Mullet looks on roaring with laughter like the Metro Golden lion.

'You beauty, mate. I was really grateful for all you did for me. When I heard that rifle being fired, I didn't know what to think. In fact, I thought me days were numbered! I better be careful though, keep me head down. Anna's likely to head up your drive and have another go at me with her broom. Like an armed tool she was. Carrying on like a chook without a head. Sticking her nose into other people's bedrooms and bathrooms. Back in Australia, we call snoops like her bloody old sheet sniffers.'

'Steady on there, Mullet! We get the point.' Dad coughs and a slight pause punctuates the conversation before the two of them chuckle.

Mullet continues, 'Those ants didn't help the situation either. I had to get medical treatment in Rome on me nether region on the way back to London.' He pauses to laugh again.

Ursula cringes and I giggle because I'm all ears but soon feel the full impact of my mother's searing disapproval. I wait for her to swipe me with her sickle.

'I itched all the way on the train from Brindisi to Rome. That didn't go down well with the passengers in the crowded third-class carriage, let me tell you. Must have thought I was some kind of a sexual deviant, you know, reaching to relieve me itchy nether region as the train chugged along.'

He pauses to hold Ursula's hand, which she rapidly drops, pretending to swat a wasp.

'When I got to Rome, geez it was embarrassing explaining the sidjo to the i-tie doctor. He didn't speak English and me Dago's bloody dodgy. Trying to explain how I got those bites on me bits. But there you go. Life wasn't meant to be easy, that's for sure.'

Focusing on Dad, he says, 'Mate, there's a cold Fosters in the fridge if you fancy one?'

'Fancy one ... do bears like honey? Go fetch one will you, love.'

Dad eyes me and away I scoot because I'm keen to get back into the good books with my parents. When I reappear, I do so with our special souvenir bottle opener with the imbedded iconic picture of Melbourne's Flinders Street Station embossed in its handle, a few glasses and a couple of bottles of Fosters on a tray. I have this balancing act down pat; after all, I've had plenty of practice.

Dad happily chats, 'Truly, Mullet, there's been many a time when I could have sold my old aunty for one of these little beauties. Mate, you have made this old bloke's day. And to hear an Aussie accent. Well, we are surrounded on all sides by bloody Pommy expats. They're fine, mate, but in small doses, if you get my meaning. The wife fits in with them but me ... well, need I say more? Anyway, the Mrs tells me you two are tying the knot?'

Mum fires Dad a dirty look. She detests being referred to as the 'Mrs', nor does she like the way his Australian accent becomes more pronounced around Mullet.

Grabbing the Fosters by the neck, Dad angles a glass up to the lip of the bottle and pours it carefully, demonstrating his skill and expertise as a beer pourer. He doesn't spill a drop as the frothy cool liquid flows into the tall glasses. 'Mrs Jo, how about you? But then perhaps not ... There's a nice bottle of Jameson for you in the kitchen. Can I tempt you with a nip?'

Mum releases a sigh as if to say she couldn't care less one way or the other, but in fact she cares very much. She, like my father with his beer, would very much like a tipple of Jameson. Mullet turns to me and, right on cue, without anyone having to say a word, I jet to the kitchen. I return with the bottle, a few whiskey glasses and a jug of water.

'Get a gander at this, will you?' laughs Mullet bursting with pleasure as he holds up the large bottle of Jameson victoriously in the air like the much-prized decapitated head of an enemy. Mum may have masterly managed a measured smile but the reality is she wants him to stop shaking, messing around with the bottle and hurry up and pour her a drink.

'Yeah, Ursula reminded me that you're partial to a Jameson and good old Pommy Cheddar. Well, we've got cheese too. But don't ask me how we got it through customs. I reckon Ursula must have winked at one of them customs officers. As you know, she is a bit of a looker and a charmer is me Ursula. She's got me hooked, haven't you, love?'

Ursula emits a dreamy smile, radiating it at Mullet as Mum cringes at his sloppy overtures. Dad half closes his eyes savouring his Fosters. He relaxes reclining back on his creaky chair and raises his glass as a gesture for everyone to stop and listen to what he's about to say.

'Well, congratulations, you two, on your forthcoming nuptials. Jo told us she bumped into the two of you. This is exciting news. It's been quite a winter. Me having to stay in Australia because my father was dying and Jo being left here to hold the fort. Without putting too much of a dampener on it, I reckon old Anna's going to be happy to hear your news too. Hey, Mullet, your latest dispatch should keep her broom in her broom cupboard.'

He releases an unapologetic laugh. 'At the same time, I bet she won't get rid of her pickling jars just in case you decide to do a bolt!' Dad chuckles like a big kid as Mum rolls her eyes in horror. Pausing, he looks at me. 'Did you say there's cheddar in the fridge? Get that cheddar and slice some bread, will you, kiddo? You know, the nice loaf Mum got at the markets today ... there's a good kid.'

I disappear and re-emerge, having followed his instructions.

In between sips, Mum pipes up, 'So, tell me about your villa hunt. You headed for Saint Marcos? Is that right?'

This time Ursula replies. 'Yes, but only briefly. There's what I think is a fabulous old villa on the edge of the village with land at the back also belonging to Mullet's mother and his aunt. The plot consists of terraced olive groves with views sloping down the hillside to Ipsos Bay. I think we can do a lot with it. In fact, with a bit of sprucing up and a good polish the old place could come up shining. Mullet tells me his mother and aunt have had the place for sale for years. They want to fund their retirement and have no intention of living here. It could be just what we are looking for.'

Mum, curious and wanting to know more, leans forward. 'When was the villa built?'

Ursula smiles and winks at Mullet. 'Mullet reckons in the stone-age! You're not rapt in the property, are you?'

Mullet shakes his head as she continues, 'But jokes aside, probably around two hundred years ago. It's a traditional two-storey place painted in a fading yellow with white shutters. The kitchen and bathrooms need to be ripped out and completely updated ... reinstated – the plumbing and the electricals redone but there's heaps of potential. High ceilings, wide wooden floor boards, expansive rooms and large open fire places. Like your villa inside, I would imagine. I'd love to have a look inside your place. May I, later on ...?'

Mum nods idly. 'Of course, be my guests.'

'And there's enough land for us to have animals. I was shocked seeing lambs in the market waiting to be sold. Waiting to be slaughtered. It's my dream to have a bit of land, an animal sanctuary. Perhaps this is my chance? What do you think, Mullet?' Her voice trails with her thoughts, doubtless floating far away to a place filled with fluffy clouds and lambs sprouting wings. Thinking for barely a moment, he enthusiastically nods in agreement.

Nibbling like a pleased mouse on cheese, Mum's certain Ursula's a couple of columns short of the Acropolis contemplating a lamb sanctuary in Greece. Who in their right mind does such a thing? Curious just the same, she says, 'If you purchase the place, how soon do you think it will be before you would be able to move in?'

Even with the beer being rapidly consumed in the heat and the bottles becoming merely pleasant memories, Mullet manages a sober response. 'I suppose we can move in whenever we like. The villa is empty. Mum and aunty have patched things up since last summer otherwise, I would have stayed there. They haven't told me what the rift was about. None of me business, I suppose. Anyway, apparently the topic's taboo.'

Mullet continues in between pausing to light a cigarette. 'But formally buying it from me relatives well, there will be loads of Greek red-tape. Females usually inherit land in Greece. I will have to negotiate with Aunty, of course. Her kid's might get narky but I doubt it. They have no intention of ever coming to Greece ... well, that's what they told me ages ago. Aunty lives in Sydney near Mum. They each own half the property. I can't see Mum being a problem and Aunty wants to get on with her life and sell. Me problem is whether or not I should apply for Greek citizenship. You know, for the land transaction to be legal.'

'Mate, you need to think very carefully before contemplating such an act of gallantry or absolute insanity.'

Slicing generous pieces of cheese that easily crumble at the touch of his knife, Dad presses the pieces of cheese with his wide fingers onto the soft insides of a chunk of bread. Before lunging into a widespread bite, he shakes his head with concern. 'I mean, no disrespect to the Greeks when I say this.'

'Yeah, David, I hear residency is complicated. We can show we have the money to live here, thanks to me windfall. The problem is I'll be forced to enlist in the military if I become a citizen. I'm patriotic, but not that bloody patriotic! Greece is on a war footing right now with the bloody Turks in

Cyprus and it's becoming increasingly tricky with the ousting of Papadopoulos. Ioannidis has inflamed the situation pushing for '*enosis*' and I can only see it blowing out. But then I suppose there is the old sneaky *fakelaki, bribe* trick, in the right hands, of course. That might get me off the hook. I could tart-up the truth and say I'm a bed wetter or hobble and pretend I've got flat feet. That might work.'

We all nod in agreement, except for Ursula. Not understanding the word, she throws Mullet a disconcerted gaze.

Dad comes to her rescue. 'Ah, yes, the good old Greek *fakelaki* trick. It's a great word for a bribe or back hander, isn't it? It sounds sleezy and it is sleezy. It actually means small envelope. But you get my meaning. Mullet, do you think you can get away with it?'

My parents throw him looks of anguish. No sooner have they found a generous source of Duty-frees than they might lose it. The worst of it is … possibly lose it to some gruesome, run-down remote stinking prison camp. What a dreadful waste of a potentially lucrative resource?

As if reading our thoughts, Mullet agrees, 'Maybe, but if I get caught, I don't fancy a stint in a rotten cell. If Papadopoulos and his mates can torture poor old Mikis Theodorakis and chuck him in a concentration camp at Oropos for his Leftist views before the French came to his rescue, what chance do I have?'

'Yep, I have to admit, that's one of the most shocking things this government has ever done. But careful who you express your views to. The place is crawling with informants. You're not an informant, are you?' Mum laughs, rubbing an itch on the caramel-coloured skin on her tired face. 'Nevertheless, getting back to bribes, the truth is,' she responds raising her eyebrows, 'you must know half the

Greek economy is based on all sorts of *fakelakis*. Apparently, they come in all shapes and sizes.'

'Indeed, they do,' laughs Dad, successfully suppressing his desire to act seriously. 'I have a friend on Samos who recently told me he was so furious about the delays involved in getting the power connected to his villa that he stormed into the central electrical company's crowded office, stood in the middle of their headquarters and yelled out, "Who do I have to screw around here in order to get my power connected?" Being a good looking fellow apparently, a few employees put their hands up. It's debatable but that could be why it's called a *FAKELAKI?*

I think this is hilarious; in fact, we all laugh. But Mum stops and gives me another one of her dark, brooding looks dripping with disapproval. I hate how her eyes hold me captive in a lesser place, like a trapped insect in some toxic dance that never ends. I'm filled with a culpability that isn't even mine to hold and I ache from the injustice of it. Thwarted by her, I wish I could pinpoint its root cause. I just want to be released from its gripping just like so many Greeks want to be released from the grasping strangle hold of this coup.

Suddenly, Mullet looks worried again. He continues where he'd left the conversation earlier. 'Well, I don't know if I like-ee the idea of *fakelaki*! But seriously, if I must join the army and become a soldier, I won't be happy leaving me beautiful Ursula. Especially once we've tied the knot. The situation's looking sticky in Cyprus; the world's turned upside down. It could all turn into an absolute fiasco. Who wants war with Turkey? And what about the Middle East?'

'Well, in my opinion, that shocking polytechnic incident last November will be the end of Papadopoulos. He's rotting in prison right now,' confides Dad. 'Jailed for killing those poor kids for simply resisting his extreme authoritarianism. In any coup, once innocent bystanders are killed, well, it's likely to short shrift anyone's career. Let's see what happens with this Ioannides guy.'

The mood becomes pensive and quiet.

'There's going to be a trial and Papadopoulos could get the death sentence. The problem is they say Ioannides is no better – both are reputedly backed by the CIA. They used to call him the "invisible dictator." So much anti-American sentiment right now. But look, fair's fair. This government has tried to get the economy going again after the wars; get industries grinding again without the strangle hold of unions. He's built schools. Every child has a chance at an education now. Electricity's connected throughout most of Greece, a first for a lot of remote communities.'

I look on holding my tongue. I'd be ripped apart if I mentioned my older brother and my experiences of any kind of a normal, formal education after leaving Australia.

Mullet sits back in our old weathered chair and nods in agreement with Dad. 'His trial is one thing, but being sentenced to death is another. How fair will it be, anyway? I'm not sure I want to be mixed up in all this political stuff. Here on Corfu, we have a fair chance of avoiding most of the fallout. But if I become a Greek citizen, as sure as the Greek Gods built the Corinth Canal, they'd send me to the other side of Greece. My living on Corfu is a conflict-of-interest. I can't be ordered to serve me country in me own backyard now, can I? And I don't fancy being dispatched close to the Turkish border.'

Dad nods in solemn agreement as Mullet laughs nervously; he knows innocent people are being shot on the streets of Cyprus right now. Perspiration sits on his upper lip. The heat gets to him, to all of us.

'Mmm, yes, you're right, Mullet. But take heart, Corfu is not known as the *Kastropolis, castle fortresses* for nothing. It's still considered to be Greece's most fortified island. That's how Corfu circumvented the Ottomans years ago. More westernised because of that. It's not all because of the miraculous powers of Saint Spyridon. Try and tell that to the locals. Oh, well, if he does have any power, let's hope his mystical influence continues to protect the island and us. If the Turks ever invade Corfu, I don't like our chances of being saved, especially after the Gallipoli debacle. But having said that, you can't beat the joys of living on this delightful Dorian doorstep, can you? Wouldn't move for quids. I know I sometimes whinge about the Greeks but ... we're hooked on island life. And it has its advantages, you know? Just check out that view. Bloody marvellous, isn't it? Outstrips Saint Kilda or Bondi Beach every time!'

Nods of consensus do the rounds of the table as we feast our eyes on the vast view of the *Neo Limani, New Port* and the sun's sparkling reflections bouncing on the rippling water beyond.

'But as you say, it's a hard one to call, this political situation. Mind you, Mullet, you need to be very careful. You wouldn't want to be masquerading around town as a Greek patriot either, then not taking up arms to fight if things go from bad to worse. Every Greek male over eighteen, some even younger, has a gun or dynamite stashed away somewhere in case the Turks invade, or the Italians or Germans. These people still bear the deep battle scars of the last war and every other bloody war before that. Yes, too many invasions have taught the Greeks to trust no one. The Civil War didn't help either. I don't blame the Greeks for wanting to protect themselves. But seriously, Mullet, nor can you build your dreams on some hastily assembled template after a few to many drinks ... you must craft these things with supreme caution, mate.'

I have to laugh or should I cry? There's Dad preaching advice he himself should have followed before we left Australia. But I say nothing. What would be the point; I'd only cop it later when our guests had gone.

Lifting the latest copy of Newsweek, he rattles it like a shining sabre in the sunlight and continues, 'With the situation in Cyprus hotting up ... there's lots of stored-up emotion and patriotic pride. It's been tense between Cypriot's Archbishop Makarios and Papadopoulos ever since the coup began back in 1967. These days old army uniforms resurrected from ancient wooden trunks, stinking of mothballs are laid out ready for action. The Turks, Greeks and Cypriots, its one unholy mess. Look, anyway, if you decide to become a resident, there's little joy marching with the rest of us expats to the alien police station for the annual 'line up, shut up and suck it up'. We don't get treated well. Between you and me, the Head of the Alien Police is like a Nazi SS officer. He forgets about all the Greeks living in Australia making a good living, and all the income foreigners bring to this country. You have lots to think about. So, mate, don't make any hasty decisions.'

Rolling her eyes with exaggerated happiness, Mum butts in. Her long creative fingers imitate crabs' clippers, delicately popping cheese in her mouth. She swallows to speak. 'Mmm, let's change the subject. All this talk about wars, student uprisings, the Greek alien police and invasions ... it's all terribly depressing. May I compliment you on this fabulous cheddar? Well done; I'm in gourmet heaven. So, tell me where are you staying and what are you doing for Easter?'

Delighted by her obvious enjoyment, Mullet smiles with pleasure as a couple of whirling dragonflies propel past on their way to a row of large heaven-scented blooms in terracotta flower pots close by. 'We are staying at the Cavalieri. We haven't thought about Easter.'

'Ah, the Cavalieri. Such a convenient location. Close to the Liston. So central. You will have a bird's eye view of pots being thrown from windows on Easter Saturday morning. If you are walking around town, watch your head. You might get hit by flying pottery. Be on the watch for road kill too. Many a mutilated body has been found beneath layers of tossed pottery at Easter. Some say it's a pagan practice, others reckon it's a flow on from the golden days of Byzantium. Who knows? It gets busy at the hospital; I can tell you!'

Fired up by the generous amount of alcohol being consumed, everyone laughs. Suddenly feeling generous, Mum clears her throat and declares recklessly, 'Then you must come for lunch. It will be an open day on Sunday from midday. Perhaps you can catch up with some familiar old faces from last summer. That should be fascinating. But, Ursula, be mindful lamb is on the menu. Our family can't wait to tuck into lamb cooked specially on the spit. We've asked Anna and George to slaughter and prepare a lamb for us. She assured us she'd pop in and show us the lamb she's chosen for the slaughter when she picks it up from the market. Really and truly, I don't want to view the poor animal before its demise, but she's insisting. It's all so gruesome.'

Ursula nods in horrified agreement but Mullet jumps in before Ursula can respond.

'That sounds beaut! Yep, so long as youse don't mind if Stick and Took come too? They'll be arriving in the next few days from London with me new yellow Lotus. It's me fancy sports car. Yep, got a snazzy sun roof and deep leather bucket seats and all. When it gets here, I'll take youse all for a spin?'

I'm excited; in fact, we all are. What a treat.

Dad's looking confused but laughs to spite himself, 'Yes, Mullet, I suppose they're welcome. But who are they?'

'Ah, right. Stick is me brother and Took is his partner. They are travelling across Europe in me car as I speak.'

'Well, that's fine. Of course, they can come. Ursula, are you okay with lamb being the main event on the menu?'

'I can always have salad or vegetables ... whatever.'

'No, no. Fair's fair. I'll take care of that. I've got plenty of fabulous quick and easy vegetarian recipes up my sleeve. I'm a whiz with beans and lentils,' brags Mum as my heart slumps.

Oh, no! She can't be serious. Our lamb on a spit had better not be cancelled.

After the initial horror of possibly losing our lamb roast on Easter Sunday, the day reclines into a relaxing one with an amusing collection of mellow moments that linger long into the evening. The adults continue in the same vein, quenching their unsatiable thirsts until the Jameson and Mum's stash of last resort *retsina* run dry. Meanwhile, no one's noticed me nibbling on the large blocks of Cadbury milk chocolate before my little brother gets home. Scientists have often remarked with amazement how much a single weakened locust consumes in one sitting. I justify my ravenousness by confessing it's the first time I've felt the presence of the chocolate Easter Bunny since we moved to Greece. Nice and early too. I've missed him and for this reason alone I'm not letting go of him, enveloped in plain silver paper, for all the worry beads in Greece.

Chapter 24

Stick and Took

Stick and Took take us by surprise. They arrive on the island later than Mullet expected, the day before Easter. Our clever chickens who have been given a rare opportunity to free-range at the new villa avoid a pre-emptive strike on their dodgy tickers by ducking down the back garden when they spy Mullet's yellow Lotus pulling up. Dad laughs at their squawks and flapping wings.

He jokes, 'How considerate of our chooks to warn us about the impending danger of the big yellow, genetically modified chicken on wheels in the drive-way. Giving us the heads up to get the hell out of the way before we're all eaten alive by Mullet's fast and fabulous Lotus.'

The big yellow monster, however, is as benign as it is beautiful, smooth and slick. Mullet, Ursula, Took and Stick pile out of its luxuriousness as Mullet shouts, 'Anyone for vodka?'

Sitting beneath the olive trees amidst an orchestra of singing cicadas in the garden, my parents' ears prick up, their faces expressing poorly suppressed looks of wonder and joy. Our new arrivals come heavily laden with more bursting bags of Duty-Free goodies. With his free hand, Mullet flashes an enormous bottle of vodka in the air.

Upon seeing it, Dad cries, 'Nostrovia! Hail to the proletariats. Da, comrades, nostrovia,' in what seems like fluent Russian. No one is more surprised than I. This is a latent talent if ever there is one. Where did he learn Russian? But looking at the book on the old outside table he's reading titled *Russian Gulags*, nothing more needs to be said.

Dad urges Ursula, Stick and Took to ease themselves into our faded canvas chairs, forming a snug circle beneath the olive trees. Mullet sets about with excited purpose introducing his guests.

'Come and meet me mate! Yeah, the famous author David and his real beaut wife, Joanna. David, Jo and their kids have lived on the island for a few years now. Gave the Melbourne rat race the flick. Hey, Stick, you and Took should think about this. Copy Ursula and me. Get off that bloody rat race roundabout. But here's the thing, I'm no writer and neither are you!'

Mullet's quick to laugh at his own humour while we smile nervously. After all, perhaps they could become writers. Who knows, stranger things have happened. Unlikely people can become best-selling novelists.

Mum suddenly feels sick, so does Dad. That's all they need, these two bozos becoming successful writers. She lights a cigarette to try and calm herself while her rapidly thumping heart pounds madly beneath her threadbare pale blue denim blouse.

'And over here are the rest of their clan. Their kids.'

'G'day, g'day, g'day.'

Cheeks collide as my brother and I politely kiss, side-swiping faces and hands briefly touch. Ursula, seeing me, sits close. There's a comfortable familiarity in Australian get-togethers like this. These Aussies liked Greece and didn't keep harping back to how marvellous Australia was compared with anywhere else. How many Aussies said that my parents were nuts leaving the pleasures of suburban Melbourne for the Greek islands? – telling Dad he was 'pissing in the wind trying to write a book while supporting a football team and a wife on his pension?'

With the sun spilling in, filtered lines cast refracted shadows on the olive leaves, along with the vodka bottle. Another bottle of Jameson is plonked on the table. I sense this is going to be a long day.

As brothers, Stick and Mullet are very different from one another. Mullet is thinner and shorter. Stick is tall and muscular. I think Stick looks like a matinee film star with his slicked back hair and handsome chiselled looks. He's also less bogan. Took is small and slim, a Yoko Ono look alike and I envy her delicate features. Nor does she have freckles on her nose and cheeks like I do. The one thing they all seem to have in common from what I can tell so far is their shared fondness for alcohol. Like illicit worshipers admiring their stockpiled stash, bottles are opened and our humble offerings of bread and *tarama salata, fish roe dip* pales into insignificance on the table. But they don't seem to notice. To Mullet and Stick at least, our dip is a delicious reminder of their heritage. For Took it's a novel culinary experience.

More remarks are made about Reds under the bed, gulags and comrades while Mullet takes command and pours vodka.

'What's the best thing about the Russians?' Dad invites, throwing the question into the air. But before anyone can answer, he quickly says, 'Their writers of course and their bloody marvellous vodka. Let's drink to that! Cheers, everyone. *Nostrovia!*'

As the vodka bottle is rapidly drained, our guests sit back enjoying the view and the glorious spring weather with the dappled sun fused through the gently swaying canopy of olive trees.

Stick comments, 'Wow, you've got quite a property here and your view of the *Neo Limani* is spectacular. I gotta ask, why did you move to Corfu?'

Dad, now comfortably settled in his seat, and having taken another generous sip of vodka, cheerfully replies, 'Well, you just said it, really. And no, it's not a bad shack by any stretch of the imagination. But seriously, like Mullet said, we wanted to escape the common herd as my wife often jokes. And I have to say our lives haven't exactly turned into complete chaos, yet!'

Now smiling, Dad jokingly becomes animated and forthright in his speech, 'But back then ... reading about Aussies who'd bitten the bullet and moved to London or Greece to write – you know the ones the media always yap on about – people like Germaine Greer, Barry Humphries, Clive James, Charmian Clift and George Johnston – well, they inspired us. We didn't want a shackled life so it was a case of shoot-through before we take root and rot. Life's too bloody short, isn't it? We escaped the rat race in late 1969. Anyway, I wanted to write a book. Well, not exactly. Jo thought I had the makings of a novelist. She thought I could win the Booker Prize for bullshit! Didn't you, dear? Truth is, I'm still searching for that novel. It's in me somewhere. I suppose I just have to keep digging till I find it.'

He releases a generous comical laugh, suddenly pretending he's looking for something, then he leans forward, grabs a cigarette and lights it. Mum lobs him a dirty look as he continues, 'At first, convincing the kids wasn't easy. You know, and our parents were against the idea. Reckoned we were reckless and Greece wasn't safe. Look, I have to admit at first, I was skeptical about the place too but my beautiful wife here tempted me with just the right number of incentives. You know ... the must-have factors wrapped in lots of carefully woven spin. But seriously, the temptation of cheap grog, ciggies, promises of *kourambides,* and *calamari,* I reckon we made the right decision.'

Everyone laughs, but the truth is we have fallen into a life that is certainly comparable with the infamous Lotus-Eaters. It's not helped by the Greek mantra *avrio, avrio, tomorrow, tomorrow* either. And as much as Dad may rave on about the ease in which we left Australia, it wasn't really like that, but I allow my father to indulge himself. He's forgotten that there were many dark nights, so many times when anger and fear gobbled up the joy in our lives. Now he's latching onto what relics remain of this evaporating dream. How I remember my mournful grandmother pleading for us not to leave. She confided that my grandfather, Dad's dad, was dying after being diagnosed with cancer. But Mum reckoned Gran was lying to keep Dad from leaving and now Grandpa is dead, Mom never expressing the slightest regret, grief or guilt over anything she had said about Gran or Grandpa. Or the profound hurt and guilt Dad tells me he feels now about leaving them.

I let my father continue with his happy-ever-after version of the story. He looks happy and even convincing telling it. 'Yep, by doing that, I reckon I created enough pulling power to smooth the furrowed brow of any of the many cynics in my family.'

'Really?' I ponder in amazement while Dad window-dresses our lives.

I remember that night back in Queenscliff when Grandpa raged, 'Mark my words, son, life soon makes a mockery of those who don't knuckle down and conform to the norm. You will be made to pay. Life has an unfortunate way of biting you in the arse. It's not like you don't have responsibilities ... so grow up, son! Right now, there are tanks rolling through the streets of Athens. Rein in your bohemian ideals and your wife before it's too late.'

But Dad, invested in his fabricated past and winking heartily at Mum, theatrically pauses to pass the pale pink dip and sizable chunks of crunchy bread around our wobbly table as he happily carries on mythologising.

'Our next giant step for mankind was to sell most of what we owned. Then we packed half a dozen tea chests with our few remaining valuables and put them on a ship bound for Piraeus. In the meantime, our menagerie of seven boarded another ship setting sail on a gusty northerly wind destined for midwinter Southampton. A few frozen months later, overland in early spring in a couple of cars in transit heading for the Greek dream, a dream imbued with new and simple beginnings; a life pared back.'

'Mullet says you've been here a few years now. You must be well into your novel. What's it about?' Stick asks, eyes flashing with genuine interest as Dad begins squirming uncomfortably in his creaky sun-bleached chair. He motions for a top-up of his drink, indicating his throat's dry.

Mullet happily obliges as Mum butts in, 'Donkeys, Goats and bloody Greeks, that's what it's about! His book ... don't be so ridiculous ... he's hardly written anything except a pile of old letters home to his dearly beloved mommy dearest since we arrived. The 'book' is a cacophony of crap as far as I'm concerned. He needs to pull his finger out otherwise he's busted.'

We look on uncomfortably. 'Mmm, sounds like I've entered contentious territory! Should I wave a white flag,' offers Stick, giving a nervous laugh to try lightening things up. 'Retreat from this touchy topic?'

'Well perhaps you should. I for one can hold fire until you all leave,' Mum asserts theatrically. 'I've been doing it for years. The point is, the stupid man has lost his mojo. He's got hooked on the local slosh instead. Or whatever is on tap, haven't you, dear?'

A sarcastic smile lurks dangerously like a viperous snake coiling around Dad's mouth. He fires back mockingly like a retaliatory youngster in rhyme. 'Golly, my muse has a short fuse. I may be no Shakespeare, my dear, but kindly remove your offending spear!'

Now it's on, and the situation needs saving before it escalates into a battle. I thought the Greeks and Turks were bad.

Mullet jokes to ease the situation, 'Geez, youse two; I sense friction and it's not fiction.'

I laugh nervously as do our guests. Fortunately, the moment is saved by the sound of a noisy truck rumbling up the gravel drive, its gears being torn to shreds. Only one person I know drives like that. As it abruptly comes to a smoky, noisy halt, out bounces Anna. Waving excitedly, she retrieves two lambs from the back of the truck. She's returning from the markets with the much-anticipated Easter sacrifices. Tethered to thick ropes, temporarily collared with metal sheep's bells that dangle despondently from their thin young necks, she leads her trembling captives toward us as her cumbersome gumboots squelch with every wide step.

'*Yassas*' comes the familiar singing sound of her voice. Today she's wrapped head to toe in full mourning attire. I look at the lambs with sadness – she's already dressed for their funeral; well maybe not with the gumboots. It won't be long now before these little cuties meet their Merino maker. Perhaps their throats will be slashed. Who knows? I just hope Katerina's mother is not lingering on the sidelines ready to step in with her trusty brick.

'*Yassou*,' we collectively reply, relieved the focus has shifted. In a flash, Anna's eyes zoom in on Mullet and Ursula. Mustering what strength she has left after thirty-nine days of strict fasting, she leads her lagging lambs to where we sit. She greets Ursula with enormous pleasure, throwing her arms wildly around the young woman's narrow shoulders. All the while she constrains the trembling lambs with an unyielding grip. Mullet, however, gets the evil eye. Still holding his gaze steady, she shouts venomously like she's just seen the devil, 'You, you! I see you have finally found some clothes!'

Mullet reluctantly stands to greet her but she's backing away from him cautiously as if he's contagious. Dad pipes up. It's his turn to ease tensions. 'Such good news, Anna. Mullet and Ursula are getting married. And this is Mullet's brother Stick and his partner, Took.'

Anna stands stiffly, neither impressed nor congratulatory. She ignores Took and Stick, and looks squarely at Mullet then fires. 'Well, I am glad you're marrying Ursula. She's a good girl. When is the wedding?' she demands like an SS officer. Under this intense interrogation, Mullet smiles bravely. In truth, the woman frightens the hell out of him.

'Now, Anna, I don't want any trouble between us,' declares Mullet tactfully, powerless to shroud the quiver in his voice. 'We propose to live on the island. I want us to be friends. We're not sure of the wedding date ... yet. Me mother Irene, you know her, has to come from Sydney and Ursula's brother from Sweden. Ursula has to be baptised in the church; there's lots we still have to organise before things are set in cement.'

Then he adds as if lavishly handing out complementary sweets: 'And of course, you and George are invited to the wedding. I'm serious about wanting to make amends over our slight ... misunderstanding last year.'

Still superstitious, her large almond eyes volley darts at him as if he's an armed invading Turk. She spits her words and raises her milk chocolate-coloured hand. She places her palm close to his distorted shocked face. 'It was no misunderstanding. I know what I saw. *Na,* this is for you, knucklehead, if you do not keep your clothes on and fulfil your oath of marriage to Ursula. You know you must marry her now that you have given *logo, your word* in front of all these witnesses.'

'So, no pressure then?' jokes Mullet like a jittery child trying to make light of the situation yet feeling her powerful curse take immediate effect. And he's right to worry.

We all watch intrigued. Her hand movement accompanied by the *'Na',* is an insult and warning. And Mullet knows it. These types of curses take him back to his childhood in Sydney with stories his mother told him about his *yiayia* and the *old magisses, witches* back in the village. He'll need eyes at the back of his head from now on to prevent her lurking, watching his every move. But he's lucky. He could have been given the two-handed version which would mean he'd be doubly cursed. And as curses go in Greece, worse still she could have called him a donkey and then the battle lines would be drawn. We could have had a duelling match on our hands in the clearing of our very own front garden. This time it's Mum's turn to save the day.

'Anna, *ella, come, ella!*' And she pats loudly an empty seat beside her. 'Can we offer you a drink, or some *tarama salata*? There's plenty here. Please, Anna, come sit down and join us.'

Jutting her generous agitated nostrils into the air as if sniffing out trouble, she makes a clicking 'tut' sound with her tongue as it taps the roof of her mouth indicating a firm '*oxi, no*'. And in so doing demonstrates to her audience she's a paragon of shimmering white virtue, only dressed in pitch cemetery black. She glares at us as if she's entered a den of iniquity hosted by none other than Sodom and Gomorrah. With her square jaw firmly fixed on a refusal, she won't be tempted into the fold of this pagan gathering. Ursula wants desperately to pat the tiny, trembling lambs, give them a gentle cuddle before death, but decides it's best not to. She remains seated; sends the braying lambs love telepathically.

Anna's look is chilling as she continues defensively, 'Of course, like all good Greeks I'm still fasting for Easter. There is olive oil in your *tarama salata* and of course, fish eggs. *Po, po, po*, I took holy communion this morning!'

She points her long pointy finger in the air at us as if it's a jittery gun about to go off. 'You should all go to church and try and wash away your sins! Today is my thirty-nineth day of fasting. Tonight, at midnight, I can break my fast. But not before. I just wanted you to see the lambs, to select one before George slaughters them. If you don't want to pick one, I can do this for you. So, if you don't want to select one, I will see you tomorrow when we bring the *souvla* lamb. Mrs Jo, I must go now and help George prepare the lambs. Then I'll go back to church for the next service.'

Looking directly at Mullet, she raises her voice, firing, 'And strict fasting from sex, like all good Greeks for forty days and nights would do you a lot of good too. *Yassas, kai Kali Anasasi, goodbye, and good resurrection!*' She leaves mumbling something about raging sin and yellow sports cars not impressing her.

After she's lifted the docile but doomed lambs into the back of her old rusty truck, she departs with a loud grinding of the clutch and a thick blast of black smoke from the wobbly exhaust pipe. The fading shape of the truck disappearing down the hill casts a feeling of encroaching doom over all of us. Like scolded children we sit taking in the gravity of her words and what she and George are about to do. Now, with the sound of tinkling sheep's bells and truck engine diminishing, we each sit deep in thought.

Moments pass and at last Mullet speaks, 'Oh well, forty

days of fasting will do that to you ... especially doing the no sex version of the Greek Orthodox Easter Fast. Food's hard enough! But gee whizz ... sex too? It'd make you more than a bit narky! Cranky as a bloody cut rattle snake. Just like Mum. Don't you reckon, Stick? That old battle axe, she's nothing more than a frustrated old sheet sniffer, sticking her nose into other people's lives. Oh well, the day is but a pup. Where's that bottle of vodka, Stick? I reckon we all need a top-up. What did you say before in Russian, David, '*Nostrovia?*'

Chapter 25

Tickling Time Bombs

The winding-up of Easter fasting in the Greek Orthodox Church is distinguished with joyous exuberance and celebrations heralding back to the very beginnings of Christianity. It arrives each year as sated buds burst forth with brilliant colour and alluringly hypnotic perfume that magically undulates. There's a gulf stream of movement everywhere, even in the contours of a war that menacingly shadows our lives.

I pause to take in the famous view of the eastern side of the Spianarda Square close to the arches of the Palace of Saint George and Saint Michael near the Liston. This place is revered for Sunday afternoon promenades, relaxed dining and the occasional cricket game. All around music and movement merge as the powerful magnetism of the occasion draws in locals from all over the island. Soon, at the stroke of midnight on Easter Saturday night, Christ's miraculous resurrection will be celebrated. Whether at war with Turkey ... or not, Easter will not be stopped.

In the crisp clear evening air, Corfu town is an illumination of lights as the island's famous uniformed marching bands parade in a procession in not-so-perfectly lined brightly coloured squads like revered roosters and hens, their heads adorned with shiny silver or brass helmets; their shoes spotless and gleaming black. In step, then often out of step, they revive the solemn paces that were taken along these same paths centuries earlier by previous generations. Breaching the uneven sides of the narrow footpaths below the gracious Venetian townhouses and shops, the bands compress the curious onlookers against the sides of time-worn buildings. With self-importance, these musicians thrust, bursting through the crowds, their showy tasselled uniforms with highly polished instruments and gold buttons flickering in the light.

Along the tapered streets, shutters are flung open everywhere as heads arch and swivel, hoping to get a better view of the excitement below. Church bells pause until that charmed midnight moment when they will all harmonise, bells ringing together in jubilation. All the while crowds clap and cheer in this vibrant carnival atmosphere. Swallows circle above wondering at the masses of lights illuminating their night sky.

Now as the darkness of night settles, fireflies hover like tiny orbital Hellenic helicopters as if on cue to play a magical role in this legendary biblical event. Soon the town will explode with fireworks, the swallows will scatter, or fall dying from shock at the bursts of noise and flashes of light that have desecrated their aerial world. Yes, that pivotal moment when the clock strikes midnight ... it's as if everyone has been holding their breath for forty days, waiting in suspense, poised for this momentous moment to arrive. Now all the pent-up frustration from fasting is joyously released into the air as a final outpouring of emotion is expressed. *Xristos Anesti, Xristos Anesti,*' *Christ has risen,* words that will be repeated over and over to friends and strangers alike, each reaching to the other. It's as if a universal human bond, a blessed moment of peace, is bequeathed to all humanity. With loving hands and generous hearts paper boxes daintily tied with thin string or bright red ribbon ties filled with Greek *glyka, sweets* are gifted or received.

As Church doors thrust open, forced by the compressed pressure of the widening crowds, the light of Christ flows out symbolically carried in hand-held candles. These raised beacons begin their journey, weaving like unwinding white flickering ribbons of light merging into the night, a sea of ambient candle lights swelling in numbers as flames are shared, passed on with blessings through the masses. Once lit, the candles are clutched diligently, sheltered from the wind with great effort on the backs of donkeys, in cars, gripped by pedestrians, or go riding on motorbikes along cobbled pathways through villages and along waterfronts. From a single light a steady stream of candle flames begins to ignite all corners of the island. For centuries descendants of the faith have travelled these beloved and worn paths heading home to celebrate with candles proudly held aloft and alight as they do now. Those who've miraculously brought their candles home still alight without it having been extinguished on the journey are told they are lucky. '*Kali Tixi, good luck* till this time next year.'

It's now well after midnight; any other night most locals would be fast asleep in bed. But not on this holy of holy nights. Villas large or small reverberate with laughter as feasting begins and most won't see bed until after three am. Others will party all night. Games involving cracking red eggs will be played, meat eaten and desserts attacked with uncompromising relish. However, in our part of the world things are proving to be less celebratory after Mullet, Stick and partners eventually hit the road.

'What do you mean you don't feel well? What's wrong with you? You were fine earlier today,' moans Mum, fumbling in the night to light a cigarette and slam the lighter down loudly on the bedside table. She hates being woken. It's been a long day for her: entertaining guests then darting off every so often to prepare food and tidy the house for Easter Sunday's festivities was not easy. The last thing she needs right now is a whinging male putting a stick in the works and ruining her precious quiet time.

'S'truth, love, I think it's my heart. I think I'm having a heart attack! I hate to say this, but you'd better call a doctor.'

Annoyed and now sitting upright and stiff in bed, Mum continues, 'It's probably indigestion. Try rolling over and going back to sleep. Anyway, every doctor in Greece from Santorini to Sparta is out celebrating tonight. No doctor in their right mind and who's diligently fasted for forty days is going to give up their precious partying tonight for you! You could have timed this better. It's going to cost a fortune even if I can find someone at this unholy time of the night. It's a bloody public holiday.'

'Christ, as if I timed this. I don't care how much it costs … just get me a doctor, will you, woman! For fuck's sakes, I think I'm dying!'

As Dad dramatically grasps his chest, falls back on the bed red-faced in a pool of sweat, she gives him the evil eye. She's not impressed.

'Oh, for God's sakes! Okay, okay, I'll go next door to Chrissie's and see if she can help, or use her phone. But I warn you, Chrissie could be anywhere tonight. You better pray to God someone's home because they're the only ones that I know of with a phone around here.'

Mum, Took and Ursula stopped drinking shortly after dinner and headed inside where our two female guests spent the evening admiring our villa, drifting from room to room and preparing food for our Easter Sunday feast. However, much earlier in the day the men, seduced by the delights of the gorgeous spring weather, foolishly pulled their fold-up chairs out from under the shady olive trees to catch the sun's rays while they relaxed, drinking until all of the duty-frees were gone. Later Mum chastised Dad as she angrily helped him to bed while Mullet and Stick sang the worst version of *The Pub with No Beer* we'd ever heard as they exited with the assistance of Ursula and Took.

It was Ursula who drove the bright yellow sports car to town, squeezing it through the crowded narrow streets to park behind the cricket ground adjacent to the Liston. The women assisted the two drunken men along the pathway to their hotel. A couple of young Greek men, thinking this was a joke, came to the service of the two attractive young women. The men, keen to show their strength and virility, fire-lifted Stick and Mullet to the front steps of the hotel. Calling for the night porter and wishing the women '*Xristos Anesti*', the men drifted off into the crowded night waving and laughing as they went.

In the meantime, Mum's followed Dad's instructions. She's raced next door to Chrissie's villa for help. A million thoughts go through her mind. Perhaps Chrissie and husband Nikko aren't home? They could be anywhere in town on a night like this. What if Dad dies? If that happens, we'll be stranded in Greece again with no money! Mum's heart pounds as much as her head thumps. She hears laughter coming from Chrissie's alfresco area. The smell of lamb cooking on the *souvla, over coals* is a hint of tomorrow's lunch in the now.

'Chrissie, Chrissie,' Mum calls as she shifts through the beacons of light from a very generous moon shining from the night sky as if specially to guide her through the troubled night into her neighbour's lantern-lit garden. But it's Nikko's frame that emerges from the kitchen, not Chrissie's. Mum's caught sight of a brunette woman leaning into him in the shadows. 'Oh, *Yassou*, Nikko, sorry to intrude. There's an emergency. David, ridiculous as always, thinks he's having a heart attack. Probably just the drink!'

Startled at first, Nikko moves quickly away from the side of the woman. Sounding like the dramatic Cretan that he is, he replies, '*Po, po, po*. Yes, yes of course, *Kiria*, Mrs Jo, you must come in. *Ella, ella*. Chrissie is not here. She would of course help you, after all she is a doctor of sorts. She would have some idea of what's wrong with *Kirios*, Mr David, but she's still at church.'

Nikko, flustered by her arrival out of the darkness of this holy night, fails to introduce the woman. The brunette stands looking on, unmoved, drawing deeply and seductively on her cigarette. A flash spins through Mum's mind that perhaps there's something going on here that Chrissie doesn't know about. After all, Nikko has the reputation for being quite a ladies' man. How many times have we seen him take tourist girls out in his flashy speedboat while Chrissie's in town working? He whizzes his women around the next bay to a restaurant for lunch or dinner. Then whizzes his lady friends back before Chrissie gets home, disposing of his passengers near the ferry terminal before mooring his boat and racing up the hill. It's as if he has an informant planted at the hospital who warns him when his wife is leaving work. It's for this reason the locals call him the '*Cretan pontikos*,' *Cretan fox*.

While adulterous thoughts swim through Mum's inquisitive mind, Nikko has been spurred into action and found a doctor's number in a matter of seconds. 'Here ... here ... this is the emergency number. Let me call the hospital. They're supposed to be there twenty-four hours of the day. Even today, perhaps? But I cannot promise this.'

With this disheartening news thumping in her head, Mum grips the moment and prays to the God she'd abandoned years ago. She's made deals with him before and even though he's always let her down, perhaps this time he'll look favourably upon her. She holds onto this hope as Nikko lights a cigarette before attempting to make the phone call. It's as if he's seeking strength to face the failure of this act of neighbourly kindness.

'Of course, I am not sure anyone will answer the call because today is a special day in the Greek Orthodox Church,' he confides in his strong accent.

Right now, she is not in the mood for a lecture from him about what day it is. She knows what day it is. Damn him.

But he seems oblivious to this and continues. 'It's a very important day. This is because we have fasted for forty days and nights and now, of course, everyone wants to party; to celebrate. Even to have sex!' Eyeing her with a lazy knowing gaze he continues, 'You must understand this. But I will try this number and hopefully someone will answer.'

Frantically, she thrusts the receiver into Nikko's hand and indicates for him to hurry up and get dialling. There's no time to dilly-dally. The phone rings, and rings, echoing into the night.

Back at the Cavalieri Hotel, Mullet's showing similar symptoms to Dad. His head pounds, his heart thumps. His chest feels as if it is about to burst through his ribcage and he's broken into a sweat like a pumping reticulation system.

'Ursula love, I don't feel too good. Geez, I think I need to see a doctor! It's me chest. I feel like me ticker's going to cut out and I'm going to cark it!'

Ursula's not amused. She's tired. The all-night partying and celebrating around town with cars horns blowing, fireworks exploding, motorbikes revving, thumping music and laughter invading their hotel room above Kapodistrias Street near the Liston has made her uncharacteristically irritable. 'Oh, Mullet what do you want me to do ... shall I call reception?'

'Yes, love. I feel like the back end of the local tip. I think I better scoot and talk to the toilet for a while.'

As Mullet does a convincing job of looking like a dead man crawling across the bedroom floor to the bathroom, Ursula reaches for the telephone and dials reception. It rings and rings. Her heart sinks. Will no one answer the phone?

Chapter 26

Easter Sunday

Mum hasn't had any sleep. A short and crusty doctor with an enormous twitching Groucho moustache arrives at 2 am and, after elevating himself with effort and royal superiority up our wide winding wooden staircase heaving an oversized medical bag in his hand, he gives Dad a quick examination. Having executed a few fundamental tests, he deems him fit as a fiddle – well almost.

Less interested in Dad's health, the ill-humoured doctor suspends any pleasant bedside manner he might have to sanctimoniously lecture Mum about his night being exasperated by numerous patients presenting with similar symptoms, conditions all mysteriously attributed, in varying degrees, of course, to excessive alcohol consumption, leading to self-imposed states of semi-induced delirium.

'And they are all '*xeni*,' *foreigners*! One of them was an Australian like your husband. Do you people have something against living? *Po, po, po*. From now on, be careful of Corfu's potent and alluring spring sun … and stay hydrated. Your husband has not had a heart attack, he has severe sunstroke and alcohol poisoning! I advise he get his liver checked.'

Wrapping her dressing gown tightly around her as if to guard herself from his unruly style, she suppresses her relief, delighted she's got plenty of ammunition to make Dad's life a living misery when he recovers, which, according to the doctor, he will. It's all too delicious for words. Now she can get days, perhaps even years of revenge out of this scrumptious little incident. Him dying would have been a nightmare, of course. Indeed, there's no denying this. It brings back haunting memories of when he nearly died of pneumonia on the ship when we crossed from Australia to England. When that happened, the ashen-faced remorseful captain told Mum she'd have to face up to the fact that Dad would be buried overboard at sea. There was no morgue ... with a freezer. Just like back then, she'd have to tolerate the self-effacing criticism and endless lectures from her family as they chastised her for stupidly moving to Greece ... of marrying Dad. Their list of grievances would no doubt go on. And, as they hauled the last vestiges of dignity from her, she'd have to beg them for money ... and with no home to go home to. Australia effectively a symbolic place, a name only. A passport, nothing more. Yes, she could see all the naysayers; they'd be lined up to stick their bit in and remind her of what a loser she is. Then there was that deep dark secret of hers that she kept so well hidden from everyone. Well, not everyone. The heartbreaking thing was that her most dangerous secrets are held in the hearts of those she most mourns. No, she could never return to Australia.

She attempts to loosen the stiff, agitated doctor a bit by joking. 'Hydrated? Hydrated! You'd think he'd be overly-hydrated. Between he and his tourist mates, they consumed numerous bottles of vodka, then attacked the Jameson. When that ran out, they had the audacity to steal a bottle of my lousy cooking wine from under the kitchen sink. I mean, who does that?'

'Well, it's not for me to judge good or bad behaviour in my patients but I would advise your husband to rest in bed. Try and flush the alcohol from his body with lots of water. Yes, only water ... nothing else unless it's unadulterated lemonade.

No alcohol. But most of all, you must keep him out of the sun!'

The doctor compounds her nightmare by placing a substantial bill in her hand then disappears with a hollow slam of our front door. She is left in the remaining darkness of the night with the curt and empty echo of his agitated '*Xristos Anesti.*'

'*Xristos Anesti* to you too!'

Surveying the unsavoury deluge of dirty glasses, ashtrays, empty bottles and plates left from last night, she takes a deep inhalation of the thick smoke, choking on what little fresh air remains in her small dark cellar-like kitchen. Happy Easter indeed! Her head throbs and Easter celebrations haven't even begun.

Returning to their bedroom where my father lies stretched out with sheets in muddled disarray and snoring loudly, she lies awake dissecting the situation, unable to go back to sleep. The hospital is always appealing for blood donors. Desperate locals and sometimes tourists loiter around for hours, sometimes for days at the entrance scouting for a donor and a blood match. Then a bidding war may ensue as each bid against the other for this life-sustaining scarlet liquid ... could this be an option? Line up and sell our blood? Hours later as the sun pushes away what is left of the night sky, there's the sound of a familiar high-pitched voice.

Kali mera, kali mera, good morning, Joanna. Is everything okay? How is David? It's me Chrissie ... Chrissie from next door.'

It seems impossible that her head could feel any worse but suddenly it does. Mum swears under her breath, 'Blast it, it can't be morning'! How can anyone be so cheery at this time? – it defies human logic. Quickly dressing in a baggy cotton shirt, loose denim shorts and floppy army surplus khaki green sun hat to hide her bad hair moment, she tiptoes with care on bare feet across the creaky spring of the old wooden boards.

With the tiles down the main hall providing a soothing touch underfoot, Jo releases her elegant wide framed wooden front door from the ritual of its nightly unlocked closure. Quickly, she suggests they sit under the welcoming umbrella of olive trees. 'Please ... please, everyone's asleep. He's fine ... he's fine. It wasn't a heart attack. The stupid man fried himself like floured calamari in olive oil only under the sun and, of course, drank far too much. He's still sleeping ... hopefully regretting all the fuss and expense he's caused us.'

'I don't like to gloat about the old traditional Greek practices, Jo, but perhaps following the Greeks with their fastidious fasting would have saved him a lot of suffering. *Po, po, po!* Fasting is not just good for a man's soul, it's good for his head too.' She laughs at the irony of the situation. Her own husband is no better. 'God is all-wise, all-seeing, you know.'

Mum laughs in agreement with the woman despite her throbbing head, salty eyes and lack of belief in anything. In fact, she wishes her kind but patronising neighbour would leave her to wallow in misery and privacy. As if in a momentary daze, she watches her neighbour's jaw move up and down. Why does she want to know which doctor attended and all the other irrelevant information, it happened hours ago ...? Still, the woman's mouth won't stop moving.

'Even though I lived in the States, I still love the traditional recipes at Easter.' Blah, blah ... blah. 'What about *avgolemono, egg and lemon* soup? I made some yesterday ... it lines the stomach after fasting. I can race next door and get you a bowl?'

Mum fans her melting face with the latest copy of Newsweek as her tired body fuses to the flimsy, rickety seat. Flushed from an atrocious combination of heat, hangover, menopausal hormones and a distinct lack of sleep, she is dreading the day ahead. Not to mention all the other irritations confounding her life, including the prospect of this woman continuing on and on about food.

'No. Thanks all the same, Chrissie. Fabulous though it is, but definitely not right now. No offence, but I think I'd vomit ....'

'But it's a great rescue remedy.'

'Look ... please, no. By the way, here's something small for you and Nikko.' She manages a limp smile. 'A miniscule gift ... but still, quite a valuable commodity around here.' She reaches and smacks an attacking insect on her lower calf without looking down, then passes her guest a large jar of peanut butter.

'Ah, I adore the stuff ... crunchy too. My favourite, thank you.'

'Well, I don't know what I would have done without Nikko's help last night. By the way, you seem much happier this morning, happier than I've seen you in a while. Any particular reason?'

Sweeping her fingers suggestively back and forth across the top of her newly acquired and much-revered peanut butter jar that now sits alluringly in front of her on the table, Chrissie releases the kind of giggle usually attributed to naughty pixies. 'Well, of course, I'm happy! Last night we feasted until our eyes bulged at my friend Nina's house. Between you, me and Spiros's *kafeneio*, when I returned home, I made wild and passionate love with Nikko after forty days of abstinence. I was like a wild ravenous beast!'

'Oh, yes?'

'Nikko was not keen at first, put off by my mother's old icon of Saint Nickolas with huge piercing eyes hanging above the bed ... said it bothered him. Never has before. I removed it from our bedroom so there could be no excuses.'

Lighting a cigarette, she continues laughing unable to suppress her joy like a delighted but rebellious child. 'Then I put it back above the bed afterwards. May she rest in peace. Maybe he thinks as we get older there are some things a mother's icon should never see ... Or, any of the saints for that matter; heaven forbid.' She pauses, crossing herself three times while mouthing a rapid silent prayer. Then her eyes shoot skyward. 'She died here in the villa many years ago, a few days after the start of Lent. It was too much for her. In Greece, it's amazing how many people die before Lent, or a few days after it begins. When they get old, they think they have suffered enough in life without the misery of another long Lenten fast. God rest their souls but you can't blame them, can you?'

Enjoying the fact that her confidant is amused, Chrissie confidently continues, 'Are you expecting many people today for lunch?'

'Along with my family, maybe five or six others. Tell me, Chrissie, how long will it take David to recover from sunstroke?'

'It depends on how much water he drinks and how much rest.'

'All of them could have done with a good serving of church yesterday, as you say. I think when it comes to having a good time, David usurps even Dionysus.'

'Nikko's the same ... and all his women.' Chrissie pauses; looks sideways at Mum, giving her a knowing look. 'He thinks I'm stupid, that I don't see what's going on right in front of me. The man is leading a perilously dangerous life taking strange women out in his speedboat. There will come the day when one of them will push him overboard ... and he can't swim. Casanova will end up a drowned rat. At least David is faithful and doesn't chase empty-headed tourist girls. He may drink a lot but he's still a good man. He loves his family and he loves you.'

Chrissie's right. Dad is a good man and he loves her, but why should Mum admit it? Life has shown her a woman has to stay tough, not let emotions get in the way. Treat men mean to keep them keen … it's a safe mantra. Well, not her sons or any boys that look like her sons.

Mum considers the woman lurking in the shadowy kitchen light with Nikko last night but decides to say nothing. Why get involved, least of all cause Chrissie any additional grief about her philandering husband. Especially on Easter Sunday, so she laughs and says, 'David, huh! The fool can't afford another woman … can't pay the bills as it is. And look at this one from the doctor … how are we supposed to pay this?'

She pulls a crumpled bill from her shabby shorts. 'After today, another six months of lentils and beans should raise enough drachmae from my meagre shopping money. The kids are going to love this. If only the Australian dollar would go up, Greece's inflation down and Greece's residency laws didn't restrict us from earning a living. David writes his bloody novel. Oh, Chrissie, I wish for so many things, things you could never imagine but I keep them locked away in my heart until I drop off this mortal coil.'

Hoping she's about to divulge streams of deep lurid secrets about the past, Chrissie leans forward, gripping the sides of her flimsy chair in eagerness. 'Ah, was there once a great love in your life and you pine for him?'

But Mum laughs despite feeling a desperate need to scream and spill her twisted and tormented story. Give up her long torturous struggle … tell the world her shocking, suffocating secrets. But she's been stuffing her feelings inward for far too long to release them now. Anyway, what would be the point

… it would only shock and horrify her neighbour and everyone else because it wouldn't stop there. Hers was not the type of secret that stays a secret for very long. People love juicy stories. And David … how would he react if he knew? He'd want out. And the kids … would they disown her? Hold it over her? Anyone would, especially since she's been dishing out dirt on others for years.

She is about to make a joke to craftily distract her inquisitive guest from the hot topic when they are disturbed by the sound of a car cruising up the tree-lined drive.

Like a dramatic scene from a 1950s movie, Hilary emerges with a long black cape swirling around her Venusian body. One hand clasps a heavy demijohn of cognac and Georgie, her new and obnoxious poodle on a lead, her other hand clasps a half-filled glass of cognac which she sips intermittently as she floats ghost-like toward the women. But, as a barking competition between Patch and Georgie ensues, an excited Georgie tugs at Hilary, hastening what was supposed to be an elegant entrance in the direction of the women under the trees into a series of jerking unladylike, uneven steps. Still, the contents of her glass remain intact but rise perilously close to overflowing like furious waves within its constrained confines.

Her sweeping deep American accent reverberates in the morning air, 'Hello, Australia! Happy Easter … Gee, I had one shit of a night ….' Her irrepressible bluntness operates at its normal unrestrained level. Most of us have toyed with the idea that it is just a matter of time before she's deported for her brazenness. If the government is willing to clamp down on mini shirts and long hair … well there's no reason why Hilary can't be carted off with the rest of them. As for her ending up with an Irish alcoholic, well, we remain mystified by the attraction.

She continues, 'I've got *loukoumi, Turkish delight* in a bag in the car for the kids. Are they around or out somewhere? Gee, I wish my kids were like yours ... off most of the time ... not poking their snotty little noses into my affairs ... spying on me for their shit of a father. Anyone who supported Tricky Dicky at the last election has to be a shit as far as I'm concerned. That's why I divorced Harry, you know? He voted for Nixon. That was grounds enough for divorce if ever there were grounds for divorce. Anyway, I sure nailed his fat arse!'

Coming to sit under the wide spreading arms of the olive trees with her excited Georgie, demijohn, and tall glass with contents still remarkably intact from her waddle and jerky arrival, she shuffles her generous rear end into the sun-bleached canvas of one of our chairs. Her substantial squirming bottom shapes the fabric in a downward direction quickly giving way to gravitational force.

She lights an American cigarette; Mum wishes she'd be a sport and offer her one. Greek Pallas cigarettes are fine, cheap and cheerful and great value but there's something magically elusive about Western brands. Yes, Western brands ... those wonderful aromatic European brands like the Matisse-blue wrapped packets of Gauloises, Gitanes or those deliciously exotic Black or Cocktail Russian Sobranies. Mesmerising suffused with intoxicating aromas of the Middle East, her mind drifts, whirling off to another place. Yes, another life when on happier days she could remember herself in the company of Melbourne's avant-garde in the late 1940s, briefly Yehudi Menuhin ... modelling for artists, sipping glasses of expensive champagne and think nothing of it.

'Yes, well on that point I have to agree with you. I've always been right of centre politically as you well know. Dreadful lying little shit of a man. I'd divorce David if he ever swung left of field. Bloody load of Communists, if you ask me. I've always instilled right wing values in my children and woe to any of them if they ever shifted to the centre, or left. Australia swung to the left after we left the country … in the late 1960s. I always joke with David saying that's why we left!'

The women laugh, but there is much truth in her joke, but she'd never be stupid enough to get into detail about it. Especially those particular laws that are changing in Australia, laws brought in by interfering politicians and so-called 'do-gooders' – laws that she needs to keep evading at all costs.

On a political level, these two women have much in common: their white supremacist views, husbands with military careers and children who run wild and free with little or no supervision when they're on the island.

'I've had one hell of a night,' Mum complains, searching for sympathy from her friend and frantically begins fanning her flushed face again.

'She sure has,' agrees Chrissie with heightened empathy, illuminating her classically beautiful face.

'Well actually, ladies, you could give me a hand in the kitchen? I was up all night with David – thought he was having a heart attack. Turns out he's got nothing more than a bad dose of sunstroke and alcohol poisoning. And the doctor … all that primal gesticulating with his stethoscope. I hate to discredit your profession, Chrissie, but I'm sure at some stage, possibly as early as conception, he evolved from a bit of mutated DNA concocted in a cracked and contaminated petri dish in some dark laboratory. Men in starched white coats … I loathe the lot of them. A prime example of one of those dreadful retro alfa Greek males. But back to serious business, ladies, there's party residue all over the kitchen table taking up valuable space. I've got people coming today and …'

Shaking her head, Hilary laughs outright, lifting the weighty demijohn from the weathered table with effort, but still teasingly swings it from side to side in the air. 'Relax, ladies, relax. This is to calm all our nerves. We've all had a long night. How about you, Chrissie? Fancy a tipple?'

'*Po, po, po, oxi*, not for me. But I can help in the kitchen, Jo. I don't mind doing a bit of tidying up. Nikko's hard at work in my kitchen as we speak. Besides making love, it's probably the only thing he can do well. His career's been a flop. I'm the one keeping the engines running financially ever since I married the stupid man. You think you are the only one suffering from family budget blowout disorder?'

The women laugh even though money, when you're broke, is no laughing matter.

'No, no, Chrissie, you stay here. Look here comes my daughter. She can go on kitchen duty for a while. Give her something to do. Ah, there you are, dear. Be a pet and get your mother some glasses and then have a look at the kitchen for me? I've been up all night. Your poor battle-weary mother is exhausted. Kitchen needs a tiny tidy up before our guests arrive ... remember, we're having lovely lamb today.'

I smile at our guests and the thought of lamb as I drag my feet reluctantly to the kitchen. I'm annoyed. If Mullet was here, I reckon he'd say, 'The day is but a pup.' It sure is!

Chapter 27

The Day is but a Pup

With Chrissie beckoned by an impatient Nikko, his voice calling weakly, probably run out of steam from his many recent extra-marital entanglements, the pair disappear behind a large flowering oleander bush and into their villa. They leave the women sitting idly beneath the olive trees in the tepid morning breeze enjoying their unimpeded view of the *New Limani* and wide breadth of a flat turquoise and blue-tinged ocean reaching toward the jutting grey mountains beyond. Hilary's demijohn rests high on the sun and windswept table as locally crafted pottery ashtrays sit overflowing now with extinguished and semi-smouldering butts exposing the bright tell-tale signs of where Hilary's red lips have been.

'What do you think of this cognac?' Without waiting for a reply, Hilary's high pitched voice rushes, 'It's from Hoppy's *kafeneo*. Yeah, it's not a bad drop. Oh, honey, I got to tell you about what happened yesterday when I popped into Thanasi's butcher shop. I don't know if he was reacting to a sex free forty-day fast, or if he'd been on an ouzo trip but when I went to pick up my ongoing order of lamb chops and beef steaks ... um ... he kind of chased me around his shop. And you know how small his shop is? He pursued me with these circular things on the end of a souvlaki stick.'

She pauses to take an unladylike gulp of her cognac and finally offers Mum an American cigarette. Delighted, Mum's face lights up like the Marlboro she's igniting and she inhales it as if savouring some exquisite delight, then slowly exhales a long grey veil of smoke from her lungs. A satisfied sigh of contentment is released at the same time.

Hilary responds, 'You know, I consider myself to be an open-minded woman. I've been around ... you know what I mean? But he officiously shoved those God damned round things on the end of a souvlaki stick at me. It was like a one-sided sword fight. You know, 'touché' without the 'ole' if you get my drift ... like he was daring me. They looked familiar in a creepy kind of way. He insisted I try one and I wasn't keen. But he kept insisting, laughing all the while as he thrust those crispy grilled orbitals at me, urging, jabbing, grunting as perspiration dripped down the side of his fat piggy face, eyes bulging, saying, "It's very nice, very nice. It's good for you. It's for Easter. It's a delicacy. We Greeks love them!" Well, honey, I got to tell you, I like to support the local customs as much as the next guy, so I reluctantly took a bite of those round bits on a stick ... you know, to be polite. And well, I knew the moment I sunk my teeth into the God damn thing. You wanna know what they were?'

'Oh my god, tell me.'

'Well, it was a fucking lamb or goat's testicle, sweetie! That's what it was. Well, I nearly regurgitated the whole damn thing up right there on his shop floor. All the while he continued thrusting that God damn souvlaki stick at me so I'd try another one ... that son of a bitch thought it was hilarious. Well, I won't be buying any meat from that little weasel anymore. Here, honey, have another cognac. I don't know about you but this stuff helps me rid the taste of that revolting thing out of my mouth. God damn it, it's a much-needed medicinal remedy as far as I'm concerned. What do you reckon? Whoever invented this liquid gold was a genius ... an unadulterated genius.'

Smacking her lips and glancing quickly at Mum's horrified face, Hilary pours more cognac. 'Yeah, it's the tale of the terrible tasting testes. Well, honey, I gotta tell you that's just how I felt. As I said earlier, I nearly regurgitated that damn thing right up on his shop floor. You know, I reckon he's lost his best customer ever. In fact, I wouldn't be surprised if it was my meat purchases that kept his shitty little business going all through Lent. I mean, you guys live on lentils as do most of the Greeks during Lent. So, who bought his meat? Me, that's who …. Shall I pour a bit more, honey?'

'Wow, slow down. I have a whole day to get through …! So I take it you are off meat?' laughs Mum.

'As I've always said, I like to participate in the local customs … shows you're interested … you know what I mean, honey?'

Hilary draws more smoke from her cigarette into her lungs, the suction power of her powerful lungs pulling in the hollows of her cheeks with their fury. Upon exhaling, she says, 'Well, should we pour a brandy for the patient? Might help resurrect him.'

'No, that's the last thing he needs right now, but I need a miracle to round off Easter. David's doing a very convincing job of imitating an embalmed corpse as we speak,' laughs Mum, and then a thought suddenly comes to her. 'Well, we could stuff him; he's already partially dehydrated from alcohol … semi embalmed, so to speak. Alcohol might be just as effective as natron, perfectly performing the same role as the ancient Egyptian preservers. We could prop him up in a glass case, turn him into a god and sell tickets. Call him Dionysus the great, great something or rather … and make a fortune out of him.'

'Good grief, you are desperate. But look, if you thought you had a bad night, I did too. I didn't get much sleep because the locals partied all night. Then when I slept, I kept seeing oversized *souvlaki* testicles coming at me. Talk about a nightmare. So, this chick needs to resurrect herself. And not the kind of resurrection I think Thanasi had in mind either.' Her booming robust laughter fills the warm morning air. 'You don't have those damned lamb's testicles on the menu for lunch ... cos I'm not falling for that one again.'

'Well, Hilary, as a matter of fact, we probably are. Anna's cooking our lamb at her place then they'll deliver it here and join us for lunch. I have to say, it's very kind of them to do that. Not sure about the testicles though. Although, Anna will probably make *kokoretsi*, so there could be lots of all sorts of bits of awful offal rotating on a stick. I'm giving you the heads up now – I'm giving anything that's orbital and on a stick a wide berth.'

'Good girl,' laughs Hilary with satisfied delight and she settles back cosily in her chair.

'Look, Hilary, I didn't get much sleep because David thought he was having a bloody heart attack in the middle of the night. What is it with men and their timing? And the drama ... you have no idea. Trying to get a doctor and then finding out it wasn't a heart attack, only heat stroke from too much sun and alcohol. Now we have a whopping medical bill to pay. He's in the bad books with me ... out of revenge, I feel like revving up the record player. You know ... really make him suffer.'

'Ah, yeah, revenge is sweet but if you're tired, what about your head? You won't be doing yourself any favours.'

Hilary's right.

'Well actually, I feel better already, your company has cheered me up. And of course, this very nice cognac.'

The two women laugh. 'So, is David, okay?' asks Hilary, cocking her head to one side to avoid a large bumble bee in mid-flight.

'Hah, he'll live to drink and be stupid another day. Anyway, I'm not speaking to him. He knows we are having guests, its ages since we've had lamb, he's ruining everything.'

Hilary thrusts out her generous chest and declares, 'No, he won't. We'll party without him. I never let a guy stand in the way of my having a good time. Hell no, so, why should you? How about we bury the bastard in the basement, I can get the record player pumping and screw him? Not literally, of course.'

Mum smiles at the idea. She stretches her long neck like a heron as she releases a vengeful laugh aiming it squarely at the upstairs windows of our villa. But, realising the morning is wearing on, the two women begin setting the table and chatting as they go.

'Did you hear Mullet's back with Ursula? You remember the Swedish girl that was staying at Anna's last summer? The one that got sprung with a man in her room … that dreadful naked man David found under the oleander bush in our garden back at Pyrgi?'

The two women laugh.

'I haven't heard this one,' chimes Chrissie smiling effervescently as she springs suddenly from the bushes, keen to join them and hear the latest gossip.

Hilary pipes up. 'How can I forget? Reminds me of when my kids are here. Springing me every time. They need to learn to knock on my bedroom door … not barge in. Shit, I'm single now and can screw whomever I want, whenever I want.'

'Well, that's telling it like it is!' laughs Mum, not at all surprised by Hilary's candour.

'You don't mince your words do you, Hilary?' agrees Chrissie promptly sitting down and slapping her black-skirted thighs with obvious delight.

The morning flashes by and soon a noisy white Fiat makes its way past the tall cypress trees edging the long potholed drive to our villa. Our friend Dimitri jumps out and, with arms piled full of wrapped gifts, he heads for the table where the women sit in an informal circle. He's become a welcome addition to our family since I met him on the beach a few summers ago. He'd tried to chat up me and my cousin who was visiting from Australia. As charming as he was, we had given short-shrift to his invitation to his villa on Gouvia Bay and a very tempting afternoon of skiing from his private pier. Though in his mid-thirties, with incredible blue sparkling eyes and a wicked sense of humour, he's adopted us, and we him. He exudes a unique, inexhaustible, overt sexual magnetism, an energy that oozes from every one of his golden-tanned pores. It comes from an inner confidence as opposed to movie or rock star good looks. With the heart of an angel, he's a hard man not to like; even when he's behaving wickedly around women. How many times has he made a big scene out of suddenly getting an untimely erection at the most inconvenient times and he'd have to suddenly grab anything handy to quickly cover his rising crutch. That's why he'd seldom go anywhere without a newspaper or his briefcase. We thought this was hilariously funny because a boyish grin would spread from one side of his face to other while most of the women blushed and looked away. Now whenever this happens, we just smile, roll our eyes and ignore him much to his disappointment.

As time has gone on, Dimitri's shared painful stories about his impoverished background growing up on the Greek mainland near Igoumenitsa, a place devastated after the Second World War but is now Greece's second largest passenger port. Dimitri was forced as a child to leave school at the age of nine and from there he made and sold wooden coat hangers on the side of the road to earn a living. What he earnt was beaten out of him by his stepfather; his father tragically had been killed during the war.

Over time, the young lad learnt to make furniture. Eventually, his stepfather's abuse was so bad he had to get away. There was nothing his tiny defenceless mother could do; she was too poor to leave her new husband, and no doubt the shame of it would have been too much for her. Dimitri fled the mainland, settling close by on Corfu. This turned out to be an auspicious decision as his *kafeneo* and restaurant style chairs sold faster than he could produce them with the booming expansion of tourism in the 1960s and early 70s. Dimitri freely admits that, since coming into power a few years ago, Papadopoulos' government has given very generous loans to businesses like Dimitri's and he, like many others, took advantage of them. He had to – he had little choice. It was either that or fall even deeper into poverty. Now he successfully exports his exclusive taverna-style furniture all over Greece and Europe. His factory or, as he prefers to call it, 'his *furniture fucktory*' is located close to our villa in the quaint historical boat-building village of Mandooki near the New Port. The factory's location is part of his export business's success story because he can easily access imported wood, produce and assemble his furniture, and then export his chairs and tables via the port with rapid efficiency. As his entrepreneurial and free-loving spirit is as unconventional and unconstrained as Hilary's, this could be a meeting of minds and bodies.

'*Xristos Anesti*,' Dimitri's warm musical voice resonates across the garden as he moves quickly from his car to sit at the now informally set table under the trees.

He places parcels on the table and, upon hearing his voice,

I race to greet him, giving him a sisterly kiss on the cheek and, right on cue, he pinches my bottom. Treating him like a rebellious brother, I push him away and pretend I'm angered by his actions. But I've already forgiven him for his keen, crab-like pinches into my rear. How can I not forgive my friend. His engaging, flirtatious grin and dazzling white teeth delivers a smile that could melt the South Pole, a smile against a backdrop of striking golden skin, with an adorable deep dimple sitting in the centre of a square muscular jaw – not to mention his athletic frame in 'tight tzeans', the consequence of his passion for water skiing which he does daily in summer around Gouvia Bay.

'Well, hello and happy Easter to you too, handsome,' croons Hilary in a deep drawn-out drawl before Mum can formally do the introductions. Craving the novelty of a new man for company over lunch, Hilary eagerly pats the seat next to her and thrusts forward her generous bosoms, flinging aside her black cape to reveal a plunging neckline. As yet, no one knows about her fallout with Paddy. She's decided to remain tight-lipped about it until something needs to be said. Continuing to pat the seat next to her, she insists Dimitri should sit beside her during lunch. His brilliant blue eyes twinkle with unashamed delight at being in close proximity to this strong, gutsy American woman. His extensive American Playboy magazine collection is testimony to this preference for North American women. Yes, the day is but a pup.

Chapter 28

Easter Sunday Afternoon

I wonder if perhaps our lives are at the tug and turn of the tides. What a wonderful thought if the tides are unhurried and calm and this Easter turns out to be a joyous and peaceful one.

With the tides now possibly on our side, the day that started off on the back foot slowly evolves at a seductively sedate pace requiring little effort from us mortals to do anything apart from imitate Lotus Easters and so we eat, drink and enjoy the sound of a timely Maestro sweeping through the undisciplined arms of the olive branches dancing above our heads. In the background is the vibrant hum of cicadas performing songs intermittently between our records being flipped, us singing badly, and the rhythmic idle chatter circling the table. Casting our eyes through the groves, the beautiful Ionian spreads before us like a wide blue fan expanding all the way to the straights to Albania where mountain peaks mirror deep into the depths of a million merging diamonds and sapphires dancing on the water's surface. Intoxicated by its beauty, we lazy, indulgent, Corfu converts sit lingering over lunch long into the afternoon.

The much longed for lamb has been served and I watch my family enjoy our first meat meal in what seems like years but, in reality, is many, many months. I wonder how Dad feels and if he could be tempted.

Out of curiosity, I wander the insides of our long hallway

and mount the wide winding stairs to his bedroom to see how he's fairing.

'Are you hungry ... the *souvla* lamb is amazing.' I say this as I peer around the corner of his bedroom door, thinking he might need encouraging.

'Hello, Possum ... I suppose there's no chance of a cognac or wine?'

'Well, I could ask Mum but ... you know what she's going to say. You are supposed to be drinking lots of water.'

I move to sit on the edge of the wide bed and attempt to straighten his tossed and ruffled sheets around him in a motherly way.

Dad bursts, 'What absolute twaddle! Water's unpalatable unless you are a platypus or a duck. Do I resemble either? Water is only permissible when it's topped generously with a nip of something to give it guts. But perhaps a small plate then .... But don't put anything on it that remotely resembles beans, tomatoes or those bloody lentils. It's a wonder we haven't all died of some ghastly disease from the wretched things ... some kind of diabolical Delphi atrophy!'

I laugh as he continues. 'You know, kiddo, we have to have one day in our lives without those monotonous spartan, fartin things. As offerings, they're about as tempting as a biblical plague. Now ... am I right, Possum?' He tries to stretch a smile across his constricted red face, his teeth posing a striking contrast and resembling a row of short solemn white columns. 'Yes, a nice plate of juicy lamb for your old Dad; that will do ... I suppose ... if I have to.'

'George reckons we should squeeze lemon on yours ... stop you having a heart attack. They all laughed when he said it because they reckoned they don't want to jump-start your heart over lunch! I don't think that's funny.'

'Is that so? Well, you tell Georgie Porgy from Pyrgi, I will eat my lamb the way I want and it's without lemon, lots of salt and oozing with fat, thank you very much. I didn't have a bloody heart attack. So as far as I'm concerned, he knows where he can put his bloody lemons. Make *avgo lemono, Easter egg and lemon soup* with them for all I care.'

'You're not going to die, Dad, are you? You would tell me? I don't think I could cope if anything happened to you. I don't want to be alone here with Mum, not again.'

'Come here, Possum. Everything's going to be honky dory, you'll see. Now don't you worry. All your old man needs right now is a great big helping of yummy lamb. Now promise me you won't worry. I'm not going anywhere.'

I smile a wide smile, enjoying the feel of his solid branch-like arms. Eventually, I release his grip and turn away, my mind now reassured and focused on the task ahead. Once outside I announce happily: 'Mum, Dad wants a plate of lamb with heaps of fat, no lemon juice and definitely no tomatoes. Oh, and he wants plenty of salt on the lamb.'

'Did your father ask for alcohol?' inquires Mum and, suddenly terrified, I say nothing. 'There, I told you … the stupid man will never learn,' she declares triumphantly.

Hearing this, George, posing as a prophet, throws his arms in the air theatrically as if about to execute an *hasapico* dance, 'You see how people are? They don't listen to good advice and when things go wrong; they expect you to feel sorry for them! *Po, po, po.* This is true, no? Especially drinking too much. Drink is like sorrow; it always survives the deluge because its buoyant. Sorrow cannot be drunk away … it will still be there the next day, only worse because you have a hangover. Drink is never the solution.'

'Yes, well what can I say?' says Mum nodding victoriously, as if she's never touched the stuff.

Keeping everyone's attention firmly on Dad, Mum

continues, 'He thinks salads are for rabbits. He'd break his own code of ethics if he so much as nibbled on a carrot, crunched a celery stick. They certainly broke the mould when they created him. As for drink, well, need I say more? Give him as much fat and salt as you can pile on his plate for all I care if he's going to ignore sound advice.'

They look on as, under a reign of rutted, disapproving looks, I load fatty pieces of lamb generously baptised with salt onto a substantial plate and disappear inside.

I return as Dad sits up in bed, cantankerously trying to make himself comfortable by fiddling and fluffing with his pillows. His sunburn looks blistered and sore.

Seeing the generously piled plate, he manages to spread the beginnings of a smile across his cherry-ripe face. 'You bloody beauty. Goody, goody ... thanks, Possum!' Suddenly imitating an excited small child, he rubs his hands together in delight.

'Well, enjoy, Dad. I got dirty looks from everyone. They disapprove of your dietary and drinking habits. I think I dobbed you in by saying nothing ... work that out!'

'They can disapprove as much as they like. The meat drought's gone on far too long, so long, in fact, I don't think there's any cholesterol left in my body. So, tell the lot of them to mind their own business. While you are at it, tell them to turn the bloody music down.'

'Yes, Dad.'

'It's not as if Aussies aren't genetically programmed to eat lamb and lots of it. If anything's going to put vigour in our veins, it will be lamb oozing with fat. Who was it that said, "Aussie's don't have sweet dreams; they have sheep dreams"? Indeed, our great nation rides on the sheep's back and that means tucking into lamb chops and wearing woolly jumpers in winter and summer, isn't that right, kiddo?'

'I suppose, if you say so, Dad.'

I leave him tucking into his plate of lamb and return to the table outside. The sun dances around us flickering between the olive trees in this alluringly beautiful ancient playground. Glancing toward the Ionian Sea, I imagine Poseidon on his adventures rising out of the water accompanied by a frolicking Kerkyra/Corcyra, the water nymph. In ancient times, the island was named after her as, until then, the island was unnamed. Corfu is still called Kerkyra by the Greeks. It's hard not to imagine the two of them wrapped in love as their spirits dance as they've done for thousands of years across these very waters. The warm afternoon twists the mind to drift as a magical spell lingers in the air. The whale-like mountains of Albania, now tinged with strawberry stripes, contrasts against silhouettes of malachite coastline along the island's bays and inlets. Mountains close by crouch low with plump olive trees and spear-shaped cypresses jutting up into the deep blue sky as if to usurp any dualling church steeples. An endless dreamy afternoon drifts as if we are locked in time.

The hum of conversation moves from one topic to another. Mullet, who's miraculously resurrected himself from his sick bed in time for lunch, tunes into my train of thought, suddenly saying as if overtaken by some literary force ... 'The island's a bloody beauty, isn't it? When you come in on a *kaiki* across the bay in the morning light and see this beautiful Venetian princess take shape before your eyes, it's bloody amazing. The town ... all those magnificent shabby chic colours. Your eyes can't help but thirstily take it all in, isn't that right, love?' He looks across at Ursula who enthusiastically agrees.

'Yep, as the sun comes up in the morning over the island, I reckon its beauty catches youse right in the throat. This place, raised from its faded, yet undeniably elegant Venetian, French and British past is magic. It's as if those gentle shades of shabby chic colours springing out of the tall town houses have been plucked from a child's crayon box and been hastily coloured in. Geez, it's beaut.'

'How poetic of you, Mullet.' Now tired and surprised by the improvements he's made in his vocabulary, Jo continues with scarcely contained sarcasm, 'Perhaps you could buy a town house overlooking the harbour and become a writer? Your words seem to capture the beauty of the island so well. You'd have amazing views of spectacular sunrises every day for the rest of your life. Now, how wonderful would that be?'

She's failed to conceal her thinly veiled envy. Her heart sinks at the very thought of this man who makes an art out of being an idiot is able to buy as many homes as he likes, homes she can only dream of. Her eyes coast our large rented villa with its peeling shutters. As beautiful as it is, it's not ours, nor is this the life she envisaged back in Carlton. Even more tragically, she's forgotten exactly what she'd imagined her life would be. All she knew back then was she had to get away, away before the shit hit the fan.

Mullet interrupts her thoughts. 'I never thought that me, this Aussie odd ball, could ever afford a grand lifestyle like this. Hey, Stick? After all, you and me are just a couple of ordinary blokes. I remember back to when we were left dead poor when Dad died. Sometimes we'd have to share a boiled egg between us for breakfast, that's how poor we were. Mum did it tough in those days raising us on her own ... working late nights in Uncle Nick's fish and chip shop in Redfern. Who'd a thought our lives would end up like this? It's a bloody miracle, isn't it, bro?'

'Well,' Mum replies, eyeing Stick as he nods in agreement with his brother, 'we are all here to help you make this transition. It's not easy being wealthy; you need sound advice.

If there's anything any of us can do for you, we're here to help. That's what friends are for.'

Anna, after elbowing a sleeping George in the ribs, hastily intervenes and offers, 'Yes, yes. We'll help you too, of course. But you must behave Mullet, or my curse will block your good fortune and you will end up with nothing. But I can take you next week to see Father George, if you like? If you truly wish Ursula to be baptised, it would be an honour to help you. But first you must decide who's going to be the godparent. George and I would be …'

But Stick, responding to a sharp kick initiated by Took's foot under the table, quickly pipes up, 'Nah, that would be me, won't it, Ursula? We discussed this the other day and want to keep it in the family. You understand, Anna? No offence … of course.'

'Of course, I understand the importance of family and so will Father George. This is a good decision. I can see your wedding will be a special one. Ursula, my child, you are surrounded by much love. No matter what happens in your life, always remember this. Here, these are my father's worry beads. Keep them safe always and they in return will keep you safe.'

As Ursula is about to receive a hug from Anna, Anna unceremoniously spits three times on the ground in Ursula's direction. Dimitri laughs at Hilary and Ursula's shocked expressions. Before Hilary can say anything, Dimitri cheerfully explains. 'Don't be offended. Anna's warding off evil spirits. If she doesn't do this, the evil gods that are all around watching our every move will destroy Ursula's happiness. By spitting at Ursula, she's showing the gods there's nothing to be envious of. And hopefully they will move on and leave her alone.'

'Well,' snorts Hilary loudly, never one to have nothing to

say, 'so long as that's what's done, I suppose one can't get offended. But if you come to my villa, Anna, please whatever you do, if you have to spit ... do it outside. This lady's not cleaning your spit off my beautiful marble floors ... and it doesn't matter how much you try to convince me otherwise.' Oblivious to anyone's reactions, laughingly she fussily flicks ash that has fallen from her Marlboro onto her trousers.

'Of course, I wouldn't spit in your house. I'm not so stupid as to do this. But perhaps if I did, you'd still have your old boyfriend Paddy and your very expensive art collection ... no? I heard from a friend that that man of yours stole all your art works.'

This is news. We know nothing about Hilary's expensive art collection or Paddy's now quite obvious absence. She'd said nothing. Okay, we haven't seen him around for a while but we didn't think he'd done a swifty on her. Our ears prick up. For once Hilary has no answer. With Mum busily topping up everyone's glasses with more wine and cognac, the *bougatsa*, *custard pie* is served with generous thick dollops of natural yoghurt. Hilary's *loukoumi* is passed in its elegant box around the table.

Eventually Hilary gathers the courage to speak. 'Well, yeah, the shit did me over. I didn't show anyone my art collection because it couldn't be displayed properly. Most of my art was still packed and locked away in the spare room. I've been waiting to get the okay to have a villa built – you know, all that residency stuff – and if I got it, I'd purchase land and build a villa to display them properly when the house was completed. I didn't say anything because the Greek cops told me not to. But I tell you, wait till I get my hands on that Irish asshole. I'm gonna screw him over with the pointy end of an olive branch!'

We look on, shocked.

'Yeah, the cops want it kept quiet because investigations are still underway. The problem is there are lots of expensive private art collections on this island. They don't want to cause panic. I know you've got friends with Picassos, and of course there is Harriet Guggenheim's collection up at her villa. And for Pete's sakes, who knows what the Rothchild's have in their villa? So, guys keep it quiet. All this on an island where no one locks their front doors? Anyway, Anna how the hell did you find out?'

'Well, the head of the crime commission on the island is my cousin. Of course, he's going to tell me things he would not tell other people.'

'So much for confidentiality!' As we all look on surprised, Hilary desperately attempts to change the subject and suggests, 'Hey, Anna, honey, perhaps you should spit on my big water bed? Then maybe, the right guy will come into my life ... and into my bed!'

As she says this, she smiles at Dimitri and his grin widens with amusement and suggestion of an offer. Sex has entered the conversation. Ever since we have known him, he's bragged he's an expert on the topic.

Anna laughs, 'You cannot find a good man because your bed is far too busy. A man needs to make a booking in advance ... check for oncoming traffic. While your bedroom is like this, there can be no one man in your life. A man must feel he's the only one; special. He must feel he has won a woman, not been thrown one. In Greece, a woman's most important quality is her virtue. She must be hard to access ... you know, like Mount Pantocrator ... Everest! Unless she's rich, of course, then she can do as she wishes. All the same, men will flock to her not for love but out of man's greed and lust.'

Making a point by waving her hands in the air, she

continues, her eyes flashing knowingly around the table, 'But you must remember, a woman like this will never be respected.'

Now, looking directly at Ursula she speaks in a whispered tone. 'In Greece, every bride on the day after her wedding day gives the bridal sheets to her mother-in-law for inspection. In turn they are shown to the villagers to demonstrate the bride's virginity on her wedding night. It's also of equal importance to show on the sheets, the proof of the virility of the male. All this will prove the chaperones have been true to their task having guarded the honour of the bride during the courtship, thus maintained the family's honour. Be mindful, Ursula, my child, traditions in Greece are like ancestral footprints that cannot be erased.'

Colour drains from Ursula's gentle face because trawling creepily through her mind now is the disturbing idea that the villagers of Saint Marcos will expect this strange spectacle to be performed the morning after her wedding night. Is nothing private on the island? And as Mullet's mother sounds like the sort of woman who would insist on this tradition being upheld, she doesn't like her chances of getting out of this one.

In desperation, Ursula changes the subject because she knows there won't be any virginal blood on her sheets on her wedding night. Perhaps by staying off the subject, no one will suggest attending her 'sheet showing shower' as if it's an extension to her wedding party. Poor Ursula, will the community expect this of her? Surely not.

Ursula foists a smile and turns to Anna. 'Tell me about these beautiful worry beads. What do they mean and what are they used for?'

Anna takes a deep breath, still managing to hold everyone's attention. 'Most Greeks are Orthodox Christians but, before Greece became a Christian country, they believed in many gods. We have always believed that good and bad luck are determined by the gods, or a single god. Of course ... It just depends on what mood we are in. So, we are careful not to tempt the gods and make them angry. That is why today Greeks place an evil eye next to a crucifix and hang them above their front doors to deflect evil with wreaths of flowers on some saints' days. Especially May Day. All of these things are to shield us in case one form of protection fails and then we must rely on the other. Logical, no? But even with all this defence, the Greeks still worry. *Po, po, po,* do we worry? And so, the men use worry beads, or *komboloi* as we call them, to click away their cares. Even with all his wealth Aristotle Onassis has worry beads. Can you imagine? Perhaps he bought more pairs after he married Jackie Kennedy? They say she's a handful even for a Greek man!'

Collective ripples of laughter fill the air.

George wriggling in his chair turns and whispers in Mullet's ear, 'Now, my boy, I need to educate you on a few things. Did you know in some remote parts of Greece the groom on his wedding night will perform a type of sexual ritual with his worry beads? He will do a fast-paced rhythmic movement of backwards and forwards with the beads in his hand mimicking sexual intercourse. Yes, they say it's to guarantee *ikanopoisi, satisfaction* on the wedding night!'

But before Mullet or Dimitri can say anything Hilary, having been eavesdropping on the male's conversation butts in, 'Well, I don't know if I like the sound of that.' Laughing she signals more brandy to be poured into her glass. 'I think I'd want the real thing. Mind you, my husband could have done with a bit of rhythm on our wedding night. You know, to get into rhythm with me. Or, George do you mean it's a weird kind of Greek Orthodox rhythm method? You know, like the ones the Catholics preach but in fact propagate because it doesn't work? That's why there's so many Catholics … I'm only joking, folks!'

Unable to resist the temptation to laugh at her friend's logic, Mum responds sarcastically, 'You know, my husband never adopted those tedious mass manufactured, irritating clicking adult-soothers. He discarded them shortly after we arrived on the island. That's because he said they failed to rhythmically calm his nerves or, for that matter, magically click away his woes. He reckoned he'd given them a fair go; practised for weeks but soon discovered he needed something stronger than worry beads. Another cognac to take the edge off his worries perhaps? Maybe he should kickstart his old pair? After all, lying in bed recovering from heat stroke and severe alcohol poisoning is not getting his novel written or reducing my worries anytime soon.'

Silence fills the gaping gulf in the air. Mum's right: as our bills mount, time is of the essence. Could resurrecting his old worry beads be a solution?

As the evening wears on Dimitri and Hilary disappear together into the moon-filled night.

Chapter 29

Letters from the Edge

Time has moved on since Dad's sunstroke setback. As I kick stones along the gravelled side of the road near our old village of Pyrgi, I spy Mullet's yellow Lotus parked at the Bogthanos Hotel near the narrow potholed thoroughfare. At the same time, hanging in the air is the unpleasant smell of decomposing seaweed that has been haphazardly dumped by the tide along the shore line. It is the remnants of a storm that careered its way into the night, ruining our sunny end to spring and now early start to summer.

The stench is reminiscent of the soggy, smelly, Sardinian sardine sandwiches Mum's been concocting lately. It's another one of her cost cutting ideas. She has purchased boxes of canned sardines from a grocer friend of hers at a bargain price. I think it is only a bargain price if people actually like them ... otherwise? 'Come on kids, eat up. Try it mashed into the soft centre of bread, it will go down faster,' she cheerily recommends.

Since the dark storm clouds have now shifted from the morning sky, the seaweed sits baking in the unrelenting warmth of insistent sunshine. Long blackish brown tresses are piled high like dark, speckled, shredded potato sacks along the coastline, defacing and denying the sun-bleached pebbles lying beneath the light of day as they suffocate under this unpleasant weight. When storms leave remnants like this, I wish for summer's powerful Maestro winds to gather forces and blow the decaying seaweed away; leave the beach pristine and white again so the pebbles can whisper their mysterious stories. Old Yannis, the fisherman, once told me that every pebble on the beach has its own unique story. Some say only living things can feel pain, but if Yannis is right, each step I take is imprinted forever into the memory of these stones and within them a real heartbeat beats. We only have to listen and believe. It's like holding a seashell to our ears.

Since we've moved, oh, how I miss his smiling face, kind words and those fresh sardines from his weathered old reed basket.

Yet even with the smell of rotting seaweed, walking along the neglected road I'm grounded, rooted in the beauty of this stunning green island. The variegated shades of malachite in alluring nuances of diffusion ... it calls to me like one of Ulysses' sailors being beguiled by the spellbinding songs of the sirens. I look across to Albania, across a vast blue water to a world washed afresh and now bejewelled with sparkling sunlight dancing across its surface – a glittering clean world except for the seaweed. Now that we have moved to Villa Kapodistria, I miss living on the coast. The connection I had with its moods and sounds ... the tempo of its turning tides and the wind.

Today I've been sent on an errand, the type that has failed to appeal to any of my family and, with no volunteers, I was honed in on as the task was passed down the shortened family line. Giving in to pressure because everyone else seemed to have worthier excuses than I, I find myself the prodigal in Pyrgi. There comes a time when asking for credit becomes an overtly odious task, only because it seems to go on and on even after Dad's return from Australia. It's a weighty responsibility having to come home with the essentials for our family's survival. But my friend Hoppy's sticking to his record of being kind to me so, in this way it's not so bad. He always gets paid, eventually.

Because of the small apertures in the *kafeneo's* whitewashed walls it's often darker inside until the sun shines at a certain angle. The air as always is charged with fine irregular lines of smoke from cigarettes and the persistent hum of men's business being discussed, dice being thrown and *travli* played against the sound of the thumping radio. Relentlessly, it plays, pumping out local hits, more butcher's music and news updates about the political situation. And again, there's the hush when I enter.

Underway is that dynamic interplay between illegitimate access to a male site and the exception to the rule because I'm a *xeni*. If I was a local woman, I would be eaten alive and my reputation destroyed. Then, as I'm recognised, the men go back to what they were doing before I entered their male world. I nod to the men I know and then carry on with my business because this is their sacred space, not mine. I'm the intruder.

I give Hoppy the list which I'm pleased to say I've written in Greek. I'm proud of this minor accomplishment because my language skills are better than my reading and writing. While Hoppy busies himself with the list, I focus my attention on his humble sweet section below the small wobbly counter. I eye the lines of ION chocolate bars with their red wrappers and pretty white almond blossoms. There's something wonderful about that chocolate, or the blue-parcelled, dark chocolate version. I juggle an internal debate about their cost compared to the simply packaged sesame and honey bar … decisions, decisions.

The sound of a strong Australian accent catches my attention. I turn to find Mullet and Father George motioning me towards their table in the far corner of the *kafeneo*. In the semi darkness of the smoky room, I hadn't noticed them when I walked in. Both smile as they acknowledge me and I nod back. I move to where they're seated and kiss the priest's hand. I do this because I feel an overwhelming sense of duty as if it's expected. I'm not an Orthodox Christian but here in this place I sometimes feel like one. Religion and faith are so entrenched, it's virtually a natural response. I can't help but get swept up in it.

I notice Father is walking without the aid of his crutches which is good to see, Byron, that offending billy goat, now a far-off memory.

'G'day there. I see you know Father George? How you been, kiddo?' smiles Mullet. Pausing, he surprisingly pulls a chair aside for me to join them. I hesitate for a moment not knowing what to do then decide to sit, otherwise it will look rude. I'm also aware that he's going to be a neighbour of sorts and perhaps a good source of future supplies of Vegemite and peanut butter. That Cadbury chocolate was pretty good too. I'd be a fool not to be pleasant. 'Would you like a drink, an orange juice or a *gazzoza*?'

'A *Gazzoza* would be nice, thanks, Mullet.'

'A *Gazzoza* it is then,' and signalling Hoppy, a *Gazzoza* is swiftly delivered to our table.

'Geez, I'm glad you've rocked up. We're trying to arrange Ursula's baptism and when that's done, the wedding. I think I'm rowing up shit creek in a barbed wire canoe to tell you the truth. Oh, yeah ... pardon me French. Father doesn't speak English and me Greek's bloody iffy at the best of times. I'm embarrassed to admit after all these years I should have gone to Greek school in Sydney when I was a kid. You know, listened to me mother instead of playing hooky on the vacant block down the road with Stick and me mates. Do you think you can give us a hand?'

I notice Mullet's Adams apple jiggling like a turkey's neck as he speaks and I hesitate. Suddenly feeling panicky, I'm aware of my limitations but at the same time I'm not bad at getting the essentials right. Anyway, looking at Mullet's face, desperate times demand desperate measures. From what I understand Mullet's Greek repartee consists of 'hells fire', in other words every swear word known to man while I'm versed in conventional conversation of the back to bare basics kind. The two of us could prove to be a formidable team talking to anyone except a priest.

Mmm, this is going to be challenging. Father speaks *Katharevuousa formal Greek and Dimotiki*, and I speak *Horiatica Peasant Greek* with the unique Corfiot Italian lilt and dialect. I feel a fiasco coming on. And, as the conversation will be spiritual, biblical and all things theological, I think departure at this stage might be the best move I've made all day. I should just grab the groceries and flee … still. But if I stay, I reckon we need one of those rapturous epiphanies people speak of from time to time with bated breath. But I'm stuck. I can't leave Mullet trying to muddle his way through this. We need the unseen powers of God, any god, to pull us through this one otherwise we could be perilously close to organising a funeral instead of a christening. Not only that, my mind is distracted by the sweet section at Hoppy's counter.

Sitting with the bagged groceries placed next to me, I reckon I've earned it … I want my sweet reward. But with a *gazzoza* in hand I am compelled to listen in as Father George explains the very important instructions for Ursula's baptism.

Unexpectantly above the thumping radio pelting out melodramatic bouzouki music, Hoppy, overhearing the conversation, limps to our table. He pushes aside the large overflowing smouldering ashtray and cups of coffee and kindly furnishes us with lined paper, a pencil and creates space on the table on which to write. I set to work detailing all the essentials for a Greek Orthodox christening. These include a white sheet, a small white hand towel, a bottle of olive oil, three large candles, one gold Greek Orthodox cross and gold chain. Also imperative to the proceedings are a godparent or two, a small fee for the service – this will include the cost of a *psaltis, chanter* – and a smart change of clothes for the child being baptised. Sugared almonds are an optional extra but expected. When Father George discovers the initiate is a young Swedish woman, he raises his hand, ordering a couple of large cognacs. He then asks Mullet and me if we would like a drink. I smile at the good Father and tip my head, signalling no.

I realise he's never baptised an adult. This will need special strategic planning. After all, this woman, no matter how thin or slight in weight, with his dodgy leg, he won't be able to lift her in his arms. Nor can he dunk her three times into a font then miraculously lift her out of the water without divine intervention, especially with the copious amount of olive oil used in the ceremony. She'll be as oily as an eel.

Then for a desperate moment it goes through my mind that perhaps this will be too hard for Father George to accomplish. Silence falls and I wait for it to lift as he has receded into deep serious thought. Yes, perhaps it will be too hard for an elderly priest to accomplish this mammoth task let alone a strong young priest.

Mullet looks at me and our eyes meet. For the first time I see deep sadness in them. Love is a powerful force; it can make people act irresponsibly, swoon with unbridled passion, even push people into deep despair. The light dims in his eyes for a moment as we wait, almost breathless, for Father to continue with an outcome one way or the other. Then, with a wide smile the priest lifts his glass, '*Allo endaksi, me fovarse, everything is going to be fine, never fear.*'

With sighs of relief, it's agreed Ursula will meet Father George and his wife tomorrow in the village church once he's finished his regular visits to the sick. With solid handshakes all around, Father leaves to continue his daily rounds. His parting words, '*Entheka avrio, kalimara sus,*' 11am tomorrow, good morning.

Then he's gone, nodding his slow way out of the *kafeneo*.

Mullet sits ecstatic and raises his arm for a celebratory drink. His mind's racing. I gather he's thinking about the list I've given him and making a mental note of all the things he has to do before his mother arrives from Sydney. He wants to topple her apple cart. 'Hey, kiddo, get a gander at this.'

As Mullet's smile fades, it's replaced with a serious look as he pulls a crumpled letter from his shirt pocket. 'What's that, Mullet? It looks important.'

I lie. Important letters don't look as if they have been screwed up half a dozen times and retrieved from a rubbish bin. 'It is. It's a letter from me mother in Sydney. She's flying to Greece on Tuesday. She'll be here on the early flight from Athens on Friday. Bugger me, I have to get things rolling otherwise she'll be all over me like flies on a dead donkey. I was meant to pull my finger out months ago. Did I tell you we're shacked-up at the Bogthanos Hotel until we get Mum and Auntie's villa sorted out? We moved in a few weeks ago. We had to after that notorious night when your dad and I thought we were having heart attacks. Ursula got stuck into me saying town's too noisy. She needs quiet; the countryside and the sea. And she has a point. Bloody motorbikes and people partying all night along the Liston. It's like Rio Digo on carnival night, only every night but with brilliant views. You see, that's the thing, you can't beat the view of the *Palio Citadel* crowning the top of Garitsa Bay, now can yah, love?'

He has a point. It's a spectacular sight alright. He abruptly stops laughing. 'Geez, seems like we're neighbours already. I can see Ursula and me popping in to see your folks regular like … borrow a cup of olive oil and having a good old Aussie chin wag.'

I smile weakly – geographically he must be kidding. It takes twenty minutes to get from Pyrgi to our villa but I let him go on. After all, he's the one with the sports car and can afford the ridiculous cost of petrol. I'm still not convinced Mullet is the nice guy he portrays himself to be. I can't wait to meet his mother. You can tell a lot about a person by their mother.

'We have news as well. My grandmother is coming from Melbourne. Mum doesn't get on with her, so this could turn out to be an exercise in a true classical Greek domestic drama of mammoth proportions with a few tragedies thrown in for good measure – depending on which way you look at it, of course. She arrives this weekend. As Mum and Gran each want to rule the roost, it's going to be fascinating to see how this pans out in our tiny kitchen. Yeah, and wait till Gran gets stuck into Dad for not getting on with his book. I don't think he's written a single page yet, even after all these years! Oh, boy, it will be on then.'

I reach into the bags of groceries Hoppy's given me to retrieve a honey and sesame bar which seems to be his choice, probably due to credit restrictions, and take a big budget bite. No chocolate for me today. The grainy sweetness in my mouth feels and tastes wonderful. Chocolate would have been nicer but scroungers can't be choosers. Still, anything sweet is still my kind of a stress release valve, and I'm consoled.

Yes, the shit sure hit the fan when the news came that Gran is visiting again. It sent shivers down Mum's spine. She flew into a highly agitated temper and cleaning frenzy. Dad reckoned it would've been easier to move house than clean it.

And we all agreed, but the lease on the villa is for a full year and we'd lose financially if we suddenly got up and moved simply because we were too lazy, or 'creatively uninspired' as Dad prefers to put it, to clean the place. However, to his credit, having recovered from his bout of alcohol poisoning and sunstroke, he's obediently fallen into line getting into the cleaning groove with Mum.

'If your grandmother is anything like my mother, she'll still find fault no matter what you do or how hard you try,' sighs Mullet, shaking his head.

'Oh, Mullet, it's not so much my Gran: it's my Mum. Her solution is to simply pour another drink and try not to think about things … unless she's twisting or contorting something. I know it's ludicrous and Gran's a teetotaller most of the time … that is unless someone's offering cumquat brandy, of course. So, she won't be looking at our life through the same eyes as my parents, that's for sure.'

I peer through the smoke at Mullet's distressed face. He has problems – big problems too and needs time to figure out how it's all going to come together. Suddenly I feel sorry for the man. I'm not close to my mother and he doesn't particularly like his and yet both of us try to make our mothers happy. It's a hard balancing act. He's like me and so many other people juggling parental issues, and age is irrelevant. The invisible umbilical cord that ties children to their parents is never severed even when parents are long gone and buried. Who would have thought that Mullet is in this strange way, like me, only bogan and cashed up to boot? The man can't be as bad as I first thought.

'Oh Mullet, I understand your concerns. We have huge dramas on our home front too. We need Marietta, our Kamikaze cleaner, to do a complete workout on our place, especially on my mother's pickled brain. And Dad's not far behind her!' We both laugh and I continue. 'It doesn't mean I don't love them; I do. I just wish I understood them better, their moods, their drinking. It's a shame Marietta only does laundry. You know she doesn't do our laundry anymore? It's too far for her to ride Ajax, and anyway these days we can't afford her services. Whenever Dad suggests we return to Australia, Mum says no. He reckons he can borrow the money to leave if need be.'

'Here, kiddo, here's a few drachmas for your time today. I bet you could buy a few honey and sesame rolls with this or something equally yummy.' And, having said that, he hands me a one hundred drachmae note. It's a lot of money. I've never been given so much in my entire life.

'Oh, Mullet, I can't take your money, and anyway it's a fortune!' I say, handing the money back to him.

'Nah, dinkum, kiddo, you keep it. You've been a real help. Do you want to give us a hand at the church tomorrow with Ursula? It would sure take the edge off things if you were there, and anyway, youse two are great mates? Yep, I reckon your blood is worth bottling.'

'Well, I don't know about that and, if it ends up being a funeral instead of a baptism, you can't blame me. You have to understand, I'm not an expert in ecumenical matters, nor interpreting. But if you really need my help, I will.'

I say this because I'm thrilled to help Ursula and delighted at the thought of possibly earning some more money. I might be able to purchase that pair of shoes I've seen in a posh shoe shop in Corfu town. As we part, we agree to meet at the church at 11 am. I carry the groceries home in one hand and the demijohn in the other along the beach front to the bus stop for the ride home to Villa Kapodistria. This time the smell of seaweed isn't so bad. I feel liberated, richer than I've ever felt in my life. I smile to myself, enormously pleased with my trip to Hoppy's. In Australian currency, that's equivalent to just over one dollar. It's a fortune!

I've seen a pair of red shoes in one of the elegant shops in the old town near the Liston. I've secretly wanted them from the moment I saw them in the shop window. But the shoes are completely impractical for my life of trekking villages or going to the beach and besides, I don't have any matching clothes to go with them. But each time I pass and see them reflecting in the brightly lit shop window, they seem to wink at me. Or is it my imagination? Vulgar red patent leather, high heels with tiny straps. So grown up and so deliciously impractical! Like arrows of radiant love, the light dances off the two silver buckles that join the straps at the ankle. I'm spellbound. Perhaps if I save enough, I can buy them and if I begin saving again I can get an outfit to go with them. Smitten and filled with hope, I scurry home to tell everyone of my good fortune and the news of Mullet's mother's arrival. We are one step closer to becoming neighbours and strangely I'm happy about that.

Chapter 30

Momma Mia

I'm not allowed to interpret for Mullet the next day at Saint Marcos. My younger brother, who is much more proficient in the Greek language than I am, is instructed to replace me. Mum insists, 'We don't want any stuff ups.'

So, I'm ousted from the equation. I'm disappointed but Mum asserts her power by diversion and sends me on another errand in the opposite direction. My gorgeous red shoes will have to wait. With Mullet's mother arriving on Friday, Mullet and Father George decide the baptism will go ahead the following Sunday. Now staying at the Botharnos Hotel, Took and Stick borrow Mullet's car and head to town forfeiting a mellow morning of drinking at the *Pig and Whistle* in Pyrgi. Still, excited at the prospect of shopping for a Greek Orthodox gold cross and chain, three christening candles and a box full of tizzy packages of pink and white sugared almonds, they lunge into the task.

The next day, Mullet arranges for the reception to take place at the Cavalieri Hotel overlooking the *Palio Citadel*. The hotel's top chef will do the catering and this will include a special afternoon tea for his mother, aunt and their teetotaller friends like me. There will be a full bar for the rest of his guests. As money is no object, he doesn't care how much it costs. He wants only the very best for Ursula.

While they had hoped to have Ursula's christening sneakily slotted in and out of the way before Momma arrived, this plan failed.

A few days later, Ursula, Mullet, Stick and Took stand anxiously waiting for the Olympic Airway flight from Athens at Corfu airport. The place is packed, flooded with tourists arriving from all over Europe, or equally, waiting to depart. A loud speaker calls out arrivals and departures in Greek, German, French and English. There's excitement in the air.

The two men see their mother's plane sitting on the tarmac and her stepping onto the narrow metal steps as she exits the plane. The four of them move to the entrance doors. Passing through them, arriving passengers charge in different directions after being pulled here and there by pushy relatives and friends. Domestic flights are always chaotic events.

With arms theatrically thrown wide open for a hug, Mullet and Stick's mother stands in front of them and in the next moment, the two men, enroute to retrieving her suitcases, like exuberant anxious school boys bound into their mother's clasping arms. Ursula and Took stand back and watch. The affection the men are displaying toward their mother seems contrary to what they'd said about their mother behind her back.

A perplexing thought goes through Ursula's mind. Perhaps his mother has more power over her sons than she thought. She will soon find out.

After a few moments the men separate from the arms of their mother's octopus-like grip, then the men step aside for Ursula and Took to meet her. 'Now Mum, I'd like you to meet my soon-to-be bride, Ursula.'

Moving forward with an engaging smile Ursula reaches her hand out to his mother, saying, 'Your son and I are very much in love.' But her gesture is ignored. Irene, eyeing her squarely, looks her up and down, saying, 'Ah, so you are the pretty one that has stolen my son's heart?'

Ursula continues to smile widely, hanging onto the hope that they can be friends, but her churning gut tells her otherwise.

'My dear, when you have lived as long as I have, you will learn that love is a fickle thing. It moves with the wind, strong one day and weak the next. It all depends on which way the winds are blowing on the day, trust me on this.'

Uncomfortable by this first encounter, Ursula shuffles her feet, moves closer to Mullet and replies, 'Well, it's lovely to finally meet you. I've heard so much about you.'

Irene, abruptly looking beyond Ursula and Took, changes the subject; orders her sons in a military fashion to 'Get my luggage before someone steals it. I trust no one, no one I tell you! If ever something is stolen here in Greece, of course it won't be a Greek that's the thief, it will be a *xeni, foreigner*!'

As if impersonating robots, her suddenly stiff and well-disciplined sons obediently disappear into the crowd to retrieve her luggage.

'And I suppose you're Took? Well, it seems as if my sons have chosen non-Greek girls to woo and marry, *po, po, po!* I don't know what to say. In our very traditional family, everyone has always married Greeks. My sons are breaking with tradition and as a good Greek mother, of course I am not happy about this. It's only fair that I tell you this now so things are clear between us from the beginning.'

As she stands before the two anxious women having said what is utmost on her mind, she smooths her below the knee restrained sweaty black polyester dress and jacket. The heat is rising around them in more ways than one. Yet, still incapsulated in her armour-like suit, the jacket remains firmly in place.

'Ah,' replies Ursula, feeling time crawl without Mullet and desperately trying to sound wise, 'but Greece is like the rest of the world. It's going through enormous changes. The Age of Aquarius, flower power, the pill, greater freedom for men and women. It's the same for this new generation of Greeks too. Surely you can see this by simply looking around you? This is not the Greece you left so many years ago – time has moved on. When you get back to your village, you'll see this.'

'I see you have a voice and a brain. That's a good thing, at least. But what you are saying is humbug. How long have you known Mullet?'

'Well, since last summer.'

Irene releases a harrowing laugh. Took and Ursula look at each other in dismay. They back cautiously away from the woman. 'My dear girl, I have stockings that are longer than that! In Greece, we believe in long supervised courtships, and they must be between families that they have known for centuries. They must be allied with our own. Then there is the business of the dowry to discuss. Can you ride a donkey? Pick olives in a thunder storm? Carry wood on your back, a water bucket on your head and tend to the animals? Can you make a meal from very little food, wash clothes on a scrubbing board in the sweltering heat with only cold water and very little soap? These are the fundamentals for every village woman to learn and, of course, accomplish. Can you milk a goat, pickle olives, make cheese and yoghurt? Do you cook his fish the way he likes it? You need to think about these things. Most importantly, are you a virgin? I do not like to bring this up in a conversation like this, but we can't have any of what you in the West call, the 'hanky pankies', before the wedding. This is a strict Greek tradition that must be upheld! And before you are baptised into the Greek Orthodox Church, you must confess all of your sins before a Greek Orthodox priest and renounce the devil.'

Ursula's furious Mullet's taking so long to retrieve his

mother's suitcases. What's taking that man so long? She's much more opinionated and obstinate than she ever imagined she'd be. It's a nightmare. Where is Mullet?

Took looks on in shock; the woman still hasn't had the decency to properly acknowledge her.

A crawling seething silence falls between them amid the noisy chaos of the airport as if they are in a time warp until Mullet and Stick's slow return panting with their mother's belongings. As if sensing an icy cold cloud above them in the hot morning air, the two men wonder what's been said. Has Irene been rude?

Ursula motions Mullet for support and Took sticks like glue to Stick. 'Mum, have you met Took yet? Took, this is my mother, Irene.'

Hoping this time, she'll be friendlier. Took smiles a weak smile and extends her hand in an act of polite alliance. 'I've heard much about you. Welcome to Corfu.'

Looking Took up and down, once again Irene sniffs the air with disapproval. 'Of course, this is not my first trip to Corfu. I was born here the way all good patriotic Greek wives should be. That's what gives our family pride in our name. The pureness of our Greek heritage. My boys might have been born in Australia. However, I left my country because I had to. The Greek economy was bad, we couldn't survive. If I could have stayed here, I would have!'

Took's ignored hand falls limply to her side as she stoically maintains her position close to Stick. Stick looks at his mother with poorly repressed anger. The air is now thick with tension and no one smiles.

Breaking the silence, Mullet saves the moment with a grand sweeping gesture of his hand tactfully encouraging his mother toward the airport exit. The others follow in silence.

'Mum, we want you to have fun while you're here for the

christening and wedding. I can't wait to show you me brand-new sports car. I have it parked out the front to whisk you away to our hotel in Pyrgi, unless you'd prefer to stay at the house in Saint Marcos?'

Not waiting for an answer, Mullet continues enthusiastically, 'Now, Mum, get a look at this little beauty. How do you fancy a cruise to Ipsos in this? That should get a few tongues wagging around the village! This will be quite some homecoming ... what do you reckon, Mum?'

Feeling an enormous amount of power and traction over her sons and their partners, she laughs smugly and fervently clutches her son's arm as a mark of domination as he leads her towards the car. He swings open the passenger side for her and helps her snuggle into the front passenger seat carefully assisting her in and adjusting the seat for comfort. When she's contentedly seated like a monarch, he turns to Ursula, whispering in her ear, 'Geez, love, I see we have a battle on our hands but we've got to be strong. Trust me on this. Please stand by me. Stick will organise a car for youse all to follow on. I need time to talk to Mum alone ... if I don't smother her first.'

Ursula's body thaws with relief next to him as he senses her need for condolence and reassurance. Drawing her close, he recognises that she understands his dilemma. Stick and Took look on as Irene waves regally from her prime position in the front seat. As she's driven at accelerated speed onto the road leading away from the airport, Mullet's determined to give her the ride of her life.

As the yellow car accelerates into the distance, Ursula breaks the dismal cloud of gloomy silence. 'Who was it that said "you can gauge much about a person by meeting their mother." Now isn't that true? Personally, I feel sick!'

'So do I,' replies Took, clasping her stomach with both

hands.

'Let's head to the Liston ... we need to eat, relax and regroup ... take the sting out of the morning. We don't want to follow on straight away, anyway. I suppose it must be a lot for your mother to take in, all in one go,' Ursula offers generously, freeing a gentle smile from her flushed face.

'What a great idea. I don't want to be within coo-ee of Mum till she settles. Let him soften the old cheese up,' agrees Stick with an ever-widening smile.

'Yes, let's go. I'm still worried though. It looked like he was taking memos from the director of a Greek multinational company. I hope I'm wrong.'

Ursula, troubled, ignores the young Greek men whistling at her and Took as they walk with a distracted Stick to the taxi stand. 'I suppose we'll have to see who's going to win this tug of war.'

Stick nods in alliance and then strains to smile. Eventually he releases a jaded laugh. 'I reckon we're all suffering from a bad dose of terminal sickness ... hope it's not terminal. I know I can speak for Mullet; we'll win this battle. She can't control our lives forever. Now let's go and forget about this morning and have fun. Taxi!'

Chapter 31

In the Driver's Seat

'Mum, you have to stop struggling with the fact I'm going to marry Ursula.'

'Let's talk about that later, my child. I want to enjoy our drive to Pyrgi. You must remember it's been years since I was last here. So many memories, *po, po, po!* Especially of your father, may he rest in peace. His soul is floating above us now as I speak. I can feel it.'

Irene looks dreamily out of the car window. 'He was a good man. Stupid, but a good man. He did the right thing by his family and married me, a good Greek girl from the same village. Is this such a difficult thing for you to do?'

'I thought you said you didn't want to talk about it? So, let's change the subject. How are things in Sydney? And how's Aunty? We've been up to the villa in Saint Marcos, had a look through and Ursula and I are serious about buying it from youse two. All we are asking is for the pair of youse to decide on how much youse want for it? We're prepared to pay a fair price ... don't want you and Aunty to have a split in the family over it.'

Irene continues to look out the car window as if ignoring her son.

'Let us buy it and then it frees everyone up. If you want to give most of the money from the property when you eventually die to Stick, then fair enough. You don't have to give me anything. I'm financially secure. Any money you may have wanted to give me you can spend on having a very comfortable retirement. Mum, are you listening to me?'

Irene continues irritating Mullet by ignoring him.

'You can go on a world cruise if you want. Mind you, Mum, the place needs lots of money spent on it. It's in poor condition, that's why we have booked you into the Bogthanos Hotel. Even the roof on the old villa needs to be replaced, the plumbing brought into the 20th century, *and* the electricals. Honestly, Mum, the list goes on!'

'If it is so terrible then why are you buying the property? It was good enough for my sister and me when we were growing up. You should buy something nice, clean and very modern. After all, you're now rich.'

'Ursula loves the old place. Anyway; it would be good to keep the villa in the family. But geez, Mum, the place is falling down through centuries of neglect. You haven't seen the place for thirty years. You need to see it before you comment. But just the same, we reckon the place has great bones. And wouldn't it be good to keep the old place in the family? Have it in good condition for generations to come?'

'Humph, I am an old lady with old bones. Have you thought about that? Who's going to look after me when I am old like that villa and crumbling to bits? If you don't marry a Greek girl who knows she must care for me when I get old and grey, then what am I going to do?'

'Oh, for heaven's sakes, Mum, stop being so theatrical. I have enough money to more than look after you when you get old. I can get you a full-time personal carer.'

'You want a stranger to care for me ... have you lost your senses?'

'Oh, Mum, let's talk about something else. You are really pissing me off now ... The world has changed. Corfu has changed. Mum there was even an Australian family living on the Pyrgi coastal strip. Who'd have thought when you were a kid growing up here that the island would become a tourist Mecca, even attracting Aussies? Now this family rent a place up on a hill outside of Corfu town near Potamos. You've gotta see the villa. It's an old beauty. They're interesting company too. You'll like them. He's a writer. He and his wife have five kids, most of their children are living overseas now, but two are still here. His wife Jo likes to cook. Mum, you can show her some of your recipes. I can see you two cooking up a storm. Oh, and they will be at the christening Sunday week. We're all heading to the Cavalieri Hotel in town for drinks to celebrate after the big event.'

'You talk to me like I don't know where the Cavalieri is. I'm not an idiot you know. I was in the world a long time before you arrived on the scene. You need to remember this! So, which priest is doing the christening?'

'Father George from Saint Marcos. Do you know him?'

'What? Are you stupid? Everybody that is worth knowing was around in my day, except you and your brother! Greece even had a king back then but not now. *Po, po, po,* instead we have a military dictatorship! The whole country is going down the well. You only need to look around. No, I don't know this priest. If I did, I would say he's crazy christening a stranger and an adult. Whoever heard of such a thing? And how is she going to be dunked in the font? She's too big. My boy, you do this at your peril. Do you want to have the broken spine of a priest on your conscience for the rest of your life? This would never happen in my day.'

'Come on, give me a break. You're flogging a dead horse here. It happened way back when Christianity was in its infancy. Didn't Christ's own cousin, John the Baptist baptise him? Jesus was no baby when he got dunked. Right throughout history adults have been baptised. No one ended up with broken spines.'

'As if you know ...'

'Oh, Mum, if you recall, even Saint and Emperor Constantine the Great was baptised on his death bed – he was definitely no bub when he carked it. He was Emperor of Rome; he established the new Roman Empire in Constantinople. Mum, he legalised Christianity for Pete's sake! I'm sure Father George will find some miraculous way of baptising Ursula.'

'Since when did you become an expert on the Greek Orthodox Church? You don't even go to Church! Did you fast for Easter? No, I didn't think so. Did you refrain from sex? No!'

'Oh, come on, Mum, give me a break. You don't need to get personal! I found all this out because I knew you would carry on. Look, Mum, I don't want you to put a mocker on things. I'm bloody lucky Ursula's willing to do me the honour and marry me. She's a decent person; everyone likes her, especially me. If you won't go with the flow so to speak, then you should get back on the next plane, pick up a Qantas flight in Athens and don't come back. Seriously, I mean it. You know I love you, but it's called tough love and I love Ursula. So tough, Mum. My future is with her, not you. You have to let go.'

'I cannot believe after all I have been through bringing you and your brother up on my own after your father died that you can speak to me like this. You should hang your head in shame. So, not only are you breaking with all our family traditions, but you are breaking your mother's heart.'

A formidable gulf between mother and son emerges as they sit close to one another in the luxurious seats of Mullet's car. Words take flight leaving only a seething silence as the car hurries them past lush countryside. Shady olive trees, spiralling clumps of bamboo and tall narrow Cyprus trees flash cooling shadows across the roads in quick succession as the car speeds past. As the road twists and turns, on one side bursts of serene Gouvia Bay are captured like quick camera shots to the right of them, highlighting the tiny white-washed church basking in the shimmering light-bestowed bay below. Only a fragile thread of a path links land to church, the surrounding undulating land robed in a delightful visual chaos of olive and orange groves. The narrow path so aptly symbolises the frailty of their tenuous relationship. In this prized jewel of a sheltered bay, a yacht owned by a famed chocolate family sits gently rocking with the calm tide. But what Mullet hoped would be a breath-catching drive filled with excitement and a glorious revival of memories for Irene is now replaced with jarred egos ready to do battle in defence of their individual stances. It leaves their reunion torn and in tatters and the church the likely setting for the public reaping of their unresolved conflict.

Chapter 32

The Christening

'What to wear, that's the perennial question.'

Mum's hurled her comment into the smoky air of her bedroom as if it's something to be hotly debated. A generous cognac sits on Dad's crowded desk next to an overflowing ashtray. Nearby, her wardrobe stands like a dark hollow pit. Every time she reaches into it, as she does now, it seems to snap and lunge mockingly at her with uninspiring emptiness.

With no false idol made of fabulous fabric to fondle and wear, she sniffs the air. Her solution is to reach with a frustrated hand for the soothing balm of her cognac glass. 'Oh, I suppose I'll have to resurrect the same old bloody rags again. Gone are the days of shopping at any of the finer shops in Melbourne. What I wouldn't give for an oversized wallet in Georges!'

Dad mumbles something incomprehensible in return as he too reaches fossicking with exaggerated purpose into the voluminous hollowed darkness of his side of the wardrobe. He secures his dependable old black suit from its mothball-infested resting place. He follows this action by pulling his long-sleeved white shirt into the light and resting it on their expansive bed. Using exaggerated attention to detail and distracting himself from the reality of their situation for just a moment, he brushes dandruff and a few stray donkey hairs from his suit. He attempts a joke. 'By Jimenez Euripides, we men are lucky we don't worry about clothes the way women do!'

'What are you rabbiting on about now, you stupid man?'

'Men ... and our lack of concern about clothes.'

'Hah! Well, aren't you lot bloody auspicious then? I suppose I shall have to, yet again, resuscitate this cast-off. Even I'm growing weary of its lacklustre Hollywood shine. My wardrobe is like paddling through sad bits of re-claimed rags from a Bombay tip. You know what fashion is like? ... in one day, out the next. Reminds me of Greek politicians.'

'Mmm ... what's that? Okay, I know things are tight but the priest might think you're trying to do him out of a job in that gear – all that excessive Hollywood froth and flapping fabric. It's fine for cocktails but not sure about a church. You look like one of those cardinals who got lost heading to the Vatican ... why they try and imitate women is beyond me. Ironic, of course, they fail to give women any power besides the honour of praying, filling vases and sweeping floors. The men get to wear all the flashy embroidery, hats and rich fabrics ... and swing smoking appendages.'

'You do go on.'

'We do make a pair ... throw in the fact I look like I've got Corinthian column disorder in this old suit.'

'Yep, you'd scare donkeys. Animals are very sensitive creatures. I know this sounds ridiculous but I saw Marietta in town and she tells me she's considering taking old Ajax to see a psychologist. Apparently, it's all the trend now. I wonder if she's joking. Such a gentle donkey too, normally so tolerant of human frailties, but lately he's been off his hay.'

'Ha ... very funny. He's probably missing our mulberry tree or he needs a partner.'

'What?'

'Yes, donkeys get lonely too, you know, in between

nibbling on mulberries.'

'Well, I thought they got snippy because they are under so much pressure with all the heavy things they had to carry. I reckon some hefty load of human lard is snapping some poor donkey's legs apart as I speak.'

'Oh, listen to you exaggerating again. You'd out do Homer and Euripides with your tales.'

'She's deaf, you know?'

'Who?'

'Mum, of course, and the kids reckon the old duck sleeps with her eyes open. They find it really quite disturbing.'

'I suppose she's worried ... the kids come home at all hours of the night.'

'Well, don't blame me ... they live by Greek time, not your time, my time or even Australian time. Too many distractions, festivals, boat trips ... the list goes on.'

As he finishes his sentence there's an abrupt knock on their bedroom door. Opening it, Mum's greeted by Gran all dolled up and dressed ready for the baptism. She's a sight to behold in a bright pink floral summer dress. Above her wide freshly minted smile sits the point of a perfectly powdered nose. Topping her glamorous look is a candy pink, broad-brimmed hat with a matching cream handbag and gloves. She's a vision of the 1950s. If her appearance doesn't get tongues wagging in church today, nothing will.

'Good morning, dear; what's the hold up?' asks Gran, adjusting her gloves.

'Ah, nothing, Mum. Almost ready, aren't we?' She spins to view her appearance in the mirror.

Dad is doing a convincing imitation of a Thessalian praying mantis; he raises his neatly combed head momentarily to nod. 'Yes, be there in a jiffy, just tying my shoe laces. If you round up the kids, then we'll be off?'

Rubbing her cream gloved hands together like a magician, she replies, 'Righto! I'm looking forward to this ... never been to a Greek Orthodox christening and it'll be a shock seeing you two in church. Never seen that either. Not even on your wedding day.'

Pausing to size Mum up, Gran deposits a look of indignation in the smoky bedroom air. 'Gee ... open a window; it stinks like a bar after the Friday night swill ... and don't you have something other than that to wear? This is a public event!'

'I beg your pardon; Mother! I will have you know this fabulous piece of flowing magnificence was once worn by none other than the famous movie star Ginger Rogers. You know ... she's the dancer who notoriously insured her legs for millions. It was big news back then, unheard of at the time. If it was good enough for Ginger to wear, then it's good enough for me.'

'Must have been a long time ago! In fact, I'd suggest there's been a lot of water under the bridge since that outfit looked good. As everyone is allowed one fashion folly in their life, this must have been hers.'

Gran continues eyeing Mum with as much enthusiasm as a ready for action preoperative colonoscopy patient.

'Mum, caftans are very fashionable on the continent. Your problem is you've been stuck in the dreary drain of the Melbourne suburbs for too long. You need to get with it. You resemble a fossil from the fifties! ... Not even the Mad Hatter would be mad about your hat.'

Gran moves her lips into a mechanical smile. Thrusting her proud head into the air, she departs and joins us outside under the arbored branches of the olive trees.

'You were pretty hard on the old duck ... that hat is one of your mother's milder eccentricities.'

Mum and Dad both laugh.

Touches of colour softly pillow our steps as a yellow velvet blanket of tiny chamomile daisies spread beneath our feet as our five jumbled assortments of size, styles and railway lines of teeth eventually assemble beside the car. It's here we decide who will sit where, even on a short trip like this. It's like negotiating the Treaty of Versailles. Difficult though it will be with the air filled with tension, it will be salvation via separation for the journey to Saint Marcos.

After a hasty nudge from me, Gran declares after sniffing loudly the fresh aromatic morning air, 'I'm more than happy to sit in the back seat with the kids, thank you very much.'

Mocking Gran, Mum starts, 'Are you sure you want to come with us, Mother? I can arrange a lift on a donkey!' Gran holds my hand and ignores the sarcasm. 'Okay, please yourself then. Or I could organise for one of the nimble old boys from the village to whiz you up on a motorbike. Oh, hold on, what about Dippy Dop, the Singing flop? Now that's a thought. He's still around, you know, lingering … And I hear he's been asking about you. He'd be keen to lure you up into the hills. Seduce you in the groves. Ply you with more of his notoriously nasty homemade cumquat brandy. You never know, you might experience the thrill of a life time.'

Gran glares, 'I'm sure he would and I suppose you are speaking from experience? I can't wait for people to put the alfa, vita and gamma of your life together!' and she thrusts her handbag firmly under her arm as if it's a weapon designed specifically to ward off unwelcome suitors and her daughter's comments.

A look of alarm funnels its way across Mum's face but is quickly replaced by defiant indignation. 'I don't know what you are talking about, Mother! Just get into the car, David, or we will be late.'

But Gran is no throwover and tosses Mum a lingering, knowing look then hastens to settle like a nesting hen in the back of the car, fanning herself.

Ruffled by Gran's throwaway line, Mum doesn't tempt the gods by aggravating the situation any further and piles in the front. Dad, not concentrating on the conversation between the two women, and distracted by the petrol gauge, chauffeurs us to the church.

It turns out the journey to the village puts a much-needed stasis on the clouds of tension that have gathered at our home and between Mullet and Irene. By the time we reach the village, we notice Mullet standing in front of the building looking like an excited groom dressed for his wedding day. Irene is nowhere to be seen. He's gussied up like a shop front window in an expensive double-breasted suit, matching flared trousers, wide black tie and generously elevated platform shoes. There's a huge market for this style of height-boosting skyscraper shoe since the first pair arrived off a flight from London earlier in the season. Indeed, Mullet couldn't look trendier if he tried. Close by, a nervous Ursula stands elegantly dressed in a simple yellow shift-style dress. The straps of the blue bathing suit she's wearing beneath show on her pale shoulders. Stick, soon to be godfather for the first time, is also smartly dressed and clinging close to Took. She's the bearer of white and pink candied bonbonniere bundled in a basket decorated with ribbons. Stick stands with pride about to plunge into the serious role of godparent to his future sister-in-law.

They stand milling happily with the many villagers who've arrived to see the service, no doubt some hoping for a possible showdown between Irene and Ursula and curious to see how adults are baptised. Irene's curious too. Now inside the church; she's dressed head to toe in black. Having resurrected her polyester suit from her suitcase, she's balancing on sore knees before the altar, pretending to be deep in contemplative prayer.

'G' day, all!' chirps Dad happily striding at pace up the path. He'd opportunistically given Gran a brief tour around the village graveyard in the hope he could plant her there but she survived the tour. Seeing Ursula and Mullet standing together in the shade of the old church, he hurries ahead of us to join them. 'May I say this is a beautiful day for a baptism ... well, actually, a beautiful day for anything except, of course, a hanging!' He smiles.

Mullet smiles too and moves closer, finding support in the company of his older friend. Ursula kisses Dad on both cheeks and he senses her nervousness.

'She'll be right, love; there's nothing to worry about. It will be over before you know it's even happened. I once heard about a Greek priest who was so keen to get back to the *kafeneo* and have another drink that he rushed through his service as if the church was on fire!'

The men laugh as Ursula looks on. She's continuing to look nervous and finds the conversation not particularly funny. 'Thanks for coming, David. I'm not sure if that's especially reassuring though. But you are right, I hope he's in a hurry and gets this over and done with as quickly as possible. I've heard about Russian priests baptising queues of babies, dunking them like dirty plates in oily water as if they're doing a rush job on the dishes. How they manage the long assembly lines of wailing babies, wet bottoms and terrified mothers, God only knows.'

She pauses now to break into a whisper of a smile. 'As you can see, I'm nervous about the ceremony but I'm not wailing. Nor do I have a wet behind ... well, at this stage, thank goodness. With my secular background, this is all new to me.

I hope it goes off without any hitches.'

'Ah, my dear, don't worry. You look radiant. Everything will be fine, you'll see. I believe in faking it till I make it ... in fact, none of us are experts on Greek Orthodox christenings either so you're in good company. And to make our day complete, here comes George and Anna with someone I don't recognise. By the way, is Mullet's mother here?'

'She's inside. Hardly said a word to me. I feel as if I'm committing murder or something equally atrocious. You'd think I was the devil's spawn and she's attending a baptism by fire. I think I have a real battle on my hands. Look, here comes Dimitri and Hilary. That romance is blossoming. How kind of them to come.'

'On the subject of mothers-in-law, Ursula, and Mullet's mother, in particular ... I've heard on very good authority that a diet of sour Macedonian goats' milk, green Faliraki figs and extensive periods of complete and total meditative seclusion in a fasting nunnery can cure Greek mothers-in-law of their interfering tongues. I must suggest this to Irene as a beauty treatment and see if she falls for it ... God knows she could do with a drastic beauty therapy of some kind.'

Suddenly feeling better, Ursula squeezes his arm. Even so, she senses she's inserting herself into something much bigger than anything she could have ever anticipated back in Sweden. In the rising heat of the morning, Anna, smiling widely, steps forward and greets everyone while introducing Spiros, her nephew. Hilary gives Ursula a dramatic big breasted hug and a small envelope. Dimitri plunges forward, itching to get his hands on Ursula, pinch her bottom and see if he can land a kiss on the lips.

But before Dimitri can release his octopus-like grip on Ursula, Dad, thinking Gran is out of earshot, telecasts, 'And speaking of old church ruins,' he looks directly at Gran coming along the path, 'what do you think of our old crumbling wreck?'

But it's too late, Gran's hearing is not as bad as my parents think.

Throwing a filthy look in his direction, she retaliates, mumbling, 'Ruins indeed! Just as well I have selective hearing.' Turning to me, she grumbles, 'Did you know, Possum, that an almond tree once said to a walnut tree, "Hold onto your nuts because here we go!" I wouldn't be at all surprised if the walls of this old church collapse the moment your father enters its haloed sanctum.'

'Really, Gran? What about Mum?'

Gran is the most religious person I've ever met – besides Father George and Anna, of course. Well, and half the island's population. Now Dad and maybe Mum's in for it.

'Yes, it would be risky following either of your parents into a church. Let's evacuate before it collapses in on them. In the meantime, we go to the Cavalieri and enjoy a lovely high tea. Mullet said they do a very nice high tea and I adore scones, cream and jam. I must say that I'm looking forward to experiencing my first Greek high tea,' laughs Gran excitedly, rubbing her hands together.

'Me too, but I wouldn't count on having cream and scones, Gran. We've never been able to buy cream here. It's not like we haven't searched high and low for it. I miss it. The Greeks only seem to use that strange Crème Fresh in desserts rather than traditional cream like back in Australia. Gee, Gran I miss so many things, including proper milk instead of that *Nou Nou Gala* stuff from a can. And have you noticed the picture on the front of the tin depicts a woman breast feeding a baby? Took us ages to pluck up the courage to buy a tin. For ages we thought it was breast milk until Katerina kindly translated the label for us.'

Anna's nephew Spiros visiting from London and speaking fluent English with a very strong Greek accent quickly joins the conversation with Anna, Dad and Ursula.

'Hello, Ursula. It's all very exciting sharing in the exotica of an Orthodox christening with you and your friends. Oh, I can't wait for the after party ... see what the Cavalieri has on its menu. Let's hope, dear, you don't end up looking like a drowned rat from the whole fucking dunking thing. You might need a hairdresser upon re-emergence from the water. No photos please!' He giggles impishly.

Ursula, Anna and Dad look horrified. 'Now, Spiros, stop scaring Ursula. She's frightened enough as it is,' warns Anna, slapping his wrist loudly.

'Oh, I'm trying to help. I'm thinking about her hair, darling! Her beautiful hair. And of course, her outfit. What's she wearing for the after event? It's just I want her to emerge like Venus from a sea shell ... fresh, free and washed of all sin! Perhaps I should take a dip too, cleanse my many, many sins! But seriously, Ursula, darling, one has to think about these things when there's an after event. One always likes to look one's best ... well, I know I do, anyway!'

Yes, it suddenly dawns on Ursula that when Yorgan, her brother, arrives from Sweden, he's going to adore this guy's bitchiness. The two will be like a matching twin set. She takes a deep breath knowing her time is nigh. With heart pounding, she steadies herself on Mullet's strong steady arm. It's either now or never to be well and truly done and dunked by the Orthodox Church. She takes a deep breath and steps forward.

Chapter 33

Written Off

Many days have passed since Ursula's baptism, not that anyone sitting directly behind Gran saw much of the service anyway because of her enormous hat. Feeling the inescapable desire to keep active while on holiday, Gran's exercising her tongue, giving it a good workout. Her target: Dad. He still has not produced a novel.

Because of this literary shortfall, he's getting niggly about being referred to as a novelist. Yes, even I must admit the title's sounding hollow, if not downright shallow. If he's not a writer, then what is he? Good question.

I suppose writers of sorts can dress in safari suits and shorts but here's the thing, they need to write. So, is he really a writer? From a Reductionist Theorist perspective, he is in fact a writer in name only. A bit like Hilary's daughter's wedding. You know, the Greek wedding you're having when you are not having a Greek wedding?

They say writers need muses and, theoretically, this may be true but Mum, God love her, has far too short a fuse to ever be a supportive or inspiring muse. There's a critical side to her nature which is hard to ignore and it doesn't sit comfortably with Dad, or me. It surfaces too regularly and it's strange that her adoring sons seldom, if ever, experience the sting or lash of her tongue ... she doesn't hijack their happiness or hopes.

Any time a few draft pages were handed to her by Dad for comment, these were given short shrift and a blood curdling response. This was always followed by more arguments. He responds to his literary failure by clinging more closely to the local cognac, wine or whatever beverage is on hand. Slowly, slowly, I can see he's losing his mojo. When confronted he admits his writing is '*Etsee*, bloody *getsee*,' *so, bloody so*. Freely admitting, 'yep, it's a no go!'

It's been said before, but not even he's subscribing to his scribe. He calls his attempts to scribble 'A pile of rotten old dribble. My humble efforts are woeful and need to be turfed. Well, everything except my letters home, of course.'

His Hippocratic oath to produce a book is slowly fading into an old worn-out habit now. Yet, there are rare moments when he strikes a dramatic pose as if he's about to compose. Then he sips something liquid and his eyes glaze. He'll sit deep in thought, poised in front of the typewriter or wanders around the villa singing *Never on a Sunday* or *Ruby My Love!*

This lack of action is causing fractious friction between Mum and Gran too. Gran reckons if he's not going to write then we should return to Australia. But Mum's adamant we're not going anywhere. And just as she says this, another pile of Dad's prose ends up in the bin. Yes, his spin is flung into the *Nou Nou garla* bin which serves very conveniently as our rubbish disposal unit made of castaway cardboard. All that prose waiting to decompose. Is the writing on the wall? Is he a write-off? I hope not but according to Mum it's an inevitable outcome.

With a few more silver hairs reflecting in the morning light, Dad defensively reckons, 'There's nothing that hasn't already been covered by some other writer. Nothing's original anymore.'

The house goes deathly quiet while his words are digested by Mum and Gran. Truly, is there nothing he can conjure up about the world around him? Crikey, if that's the case, we're in real strife. Surely there is a tiny crack through which he can peek at the world anew? Discover something original to share. Has everything really been done? Gran, astounded at his words, says, 'The man has lost the plot – not that I estimated he had much of one in the first place. I insist you pack for Australia, pronto!'

Poor Dad. Couldn't he see opportunity in the chaos around him? Where have all his pillars of wisdom, sculptured insights and breadth of mind gone? Will there be no happy ending, like bringing home the Parthenon Marbles for the Greeks? Only in our case, Dad's marbles?

Mum says, 'I think it's not so much of a shortage of a storyline, it's keeping David away from the wine.'

Plonk is the reoccurring theme, the fault-line in the storyline. With the floodlights fixed on our lives being a fiction of sorts, it's now looking like a non–fiction drama. It's a lingering, worrying outcome. Out on the rounds of Corfu's busy expats' cocktail party circuit, he rages at Mum through clenched teeth. 'Stop introducing me as a bloody writer, will you, woman.'

'Hold on a jiffy, but aren't you?' He looks sheepishly away. 'Well, come on, man, that's hardly a loaded question. Or, is it?'

Now, whenever broached about his book, he acts as if someone's pointing a loaded gun at his temple. He winces as if he can hear the bullet shift in its barrel. Like a tortured man wearing a mask that's slipping, he looks uncomfortable, pressured and defensive. He's adopting the same characteristics as those polished politicians I hear on the news daily when they are under pressure, expertly ducking and diving questions. He's uneasy.

Is Mum's mask slipping too? She seems foxy, daring him to the edge of some deep dark abyss, trying to make him say something out loud, something that's hidden between them. She'll goad him to a point and then suddenly stop, quickly backing away from the edge of this 'something', as if whatever it is, it's too hot to handle. Too confronting. Whatever it is, it's hanging uncomfortably in the air. Well, hasn't it always …? Besides our financial dilemma, what's stopping us from leading a conventional life? Can't we become Greek citizens so we can work if we are to remain here? What's the hold up?

Out on the social circuit at parties where artists and writers crowd for cocktails and Corfu canapés through the heady days of summer, it's difficult for Dad to duck and dive pointed questions. After all, you never know who might turn up. Perhaps one of the Durrell's?

For him, it's nerve-wracking. An evening of back-slapping chit chat. 'Oh, so you're a writer too? Welcome to the club, old chap. What are you writing about? Any animals?'

'No', laughs Dad. '… just us, we are the animals.' Awkward.

But Dad, with a flush on his cheeks, is keen to talk about anything besides critical reviews, other writer's successes, the horrors of writer's procrastination and the power plonk has over performance. While all writers have their demons, Dad, with no script of his own, only hears alarm bells ringing in his head. It's a knee-jerk reaction. A bit like hitting a painful tooth or something equally excruciating. He mumbles an apology, and clambers off to the nearest bar, bottle or cocktail waiter with a loaded tray. He'll loiter in the distance until he's sure the conversation's shifted then he'll return to lead a debate on a completely different topic: Middle Eastern conflicts, the oil crisis, Watergate, global recession, inflation or the invasion of Cyprus. Always good options, all conveniently controversial enough to grab everyone's attention. The topic of writers dissipates until next time. Yes, next time …

Chapter 34

The Vice Consul's Function

Mum's in a flurry of anticipation. The invitation she's received in the post today has coated her disposition with sweet nectar from the gods. We're invited for cocktails to the British Vice Consul's official residence yet again to celebrate the Queen's birthday. It's an annual thing. Bursting with rapturous excitement at the thought of hobnobbing with the right kind of people, she inspects her wardrobe. She loves posh do's, dressing up ... but with little to wear. Again, she plucks her Ginger Rogers caftan out of mothballs. I hope this time it will be the caftan's last public performance but somehow, I doubt it.

We arrive ready for a night which for me will consist of a formidable foray of fluff and hot air-filled with formalities for us, the Antipodeans. Dad whispers in my ear, 'Look, all the usual British free-loading ex-pats are gathered at the entrance like horses about to charge from the starting line. Then once in, they scramble to assemble in a tight circle around the *meze* plates like vultures, and mumble, "God bless the Queen and hip, hip hooray, etc. etc."'

I look on and smile.

Yes, those of us from the colonies observe the formal proceedings with tongue in cheek. We are outnumbered by doe-eyed devotees to Her Majesty. Dad murmurs to me under his breath, 'Ah, God bless the little dears. It's heart-warming to see such dedication and devotion to the Queen. The rest of the year they couldn't give two hoots about the old duck.'

He's right, especially since he's here under sufferance at the insistence of Mum – just like me.

The evening starts off pleasantly enough. Lots of 'How do you do's' – a bit like the night we met Lord Alexei. The formalities are tedious as far as I am concerned. All this tut, tut talk! But the evening is not about me or what I think … the evening is about, "Rule Britannia, Britannia rules the waves."

We Aussies line up, suck it up like we always do, like good colonial subjects. Dad refers to these events as B and B events: booze and bullshit evenings. The art of mastering the two-hand fiddle armed with glass, serviette, cocktail toothpick with indistinguishable object attached masquerading as something edible etc. etc. then throw in a hand shake to really get you juggling. I glance at Mum – she's in her element. She's been catapulted from drab expat Greek village housewife living among the 'wrong people', to finding herself among the most exquisite, 'right people'. No plebs at this party. Well, apart from us. Her accent is primed so few, if anyone, will suspect her Antipodean roots. She's poised, performing to perfection, nose in the air, ignoring other Australians of inconsequence. She's on a mission, a mission to impress the best in the room.

While holding a canapé in one hand and glass of wine in the other, she whispers to me, as a reminder of other similar events, 'Now you must say, how do you do, a pleasure I'm sure and with an extension of the right paw, which by the way must be executed directly with a light, but credible grip then an almost but not quite, curtsy! Have you got that?'

I obediently nod and conform. I want to eat tomorrow. The evening proceeds as pleasantries are expressed, drinks and canapés roll up and into mouths and then are gone, splashed down with cheap wine. Then the process is repeated. The obligatory scripted speeches made, and plates of free grab-a-handful of finger food does the rounds of the room again in between pressing crowds. One big huddle eventually shrivels down to a few small groups as the evening wears on.

I tag along, dragging my polished school shoes behind Mum. Small talk here, smaller talk there. She mustn't keep still; must move along and continue making the rounds in order to meet the right people. There's chit chat about island living, local customs, Greek toilets, the complexities of the language and the gruesome horrors of the local butchers' shops. The evening wears on. The groups get even smaller as stragglers monopolise the last few available waiters. Their tray contents disappear rapidly.

An English couple ask me: 'I hear your mother has five children. Do you and your siblings go to school on the island? Or do you go to the American school in Athens?'

I'm about to answer when Mum elbows me out of the way. She side-grabs another chardonnay from the returned waiter and cavalierly retorts, 'Most of my children are out of the country now; I only have two here at the moment. Oh, well of course none of my children are academics and this one, well …' and in that space sits an awkward silence into which I'm sucked.

I'm gob-smacked, embarrassed by her silence. At fifteen, I feel as if I'm being written off as virtual vegetable matter. My heart pounds at the injustice of it because my marks at school in Australia were good. Somehow, we, her children, are responsible for not going to school; not my parents? My mind clouds with self-doubt. Perhaps I really am terra nullius on top? Surely the reality is she's not letting on that it's an economic issue rather than an intelligence problem. Why lie?

Resourcefully, she salvages the situation by moving me

aside when she sees my shocked and hurt expression and points to my little brother. She shifts him in front of her and says gregariously, 'My youngest son, George, or *Georgios* as the local Greeks like to call him, he's the smart one. He goes to the local primary school in the village of Saint Marcos. Primary school education in Greece is free, did you know? Wonderful education system for primary school children. He's multilingual now, aren't you, dear?'

Urging him in the back, she manoeuvres him to the front and then just as swiftly shifts him to one side and changes the subject saying, 'Have you ever been to Saint Marcos? Oh, it's a lovely village. Parts of it date back to the twelfth century you know, or, possibly even earlier. I believe the Byzantines established the village. Yet much of the remaining architecture was built by the Venetians. The locals built away from the coastline to avoid the ravages of pirates and of course those nasty Barbarians. And I haven't even mentioned the Turks! As you are new to the island you should go there sometime. Best in the spring when the wildflowers are out? Have you ever visited the island in spring?'

As the evening wears on the conversation switches to Dad being a novelist. Mum, with plum still firmly positioned in mouth, is ferreting on again about his non-existent novel. Standing next to her, Dad's angry and frustrated. What is she not getting? Hadn't they argued about this the other day? He responds by excusing himself and heads to the bar, escaping the discussion about his novel that's not, and may never be, under construction.

On his way to the bar, he spies something special. It's a delicious reprieve from bread and tomatoes, our monotonous Greek fast that never, ever seems to end. Like a man hit with cupid's mesmerising bow, he follows a tray of honey and soy chicken wings before they disappear under a flurry of expat fingers. In delighted abandonment, he grabs a wing here and a wing there every time the few remaining waiters swing around or circles him. Dad's eyes glaze over with joy. Out of the corner of his eye he sees Mum. Like a steam engine on full throttle, she's heading over to where he's drifted to savour his honey and soy chicken wings in peace. She's dragging an elderly man by the arm as she heads toward him.

Dad hears her refer to his novel again, 'Oh God,' he whispers under his breath, 'here we go again!'

There's nothing he can do to get out of the situation; he's cornered. He takes the chicken wing out of his mouth thus enabling him to politely converse and flings the chicken wing onto the waiter's passing tray. Then, as quickly as the tray appeared, it disappears into the milieu of the last standing stragglers and into the kitchen.

Mum's like a leopard about to pounce and introduce him to the man by her side when Dad, with his hand in the air, makes a sudden dash across the room after the waiter. Mum's furious and mumbles apologetically, 'Oh, I'm sorry about that. I don't know what's got into my husband this evening. Can't get enough of those chicken wings, I suspect.'

Half an hour passes and Dad hasn't reappeared. Mum's furious. Leaving her newly acquired friend, she rounds us up, dropping her English accent momentarily and shifts us away from curious listeners and riles.

'Where the hell's your father? Honestly, how dare he duck off like that? Wait till I find that man! All because he won't discuss his book. You know, if he'd talk about it, he might get inspired and get the bloody thing written. That was writer Kester Berwick, you know, the famous author.' She says this as if this man is the answer to all the world's literary problems.

As the Consul's function ends, the evening descends into

more receding decay for me as the sleeves of Mum's caftan are pulled up for a discrete search for our lost leader. After all, we need to get home. Drawing blanks about his whereabouts from us kids, eventually, a reluctant waiter plucks up courage and steps forward. 'I saw him going through the bins, searching through discarded food scraps.'

Mystified and embarrassed, Mum angrily demands, 'Why in God's name was he doing that? Come on, man, speak up!'

The waiter shrugs his shoulders and, seeing her combustible expression, shrinks then quickly disappears.

She murmurs, 'What the devil is that man of mine playing at?'

We are left huddled in a corner as she interrogates, discreetly, of course, anyone who knows Dad – everyone except the Consul. The Consul must not know Dad's been ransacking her bins. Eventually Mum gives up the idea of finding him in the building. She bids her host a sweeping goodnight then leads us down Kapodistria Street to the cricket ground car park to see if our car is still there. It's there; he hasn't abandoned us. Arriving at the car and seeing Dad's shape in the driver's seat, Mum pulls the passenger door open and seats herself next to him. He'd been quietly waiting for us.

But before Dad can say anything, Mum lunges, 'How dare you embarrass me in front of that interesting man. I was about to introduce you to the well-known author Kester Berwick. He wrote the book *The Head of Orpheus Singing* and he's invited us to accompany him to Patricia Manessi's villa. She lives on the San Stefano estate in Benitses. He's suggested afternoon tea. He says the house was built on solid rock in 1782. It has a private chapel in the garden and spectacular views. I wish you'd pay more attention to me.'

She continues, 'I'm trying to get you in the right circles.

How dare you disappear and leave me looking like a fool! Anyway, where have you been all bloody evening?'

All Dad can manage are a few mumbled discombobulated words, of which none of us can comprehend.

She continues her attack, 'What was that you said? Stop being so cryptic and speak up, you old fool. I can't understand you!'

In the darkness of the interior of the car, she hasn't looked at him because she's preoccupied with carefully adjusting her Ginger Rogers caftan around her like a mother hen scooping chickens under her bottom. Dad mutters again and this time it's even more indecipherable.

'What's that? What's that? Speak up, you stupid man?'

After moments of heavy stillness, he starts the engine. Before he steers the car out of the car park, he turns and looks at her. The illuminating yellow orbs from a passing vehicle flashes streaks of light across his face. In the glare of the headlights, he throws her an exaggerated toothless grin mumbling,

'My denthures, my denthures, I lost my fucking denthures on a chicken wing, you stupid woman!'

Chapter 35

Hail to the Mail - The Australian Family Greece

In our part of the island, the epi-centre of our tiny chip off the old Hellenic rock, our lives settle taking on a precarious pace after Dad lost his upper set of false teeth at the British Consul's function. As the days flit past it's becoming increasingly depressing seeing a moping, miserable, toothless father. The good thing is, Mum's backed off and is leaving him alone. This repose is giving them a much-needed break from one another and her persistent inquisitions about his book and our finances.

Gran's left too but not before she developed an enduring friendship with Kester who in her opinion is a wonderful, gentle souled man. They'd spend hours together reciting poetry and talking all things linked to literature and the arts. Gran had become very fond of him, but, him being gay, well, it was never going to be a match made in heaven. Still, she suggested he go to Australia with her so he could get his skin cancer treated. A scaly sore has developed on the side of his mouth. But with Kester, one quickly comes to learn that it's always about money and his lack of it.

Weighing the situation very carefully, Gran decided she'd had enough of spending time with anyone who'd allow themselves to be consumed by an ambitious cancer, need psychotherapy like Mum, or rudimentary dental care like Dad. She'd mumbled on more than one occasion that Dad's teeth were, however, the clincher. I suppose Gran's right; he's not a pretty picture. I wonder how many toothless authors exist in the wide world of writers? Probably more than anyone of us care to contemplate.

Placed in relative isolation from the rest of us, we're giving him a wide berth to mumble miserably under the olive trees in the garden. It's also a chance to delay visiting the Manessi's home for afternoon tea with Kester. So, until the state of Dad's teeth improves, we are reluctant to be seen publicly with him. It's not pleasant hearing him speak his limited amount of Greek without teeth. The problem is it's going to take ages to accumulate enough drachmae to acquire a new top set. The only good news for Dad was Gran departing.

A month or so after the Consul's cocktail party, a small parcel arrives special delivery for Dad. Tucked carefully in an envelope cushioned in tissue paper is his upper set of false teeth. They've arrived with salutations from the British Consul's office. The letter inside is from the chef. After Dad's teeth were eventually discovered, they were passed around as offerings to anyone who might want them and as there were no takers, it finally dawned on the kitchen staff that perhaps the Australian man with the wife in the ridiculous caftan, could be the owner. He didn't say from where he'd exhumed Dad's teeth, only that he'd found them and thought he'd want them returned. Dad can't take the smile off his face! What a relief for, as much as I love my father, it has been challenging seeing him smile without his teeth and to hear Mum moan and groan about trying to pulse his pulses without an electric blender. She'd been unsuccessfully using a pestle and mortar. With pulses clinging like sloppy projectiles all over our kitchen walls, it will be great to get back to some kind of normality. Interestingly, he makes no effort to enquire about where or how the chef found them. I reckon the truth is Dad doesn't want to know because of a wise old motto, "What the eye doesn't see the heart doesn't grieve." Under the circumstances very wise words indeed.

Now happily sitting under the trees with a full set of disinfected teeth in his mouth, he philosophically announces, 'Crafty farmers never look gift horses in the mouth and, kids, I reckon the same goes for my mouth. I don't want to know where my teeth have been! I'm only grateful to get them back to where they belong.'

We all smile cos he's smiling and a full set of teeth appears dancing magically in the sunlight. It's truly amazing what Greek bleach will bleach. It's strong stuff as all our underwear and his teeth can now attest.

Deciding to be cheeky with his dazzling dentures, he teases, 'Do you know that if you bought a set of Greek false teeth your teeth would never stop chattering? They'd go on and on just like your mother; even after death. I'm convinced her teeth are Greek falsies. Greek dentures are full of misadventures you know. And I advise anyone never to walk through a Greek graveyard at night.'

'Why, Dad?' I ask, absolutely intrigued.

'Well, Possum that's when all the dead dentures get together and harmonise in a collective chorus of *The Green, Green Grass of Home*. It's spooky stuff, Possums. But then my Aussie ones are full of adventures too. Mine are dentures that have misadventures! Hey, kids, check this out. How do I look with mine in backwards?'

'Err! Dad, that's so gross!' We evacuate the area leaving him contentedly sitting in the sunshine doing his novel impersonation of Hannibal Lecter while admiring the ships in the harbour.

On the subject of things that arrive in the post, the reality of the fragility of our lives is we wouldn't be able to live on Corfu without the Greek postal service, or its Australian equivalent and all the international services in between. Dad's dentures are a perfect example of this life-sustaining service. This is amplified by the fact that we don't have a telephone or television. In this way, the postal services are our umbilical cord to the outside world – well, apart from a few Greek pigeons and the local village grapevine. Between them, they know pretty much everything that's worth knowing locally anyway. But then there is the BBC broadcast from London …

Greenwich Mean Time and I mean all the time which drives us kids nuts. We find the news, unless it's directly related to what's happening on the island, exceedingly boring. The world beyond our world sounds uninviting and depressing. But my parents listen keenly for any skerrick of news from Australia and, of course, updates on Greece's political situation. As they can't speak Greek except for a few scant words, the BBC broadcast from London is an important lifeline with its decidedly British perspective on the world. The irony is Mum and Dad moan and groan about the Poms but they wouldn't be without the BBC.

But everyone loves the mail except when bills arrive. The only thing we don't do is get down on our knees in gratitude to our postman and say, 'Hail to the mail!' as he hurriedly flings letters in our mailbox before zooming off at speed down the road. He'd probably linger longer by our letterbox if we were not so far down the expat food chain. We are not the Rothchilds nor the Guggenheims.

You can almost set your clock every weekday morning when one of us inquisitively cries out, 'Has the postman come yet?' It's gripping stuff and usually followed up by a shuffle along the well-worn track to the letterbox. It has all the excitement of a pre-Lotto draw before you realise you haven't won anything.

Today a letter has arrived addressed in bold capital letters to **the Australian Family Greece.** As if guided by a mind-reading invisible being, the letter was sent from Australia via Athens's central post office to our humble letterbox. Upon seeing the letter, Dad gathers us around the table and announces theatrically that we are famous. Time for a group hug – well, perhaps not. It appears we are so renowned the central post office in Athens on Syntagma Square knows who we are and hence where to send this obscurely addressed letter. As the letter is passed among us to admire and um and ah over, I wonder ... are we the only Australian family living in Greece? But then, on the other hand, it could be sheer chance the letter arrived at the exact villa, in the correct village and on the right island. Surely, we can't be the only Aussies? But then perhaps we *are* the only Aussie family. If that's the case then we are indeed very famous if for this reason alone.

After opening the letter and being assured the letter is for us, we feel smug about our one and only possible claim to fame for about ten seconds and then go back to doing what we were doing before the letter arrived. Funny how fame doesn't last.

Our letterbox is a tin box with a slit in the side and a back that flips open when tapped – pretty nifty and it's manufactured in Greece by none other than my famously not handy Dad. It sits suspended by wire ties on another one of his dodgy fences. This fence was also constructed with chook wire and designed specifically to keep the neighbour's sheep, goats and any wandering gypsies out. It's still standing after a few storms much to everyone's dismay.

Next to our letterbox flies the Australian flag. It's not a big flag by any stretch of the imagination but Dad reckons it catches flies just as effectively as sticky fly paper. He means Aussies, of course. He got the saying from some Canadians who kept referring to Australians as blowflies. At first, we found this offensive and then well, it caught on. "Buzz."

Our flag is a patriotic symbol to any passing Aussies, or anyone else that notices it, that Aussies are in residence. All the villas we've resided in on the island are swiftly baptised the "Other Down Under." Under this proud banner, we attract a lot of fly-swatting Aussies doing what Aussies do naturally and that is, of course, the Aussie salute. We also attract New Zealanders, Canadians, South Africans, Poms, Irish and Americans. They're all learning to swat like Aussies, especially the annoying Greek mozzies and wasps. Our flag is a valuable commodity if measured in "company" because my parents enjoy meeting new people and are constantly inviting people to the villa. I never know who's going to be sitting at the table when I return home. It's better than television ... well, sometimes.

Our lives revolve around conversations. I definitely think we have developed the delightful Greek art of "anarchy." The concept shouldn't be seen in a negative context ... for the Greeks, it's an opportunity to debate and question everything. And we do debate everything, well, except Greek politics. Some evenings we might have lengthy debates with officers from a British nuclear submarine; another night, crew from a British battleship, over dinner at the villa. In appreciation for our hospitality, not sure about our "anarchy", they're often only too happy to give us huge slabs of delicious British cheddar cheese, butter and other British goodies. Real luxuries for us. At other times, officers from American warships join us for dinner or lunch; sometimes breakfast if they've drunk too much and fallen asleep in a chair under the trees in the garden. It's not unusual for Dad to stumble upon a body or two as he navigates his way around tattooed navel trunks as he steps outside to sip his first coffee for the day.

At meal times, our table's laden with humble offerings of

bread, beans, olives, feta and tomatoes and this is reciprocated by the Americans with candy bars, t-shirts, Time and Newsweek. Just as well our dishes are a novelty for these guys, but more than this, Mum reckons they're lonely for family and yearning for home-style cooking. She even starts a soup kitchen for young backpackers staying at the campsite at Ipsos thinking they don't have much money and need a good feed. But unfortunately, the Greek authorities stepped in and threatened her so she had to stop. They argued she couldn't legally work and locals had complained that she was stealing their customers.

The truth is, Mum can be kinder and more charitable to strangers than to her own children. There are times when I see her stare into the faces of young men as if she's looking for a lost loved one in the crowd or searching the eyes of a dusty lone backpacker stumbling wearily along the road for the spark of a certain resemblance. Is it my imagination? What can I see in her sometimes-sad eyes; she's cocooned, an aloof mystery to me. Can anyone trespass into the clandestine corridors of her mind? And so, the hordes of strangers come and go bringing with them their stories as we scrape together enough humble pickings to go around. Perhaps a United Nations flag would be more apt so if our Aussie flag ever blows away or disintegrates beneath the sweltering summer heat, we'll know what to erect.

Our postman brings fortnightly cheques addressed to Dad from the Australian government. It's his military pension cheque, the only thing that stands between us and abject poverty. At times, it's an unenviable task being our postman because if there's a mail strike in Melbourne or Greece, he becomes the bearer of bad news for not bearing anything. On days like this, we wish someone, anyone, would drop us a line. Silently I plead: someone, anyone put us on your mailing list

... please. Go on send us a poison letter with noxious news in it. Well, perhaps we're not that desperate. And I ask you, where are all the foreign correspondents? Personally, I'm inclined towards colourful postcards from exotic countries bearing happy tidings.

Glancing at Dad throwing a few crumbs over the balcony of our villa, I wonder what he's up to. But there he is feeding pigeons. It seems mundane, so innocent, but is he attempting to attract a few passing international ones so he can pick up their messages? Or when fiddling with long pieces of wire, is he secretly setting up a satellite dish so he can tap into passing radio signals? Sometimes during the long lonely rainy season when all the tourists have abandoned the crystal coast lines, there's no consolation for island isolation.

When cheques don't arrive on time, we still negotiate all sorts of deals with locals as Mum and I did when Dad was in Australia, but even prior to that they'd arrange all sorts of transactions to reimburse people when the tide eventually came in. When cheques arrive, our postman becomes our hero for the day as Dad attempts to pat his back, treating him like a long-lost war hero before he zooms off. Dad, having secured the cheque in his hot hand, races away to the bank in Corfu town to get it cashed. After determining the daily rate of exchange for the Australian dollar against the drachmae, he sits and conforms to a set of unvarying protocols which are all part of the local convoluted banking system. It's a system that drives him to despair.

First, he's instructed to sit and wait to be interviewed by the bank manager. He's advised time and time again to not go directly to a teller. When he asks why there's no reply, he only sees shrugs of shoulders and blank expressions resembling those initiated by a well-trained firing squad. When the bank manager's ready, Dad's politely escorted into his office. The manager instructs him to sit on a truncated seat facing his oversized desk while he sits in his wide elevated chair. The manager examines Dad's cheque, scrutinising it under a magnifying glass, orders coffees, talks about world politics while Dad politely listens and sips. Frequently, the manager bursts out with statements like, "All the best Greeks are dead, you know! All the philosophers, anyone of any purpose that is."

Dad recoils at the man's words wisely, refusing to be drawn into conversations like this with a character who has a reputation of being an inquisitor and a sneaky informer. If Dad agrees with him, the manager might argue, "Ah, really? Then why do you live in Greece if you think all the best Greeks are dead?"

Dad can't win. So, he cultivates a civil diplomatic tongue, avoiding debates on most topics, especially Greek politics. All the while Dad's foot, discretely of course, taps up and down impatiently as he sneaks the occasional glance at his watch as the manager closes his eyes and drinks loudly on his sweet Greek coffee. As he sips, his little finger with its provocative, protruding manicured long nail points directly at him, wriggling. Dad finds this unnerving even though we have come to discover this male nail phenomena is a common trait among elite Greek men. Yet, Dad can't help but be intrigued. Is he flashing his fingernail at me, he wonders? Is there something overtly sexual, perhaps perverted, in the protrusion of his playful little pinkie?

Dad needs to nail this. Why do Greek white-collar workers and elite Greek men have long manicured nails on their little fingers? It must be a marker of sorts? A bit of unambiguous social status screaming, "Look at me, look at me, I'm all class!"

I suppose olive pickers and fishermen have no chance of

maintaining or caring for such frivolous and ridiculous vanities. They're far too busy getting on with the job. So, what are Greek men's carefully manicured long nails on their little pinkies used for? Our minds boggle. After much lengthy family discussion on the topic, rightly or wrongly we've come to the collective conclusion that they're for picking noses or mining into the cave-like crevices of ears to excavate lurking murky earwax.

Our bank manager is also a spreader and a wide one at that. Translation needed? A man who sits with his legs extended as far apart as is humanly possible as if to say, "Get a load of this!" It's distracting, and overtly sexual especially when he's adjusting his bits and pieces. Eventually, when he's ready, he'll signal Dad to stand and follow him to the counter where he'll oversee the teller dealing the drachmae. It's like a high-rollers' table at Vegas with staff heavies hovering to oversee a winner's payout. But it's hardly huge winnings.

While personal service can be a good thing, the problem is there is too much of it. The worst thing is, the manager's English is fairly limited and spoken with a heavy accent and Dad's Greek is practically non-existent. How many times has Dad walked out of his office scratching his head wondering what the hell he's nodded and said "Yes" to, especially with that neatly shaped fingernail wiggling at him again?

Sometimes we join Dad on his trip to the bank for moral support, clowning around as kids do. We have nicknamed the bank manager Bumblebee because he's wide, round and mumbles like a bee. A trail of white icing sugar sits like fine dust on and around his desk. It's a tell-tale sign that he keeps a stash of *kourabiedes* carefully concealed under his desk. The icing sugar doesn't linger for long – militant Greek ants on a mission are on the move and it's just a matter of time before they devour any signs of *kourabiedes* ever having been there.

The fact is, we might like the man more if he'd offer us one.

Returning from the bank one day, Dad shakes his head grumbling, 'Protagoras once said, "Man is the measure of all things" and I'm quoting Plato, kids, from Theaetetus. So, I ask you, what does that make the bank manager at the bank then?'

We shrug our shoulders.

'A bloody idiot, that's what it makes him! But, fair's fair, kids, he'd make an attractive corpse.'

'Oh, Dad, that's gross!'

'Ah, now you may well shake your heads at your old man but it's true after the day I've had. In fact, I can say anything I like about Greek bank managers in the sacred sanctity of my own villa. If I asked you how many Greeks does it take to cash an Australian government cheque, you'd think it was a joke, wouldn't you. The problem is, it's not!'

He does have a point.

Chapter 36

Before the *Gamos*

In the village of Saint Marcos excitement permeates the air. The intoxicating sensation of completion, the delicious relief locals feel now the annual olive harvest has finished and their animals and crops are thriving. There's liberation from tedium; it's obvious in the upward tilt of chins, the way the locals straighten and stretch the stiff curves in their tired and weary backs. Olive oil: the precious fruit of their most back-breaking labour rests pressed in storage containers stowed in dark musty pantries or cool cellars, concealed from damaging sunlight in ancient villas, *kalivakia, barns* and the surrounding hamlets throughout this spectacular Venetian village ready for use. The locals, as generations before, use this golden liquid so laboriously derived from the earth by pouring it into practically every facet of their lives. It flows, seeping like blood through villagers' veins extending the quality of their lives by decades. Few physicians would disagree.

But the main reason for the flurried excitement is locals anticipating Mullet and Ursula's wedding. This momentous event will take place in the village church as sacred words are released through the archives of time to the present by Father George's hypnotic musical voice accompanied by chanting *psaltas*, their heads angelically tilted toward heaven. In timeless rituals, perpetuated by tradition, the bride and groom will be anointed with rich olive oil harvested from this fertile land. Soon it will shine on the young couple's foreheads in the glistening lustre of ecclesiastic light. The catalyst of communion, home-made wine once impregnated with powers beyond human imagining by the priest, to be poured from fine decanters and set upon an elegant tray. In the priest's masterful hands, the decanter will dispense its liquid contents into a sacred vessel from which the couple will take their first tentative sips, red bejewelled baubles of wine-drops to crown their lips in solemn sips at the height of the service, the air palpable as the flesh of two symbolically become one. Mullet and Ursula silhouetted in light, led by the priest, join in step circling the altar three times.

But here in the village, at Mullet's family villa miles from the buzz of Corfu town, an individual's wealth is measured by an olive tree tally and property count. This fact of village life has not slipped Mullet's mother's attention as she interrogated Mullet about Ursula's dowry weeks earlier. No sooner had she got off the plane then she began her examination. 'How many olive trees does she own? Huh, answer me this!'

'Mum, she's not Greek. Don't worry about how many olive trees she owns. I won the lottery; we can buy more olive trees than you can poke a stick at. That will make up for the fact that she doesn't have a dowry. Especially now you have your land, and Agarpe's land fairly purchased from both of you ... the place is covered in olive trees. So, what's the fuss? Her trees, my trees; it's the same thing. It was enough for you and Agarpe to catch husbands.'

'That's because we married men from the village sticking with tradition. Your wealth comes from you, not from her, to you. You should marry a local girl with land to add to your estate. Stick with tradition and you can never go wrong in life because if anything goes wrong you can always say, I did the right thing. In this way your conscience is clear!'

'Struth, Mum, give it a break. You have to be bloody

kidding! That's never going to happen. You are not setting me up with some local chick who has a big dowry and resembles the rear end of a donkey's backside. No, it's not happening. We're not living in the dark ages. This is the 70s. The age of Aquarius, freedom, women's liberation! *Capiche?*'

'Don't come the smart arse with me. And don't speak to me in Italian. You don't know what the Italians and Germans did to us during the war. Yes, you and your whole generation with your bloody dippy hippy ideas. I know all about Ursula's liberation. In fact, the whole village knows about it. You were thrown naked out of that woman's bedroom! Naked, shame on you and her! *Po, po, po!* Everyone still talks about it ... you flashing your fundamentals around the village. Imagine my shock to come back to my *xorio, village* after all these years and hear what they say about you and that, that ... *puntana, prostitute*. You shame me and you shame your whole family. *Na*, this is for you, *vlaka, stupid*! You are an idiot just like your father. You take after him.'

Angrily, she places her hand close to Mullet's face and curses him. 'You are worse than a mule when you speak to your mother like this.'

Her eyes glare, connecting with his. He grabs her hand, sweeping it aside and stares her out then bellows, 'Ha, a mule, a mule! You called me a mule! And me future wife a *puntana*! What an insult! I am Greek enough to know you can't insult me any more than you have right now! That's it, Mum! This is the end of the conversation as far as I'm concerned. Now that the villa's mine, you're lucky I don't throw you and Aunty out on your fat arses! I let you both stay here only because you didn't want to stay at the hotel.'

'How can you speak to me like this? And about your aunty too. She just agreed to sell you this property! If your father were alive today ...'

'He would agree with me. If he had his chance over again, he probably wouldn't have married you in the first place. But he was forced into it. He must have felt like I do, being pushed into a marriage I don't want. I know you have some village chick ready on the side lines just in case Ursula makes a beeline for the exit because of how horrible you are to her.'

Irene turns sharply, strides with haste from her son, covering her ears with her hands as she goes. 'La, la, la! I'm not listening to you.'

'Good, then don't. I'm going out. I'll come back later today because I have an electrician coming to give me a quote on having the whole place rewired. But after the wedding, I don't want you here. You can go back to Sydney; go anywhere for all I care, but this is where Ursula and I want to make our new life together. It's going to be the Epicurean epi-centre of our existence. If you can't deal with that … learn to love and accept our relationship … then go. I intend running a tight ship filled with only genuine relatives and friends.'

News transits along the local grapevine quicker than Thanasi can cut a sheep's throat. Irene tells her sister Agarpe about her woes with Mullet and before you know it, the rest of the village are aware of their squabble.

And so today villagers anticipate the big wedding day ahead, before and after rings are placed on the bridal couple's trembling fingers. Will there be problems with Irene? They know from their school days long ago she's fiery, animated. Life with her is either Heaven or Hades. Yet, out of respect for today's proceedings, locals keep their opinions to themselves and refrain from flinging open shutters to air blankets or shake Flokati rugs in the brilliant sunlight. Since early morning, they and their partners have been dressed in their Sunday best, shoes polished, shirts and skirts pressed. The men gather at the *kafeneo*, while the women abide in small groups along the village path, warming their backs with hands on hips, the sun's generous rays resting on surfaces in penetrating silence. The women stretch and arch, copying lazy cats on the narrow path in front of them. Hypnotised by the balminess of the morning, the giggling clusters linger, discussing wedding night dramas and delights. These are precious moments, relaxing and enjoying time away from arduous farm duties while waiting patiently for guests to arrive and then meander slowly to the church.

Irene breathes in and tightens her corset. Speckles of perspiration dot her forehead. She hasn't slept. Irritated and tired, she calls to her sister Agarpe in the next room. 'It's the bread, that blasted Greek bread and olive oil. They're dangerously delicious and now I'm as fat as a Phoenician pig! Look at me. This dress fitted me before I left Sydney. It cost a fortune too. Now, oh my God, look at me! I've taken on the general appearance of a beached whale contorted in sausage skin.'

Poking her head around the door, Agarpe laughs at her sister, 'Yes, that's an unfortunate choice, isn't it? You'll have to breathe in for the rest of the day. That is your only option. It's too late to buy something else. Perhaps you can change during the reception? You know, into a pair of elasticated stretch pants ... the type we used to wear on Christmas day in Sydney when we were in our twenties. Do you remember how hideous we used to look? I still have a pair. Mind you, it's a much bigger size!'

Irene looks away from the bedroom mirror and laughs with her sister, remembering their daggy, grey baggy stretch tracksuit pants. 'You'd never wear them on a first date ... that is if you wanted a second date, isn't that right, sis? I could kill for a pair right now and bugger the date, well, if I had one. But if I had three wishes today one would be Mullet wasn't marrying that *xeni, foreigner*, and I can wear my old baggy tracksuit pants to a reception where my son is marrying a good local Greek girl. Oh, and the third wish; I can eat whatever I want without ever putting on weight. Now isn't that the dream of every woman?'

Agarpe nods heartily and commiserates with her sister, 'Well, that's never going to happen so come here and have a tipple with me before the service. This will steady your nerves and mine before things get too crazy and out of hand.'

Agarpe pours them a cognac. She's using her mother's good crystal glasses, recovered earlier, and places them formally on a silver tray. Her sister joins her by the antique sideboard. They stand in front of an old faded photograph of their parents on their wedding day. The sisters, positioned together, clink glasses. Each takes a sip feeling the powerful liquid run through their bodies, warming their shaky insides. Their eyes sparkle, and cheeks flush with the endorphin rush.

Agarpe looks long and hard at her sister and says philosophically, 'Well, here's to you and Mum and Dad. I wish they were here. They'd be proud. We've come a long way and produced sons. They may be idiots half the time but, to our credit, they're men able to carry on the family name. That's what's important, isn't it? I'm sorry mine can't be here for the wedding. As for the wedding, well there's nothing we can do about that or your waist-line. You're just going to have to suck it up and stop acting like a princess about his choice. Ursula's not a bad person, she's become an Orthodox Christian. In this way you can't say she hasn't done the right thing even if they don't go to church as often as you would like. At least your grandchildren will have hope, a sense of connection to their roots through the church. And they bought the house from us. We can get on with our lives in Australia now knowing the property is in good hands. We can retire in comfort and not have to pick up after a male ever again by having to marry someone for money.

'Traditionally the boys should have inherited the property because we don't have daughters but Mullet was very generous insisting on purchasing the place. Stick doesn't mind – he's made a few bob out of the deal. You have given him some cash and that should do him until you die. Mum and Dad would be pleased with how we have lived our lives. So, sis, here's to Mum and Dad, *Stin ayhia sas, cheers.*'

Teary eyed and filled with emotion, the two women raise their glasses high into the air and pause, gazing affectionately at the photograph of their parents. Agarpe's chin trembles thinking of their mother and how she must have stood in this very spot and talked to her mother about marriage and the man she would marry all those years ago. Irene returns her glass to the tray on the sideboard then bends uncomfortably to put on her high heeled shoes.

She complains loudly as she again straightens her generous figure. 'Oh, my back. What I would give for a younger body. And a young man. Well, actually any bloke so long as he's got a pulse and wallet. Who's fussy these days? I'm not happy about anything to do with this wedding. And what about the caterer? Ursula's brother, the chef? And he's a *poosti, gay.* What's the world coming to? Men cooking is one thing but on top of this, act like women too. *Po, po, po,* it's too much!'

'Oh, grow up, sis – the Greeks invented gay sex ... think about Plato and Sappho.'

'Maybe, but every second word is the F word. Can you believe this? And as for that Australian woman Jo ... she's not so bad ... at least she helps but she drinks like a fish. It's not ladylike to drink like that. And she's a mother with five children. Nice people, yes, but they both drink too much. Didn't they have television when they lived in Melbourne?

Five children! Greeks sensibly stop at two at the most .... then we find reasons to argue with our partners, cut it off or turn over and go to sleep. Yes, we let our passions rot like old tomatoes left on the vine. But no wonder they don't have any money. But work this out, there's always money for alcohol and cigarettes. Who can support five children, drink and smoke unless they're very, very rich, even in Greece? They say she's a good cook but old Takis would be the best caterer for this wedding. That is because he's a real Greek cook. He knows what to do on big days in the church and for weddings. He doesn't work at the Bogdanos Hotel for nothing, you know?'

'Well, as I say, it's too late now. What do you think of my earrings? Mmm, perhaps not. They might cause a scandal in the village!' On closer examination, eyeing her image in the mirror, Irene concedes. 'Oh yes, a huge scandal. But then what am I saying? Mullet's wedding is already the biggest scandal of the day. Indeed, in this village, the scandal of the century.' Laughing, the two women pour more cognac.

Meanwhile, at Villa Kapodistrias, voices ring out in all directions in the morning air. Our ridiculously tiny kitchen has been taken over by Ursula's brother Yorgan, the knife juggling chef, kitchen hands and waiters. After the 'chef' almost fainted at our inadequate kitchen facilities, nearly causing anarchy among the junior staff with his dramatics, he settled into a state of determined stoicism for the sake of his sister's happiness. Why he's dressed inappropriately for a day of anticipated catering chaos – wearing an elegant pale chino suit with a pink floral shirt – is anyone's guess. Mind you, it's absolutely fabulous for the wedding and reception. Imitating a mother hen, he fossicks and fusses, throwing tizzy fits every so often to release tension and calm himself.

Stick's kicked the front door open and headed for the fridge with a box of pre-wedding drinks. He's managed to source Aussie Carlton Draft specially sent in from London for the event. It takes second place in the refrigerator beside bottles of Veuve Clicquot and Dom Perignon. Yorgan fusses, crowing about alcohol taking up precious room in the fridge where food should sit and Stick, with equal determination, ignores him.

Mullet's yellow Lotus luxuriates in the morning sun in the garden, gloating beside our old shabby car. We've decorated this car with garlands of flowers, ribbons and evil eye wash off stickers. Cans have been tied to the bumper bar of the car and these will rattle and roll all the way along the pot-hole pitted roads to Saint Marcos and back. I'm not sure who will come out the worst for wear, our ears from the noise, the dusty dry roads, or the hollow and malleable tins. But somehow, on a day like today, it doesn't matter.

Ever since his fall-out with Irene, Mullet's been staying in the old library downstairs in our villa. He's moved in to try and diplomatically reduce the tension between him and his mother. She would not permit the couple to live together until after the wedding, the importance of respecting local courting protocols now suddenly imperative with his mother looking over his shoulder.

But even having done this, try as he may, he couldn't repair the distance between them. Time has moved on and any healing that needs to be done will have to take place at some later date. Even so, he's developed a wonderful bond with Dad. Mullet moving into our villa has also worked out to be quite a lucrative arrangement for Mum. The usual frigging frugal food menus have expanded to more imaginative delights, like defrosted Argentinian beef mince in the form of marvellous *mousakas* once a week (much cheaper than local beef), and delicious herb-filled chicken roasts. Because he's a very generous house guest, she's tolerating his Australianness. In fact, there are times when she can be as blue-collared bogan as he with her rapid deployment of Australian colloquialisms and less than lady-like smutty one-liners. In the meantime, Ursula is back in the fold with Anna and staying at her villa so as not to tempt the gods with bad luck while, at the same time, keeping her safely away from Irene's officious tongue. It's somewhat a relief for Mullet that he can come and go freely around the village without enduring lashings from Anna's tongue or risk having his testicles cryonically preserved or pickled in a jar. In a strange turn of events, Anna's once serpent tongue directed squarely at Mullet has turned into soothing *meli, honey*.

As falling droplets of cold liquid dribble down the side of glasses, Stick occupies his nervousness by pouring beers and topping up glasses with effervescent surges of champagne bubbles with deliberate strained precision. Anticipating other's nervousness, he's taken time to consider where he'd settle everyone's drinks so they'll be within easy reach of whatever they are doing. Yet, perilously, he's tempting the gods because he's overlooking the fact that this is not the wisest strategy given it's hot and early in the day.

While Greek priests have been known to have a few tipples before a service, it's expected the groom and best man lay off the grog so they don't end up cross-legged in a christening font or marry the wrong person. They need to stay alert just in case a quick bride switch occurs if distracted at the service. Thick-laced wedding veils may have been designed for this very purpose.

Mullet nervously struggles, straining to adjust his tie. Like a father patiently teaching a child to tie a shoelace, Dad motions Mullet to move his hands aside so he can adjust and straighten it for him. Moments later, Mullet steps keenly in front of the large, Russian, gold framed mirror that takes up half a wall in our light-filled lounge to examine his image. The old floor boards of the villa creak beneath his polished shoes as he moves from side to side to view his profile on all angles. He finally moves in for a close-up, then eventually steps back, smiling admirably. He likes what he sees and hopes Ursula will too.

Back in Pyrgi, Anna's in a fluster; nothing's gone right since she got up. The gas tank on the small hot plate that sits atop the limited bench space in her tiny multi-chromatic kitchen ran out. This occurred just as she was making a cup of Greek coffee and the flame slowly teetered into extinction until the blue and red flame shone no more. Her *briki* now sits cold and abandoned on the stove top.

'George, George ... where is that man? Still in bed? ... get up, there are more important things to do today than sleep? Can your ornamental-looking handles for ears not hear me? The gas has run out in the kitchen and now neither of us will be able to have a morning coffee unless you get up and get a new gas tank connected. Have you forgotten it's Ursula's wedding today? ... come on, man!'

'Woman, keep your hat on. You don't need to shout. I'm not deaf. I'm getting up,' George mumbles irritably under his breath as he flings back the covers of their hand-embroidered cotton bed sheets.

She fires furiously back at him before slamming the front door, 'You're deaf when you want to be, just like all men!'

Leaving their villa behind, her arms encumbered with a freshly pressed wedding dress, she carefully steps, tip-toeing her way across her garden to Ursula's villa. She taps gently on the door. 'Ursula, Ursula ... are you awake, *koukla mou, my doll*. Today is your big day. Come, come, answer the door. I have your dress for you.'

Sleepy-eyed and hair tousled, bare feet touching the floor, Ursula slowly opens the door and steps back as Anna sweeps into the room.

'Quickly, quickly you must shower and then I will do your hair. *Ela, come* quickly now because for this one day only … in your entire life, you will be a queen in God's eyes.'

Five minutes later, Ursula, with a thick white towel wrapped in a spiralling hug around her head and hand holding the front of a loose scent-infused kimono, submits to Anna's fussing by obediently sitting in front of the dressing table mirror. With arms shifting through the morning air like an orchestra conductor, Anna begins the transformation.

'You know, Ursula *mou*, I always wanted to become a hairdresser but life didn't grant me any of the dreams I'd hoped. Life can be cruel to some yet good to others. Life is more than chance. I think the god's have their favourites, and I sadly I am not one of them!' Ursula looks up through the mirror into Anna's sad brown eyes as she continues, 'Yes, it's like fishing when the big one gets away and you only haul in a tiny *spari, fish*. Two women can marry. One gets the good groom; the other an idiot. I think I got the idiot and my friend Frosso, the good man. I hope you and Mullet will be happy. Having lots of money will smooth many paths for you, you know? You won't fight over bills that need to be paid or wonder where your next meal is coming from. These things are important in life. But you must be like a hawk, keep an eye on the money so it stays safe and is not frittered away by stupid, frivolous spending. Mullet likes to show off so you must talk sense into him. You must always hold the purse. This is the key to your power.'

Anna's arms move with precision, parting sections of Ursula's hair then clipping them in swirls high on her head.

'Yes, I always wanted to be a hairdresser but I was not allowed. I had to care for my sick and wounded father who'd been shot, mutilated by the Germans during the war. They took pot shots at his legs like they did to poor old Hoppy. They are a race without humanity. They treated my father without mercy as if he were less than an animal. When his comrades found him shot to pieces bleeding down a hole, he was thrown over the shoulders of a Cretan partisan ... a saint ... and taken to hospital. It is there that the surgeons cut off his legs. My poor mother, a new bride and her man came back from the war half a man. You can't imagine her horror and she tried not to show it. She worked like a dog for us until she could stand no more and died out there in the olive groves one cold morning when I was just a child. Her heart gave out. I suppose the pain was too much, the kind of biting, brutal sorrow that never mends.

'So, *pethi mou, my child* that was my lot in life. Of course, as I got older, I stayed to look after my father. How could I abandon my only flesh and blood? I married yes, and he's not a bad man, he's just an idiot so I never got to be a hairdresser. Today I will show the world my talents through you! What do you think, Ursula?'

Anna throws back her head, releasing a joyous giggle like an excited pixie and then she stops, bringing her cheek close to Ursula's. The two women look at each other in the mirror and smile. Anna has felt like the mother of the bride since she forgave Mullet and Ursula's wild night of passion and they became respectably engaged. Once the *logo, word* has been given, all can be forgiven ... unless the wind changes. Then out will come the knives. Anna's spent weeks boasting around the village that she was the one that brought the couple together. Besides her love and loyalty to her father and Mullet and Ursula's successful union, these are perhaps her main claims to local fame, not dissimilar to us being THE AUSTRALIAN FAMILY, GREECE.

'Did you know that since the time of Homer, brides have threaded flowers through their long locks. So, before we finish our work of art this morning, let me put flowers in your hair because as from today you are one of us. Now you can see first-hand what a difference a few large beautiful blooms can make to a bride's appearance? You were a princess before but now you will see you are a queen, no? Now that your hair and makeup are finished, let's get you into your dress. When you put it on you must not let it ruin your hair or let your dress touch the ground. *Po, po, po.* Quick lift it up, lift it up and put it on very carefully, we don't want to ruin or crease anything.'

Anna clucks happily as she snatches fragments of notes from an old Corfiot wedding song that was sung and danced to on her wedding day. 'Wait, wait do not move ... here your hair, your hair. Some hair spray and of course some rose water. Rose water, it's for good luck, just like my little evil eye. I will pin it into the side strap of your gown. Here, stay still. Now look, you look beautiful.'

Ursula looks long and hard into the mirror, searching her eyes. Is today really my wedding day, she wonders? 'Yes, yes, I suppose I am quite beautiful today. I never think of myself that way, beautiful ... but today I will. Thank you for being here for me and allowing me to stay with you. You have been more than a mother to me.'

The two women embrace. 'Now, now, my child, this is not a time for tears, especially not on your wedding day. *Po, po, po!* You already have your work cut out for you marrying Mullet. Is he not a handful? It's time to think about making our way to the church. Where's that stupid husband of mine with the truck? I bet he still hasn't even fixed the gas bottle. But for now, let's forget the gas; first things first, he must get the bride to the church ... is this not right?' And the two women laugh nervously as they walk outside into the morning sunshine arm in arm, embracing the golden light of a new summer's day.

Chapter 37

The *Gamos*

Wedding services can be emotional gatherings for many different reasons. Feelings subdued to save face, or agitated and ready to cause a scene, I liken them to girdles that are too tight, high heels too high, ties too tight, stockings too hot. People perspire and endure, contemplating that delicious moment when they can return home, strip down and release the pressure points.

The air today is laced with the unique combination of garlic breath, incense, Chanel perfume and musty mothballs. It adds an intensity to the weighty atmosphere of the day. Orthodox weddings are formal events because marriage is a serious commitment. Services are long enough for any unwilling participant to exit at any time. But not today.

Ursula and Mullet are joined in matrimony in front of the community with Father George performing the service without the need for crutches. They say it's a miracle, especially after the christening. Those who didn't attend still think he miraculously lifted Ursula up and down single-handedly in and out of the christening font. Imagine that, without his bad leg collapsing beneath him!

Laughing, Anna said, 'If anyone is stupid enough to think that, then why should we tell them anything different? Let them think whatever they want. They are going to think what they want anyway. God never said it is my moral duty on this earth to advise people otherwise. Am I not right?' She has a point.

There is that look of resigned horror once again on Irene's face as she now sits in the church with her sister. Resembling a stuffed crinoline pork sausage in her tight dress and trying her best to hold in her stomach with little success, her cheeks have flushed to a scarlet pomegranate colour as perspiration accumulates below a nose that is firmly out of joint. The bride she had had in mind for Mullet sits tormentingly close to her, only a few rows away. Irene shakes her head with bitterness at the unfairness and tragedy of it all. A bloody *xeni foreigner*, and a *putana, prostitute, Po, po, po*! What's the world coming to?

Sister Agarpe sits with her hair piled up in a beehive-style hairdo, about which she smugly admits to using at least two cans of hair spray to achieve this engineering feat. Her young female friends compete to see who can use the most hairspray and get their hair to set the highest. They resemble little Everests perched ludicrously large on small brown and pink smiling faces marked out even further by bright blue-eyeshadows, misty pink lipsticks, dresses far too short to be considered respectable, bare ankles, jaunty heels, and small hand-held fans waving rapidly among the neat rows of pews.

Contrary to her sister, Agarpe is savouring the excitement of the wedding. Her eyes like a fox's scan the church for familiar faces and any eligible males.

Yet again, and with more frustration than ever before, Mum has resuscitated her famous but jaded caftan – how many more wears can she get out of that thing? I've been saying this for a long time now. It's like teenage acne: it just keeps popping up on important days. And me, well, I've managed to borrow a pair of Ursula's high heel shoes. George, the famous sandal maker in town, reputed by tourists from all over the world to be some sort of Greek shoe god, has resolved to add an extra puncture in the strap at the ankle to secure them for me. A pale pink dress with thin tie straps my sister abandoned long ago was found in one of my mother's forgotten drawers. I've revived it and it looks quite elegant on me. Even if I say so myself, I'm blossoming into an attractive young lady with my puppy fat having melted away long ago – thanks to our lean diet. How lovely to have a beautiful pale pink silk slip dress clinging in all the right places. My hair's grown too. I am able to successfully sweep my hair up into an elegant bun for today is, after all, a chance to look one's best.

Dad's stoic in his thinning black suit and narrow black tie. He, unlike many of the males at the wedding, has stuck to his word about fashion preferences and is steering clear of fancy flairs and platform shoes. The truth is he couldn't afford them anyway. Besides, standing over six feet tall, he has no real need for height enhancers. We've all noticed that with these new fashion trends that many people appear taller, their shoulders broader as excessively generous power shoulders become all the rage. Or are these physical changes just more miracles on this island of miracles?

The sound of the priest's commanding words, a voice that I have come to know so well over the years, falls into a hush as *psaltis* take their places chanting in deep tones that float as if curling like candle smoke through time to the beginnings of Christianity so long ago. A few recalcitrant free-ranging roosters ignore protocols and crow in the background.

The service is mesmerising and, for a while, time seems to stand still. Then, at the conclusion of the service, a couple of fiddlers play a fast-paced traditional Corfu wedding song as rice and flowers are thrown into the air. Mullet grabs Ursula's hand and they almost run out of the church and into the bright golden sunlight. I'm mesmerised by this music and every time I hear it I'm transformed for just a moment as all my senses conspire in sending tingles down my spine. I don't know why but it invokes something deep within me as if retrieving something lamentably absent from a past life into the present.

Church bells reverberate and there's a breathless jubilant feeling of exhilaration in the air. Then, just as quickly, there's a frantic rush for the farrago of transport available to ferry the guests to our villa. Ursula and Mullet speed off into their flower-covered Lotus as our family and extra guests shove one on top of the other into Mum's old car as Dad takes the wheel like a commanding chief of a discombobulated goat herd. Even Costas' motorbike from the 1940s, with its sidecar, has been pulled out of his barn, dusted off and polished for the event. The Kolonos Kid's here too but, for once, without his rifle or even his bouzouki. His eyes keep scouting wistfully the horizon as if seeking out Gran but she's long fled the country. Some villagers are so determined to get to the wedding reception that they have even borrowed a funny looking three-wheeled vehicle and loaded it to capacity with passengers. Hefty handbags, round rumps and lady's legs flashing far too much stocking board this strange little vehicle or mounting motorbikes. This is followed by louds bursts of rollicking laughter and blushes of bright beetroot.

The expanse of our garden is a fitting venue for a wedding with grounds big enough to accommodate long tables crowned with crisp white linen tablecloths and lengthy sprays of bright pink bougainvillea reaching like elongated arms along table tops. Dad's stoic portable record player still works after years of very rough handling and has been placed on a separate table ready to bash out the last of our surviving rather dismal collection of ancient record relics. Old chestnuts like Tom Jones's *Delila* and *The Green, Green Grass of Home*, the Seekers, *Gigi*, *Paint your Wagon* and a few local Greek popular tunes along with Mullet's request for the newlywed's, *Bridge over Troubled Water*. Across the hilltop their song will boom out when the bride and groom are ready to sashay across the garden executing their first dance as husband and wife.

As soon as I get back to the villa, I career along the wide long hall. It's crowded and there's a general feeling of chaos. I pass the kitchen and curiously stick my nose into the hot steamy room. It's as crazy as it is congested and inadequate. I'm told tempers have been flaring all morning. Waiters with mountains of plates zoom past and there are elevations of food and not enough counters onto which to place the dishes. In an attempt to resolve the issue, extra tables have been set up in the old library long ago stripped of Alexei's books and now hosting Mullets temporary sleeping arrangements.

'Youse better to make sure there's only vegetarian food at our reception. There better be plenty of it. It might only be vego but I won't have my guests going hungry!' Mullet warned.

Mum and Yorgan had nodded their heads in unified disappointment. But they'd been given a very generous budget. In fact, the sky's been the limit but, as Yorgan complained under his breath, 'Unless your guests are mountain goats or ravenous sheep, who cares how many truckloads of greens are available? The hillside should be filled with revolving lambs and chickens on spits.'

Helen, our one-time spinster landlady, is beaming. She's no fool. When the bouquet was about to be thrown after the church service, she'd strategically placed herself close to Ursula. She'd tactically elbowed any possible competition out of the way and, as she flew forward, she caught the bouquet as a loud roar of cheers from the villagers erupted in the air. Caught up in the excitement of the moment, no sooner had she grabbed the bouquet than Yannis, my very dear friend, the fisherman, plucked up the courage to ask her to marry him. Apparently, he'd been in love with her since they were at school together. My very dear humble friend never considered himself good enough but today under such an auspicious sky, he does. To me at least, it seems like another miracle.

Today, much like any other wedding, after the rounds of greetings and congratulations from the guests, the bridal couple lead the first dance with their song, *Bridge over Troubled Water*. Mullet directs a wistful smile in the direction of his mother in the hope that they can overcome their differences too by also using the song as a metaphor for their difficulties.

When the newlyweds resume their seats, inspired by the magic of the moment, Frosso pulls out a record of her favourite tango songs. With her head held high, she and Lefteri set the pace amid laughter and clapping around the garden. They revive all those memories I have of them, especially her serenading her chickens as the sun goes down back in their Pyrgi hamlet. And of course, I recall how on those hot Corfu summer nights she and Lefteri tangoed through the night on their front porch as I looked on, charmed by their energy and steamy passion. They are as much in love today as they always were.

There's something indefinably special about a wedding. Perhaps it's the sense of infinite hope … a deep yearning in us all for something … something indefinably wonderful, good and continuous. Then the moment is shattered, battered as an old van noisily veers, grinding its gears, up the hill and the fiddlers who had performed at the church earlier arrive to the jubilation of the guests. A band is quickly set up.

Dad's banal array of records, along with Frosso's tango temptations, are rapidly and guiltlessly given the flick in favour of the raw vibrancy of live music. As it turns out, this random bunch of hit-and-miss players can pump out most of the traditional favourites and a few western songs thrown in for good measure even if they get the words wrong. Could this be yet another miracle?

Father George, with incredible pep in his recovered step, leads a troupe of Greek dances beneath the olive trees. We could all learn a lesson or two from him on how to dance a proper Zorba dance, especially Hilary's ex-boyfriend Paddy, the heist master – that is if he hadn't nicked off, shooting through with her art collection.

But there's Dimitri charmingly holding Hilary's hand in the dance. Dad's chatting to Irene about the glitches of bringing up children and the many problems this entails. He says he gets annoyed when we speak Greek in front of him: he thinks we are deliberately leaving him out of the conversation. Well, we are but ... Consequently, his solution, like Mum's, was to ban all Greek from being spoken in the house years ago. But now we have mastered the fine art of Greek sign language. I discovered a copy of the delightfully illustrated book *Instant Greek* by William Papas and from there, there was no stopping my brother and me. The book has been subsequently hidden from my parent's curious eyes. I can't have him working out what we are saying. But I laugh remembering the time Dad excitedly hurried off to town to buy a chicken when we first arrived on the island. He ran around the butcher's shop flapping his arms, crying out, 'Chook, chook, chook', hoping to break all linguistic barriers until the butcher finally said in perfect English, 'Oh, but surely, sir you mean chicken?'

Dad and Irene look up as the dance changes and see Ursula leading the local village girls in a set of traditional wedding dances, hands hooked or joined at the waist, slim ankles flying with a torrent of laughter filling the air of this hot and heady afternoon. The stirrings of a smile finally edge the corners of Irene's habitually austere face as she realises she's finally home. With this knowledge, her eyes overflow with tears as she releases years of unexpressed grief at ever leaving her homeland.

As the afternoon wears on, Irene and Dad agree on at least two things: the younger you are when you learn to dance and acquire a language, the better. He looks over and sees Mum in her element overseeing the catering with Yorgan. They make a good team the pair of them with their crew of hired workers all smartly dressed in black and white. They can boss the hired help to their hearts content and leave everyone else in peace. Bliss.

Plates and glasses are filled and refilled. Tables are laden with cooked soy-vlaki's and vegi-vlakis while more turn on hot fiery spits above smoking coals. Large trays of vegetarian moussakas and pasta sit warming on the sidelines. There's a general grumble among the Aussie guests, namely us, that a couple of 'chops' on the BBQ wouldn't have gone astray.

Apart from Dad having a word with Father George, what can they do? Mullet refused to be moved on the meat issue. Dad whispers in Father George's ear, 'Father is there any chance of a few miraculous lamb chops from heaven? You know, the way they manifested bread and fishes back in biblical times, only this time with lamb and a few pork souvlakis?'

The priest smiles a wide and wise smile, looks toward the heavens and slowly shaking his head sadly replies via Stick the translator, 'No *fillos*. God is very busy fasting from meat today for some reason ... and for this, we are all very, very sorry!'

The three men laugh. But here's another miracle ... Christian and atheist clicking glasses.

Greeks are a dab hand at vegetarian dishes even if it isn't Yorgan's forte and, irrespective of the fact that it's his sister's wedding day, it hasn't stopped him throwing the F word around with agitated vigour. In his strong Swedish accent, he raves at Mum, 'I never wanted to cook this fucking vegetarian food, darlink. The whole fucking wedding party is a disaster! A fucking disaster. But, what can I do? I am fucking helpless, darlink, absolutely helpless.' While wailing theatrically, he throws his arms up in the air and seconds later recovers enough to reassemble himself into a dignified unflinching regal pose.

Laughing, Mum whispers: 'Well, darlink you better suck it up because there never was going to be any meat here. The cooked type or otherwise! Focus, man, focus. Your problem is you've been pinching too many artichoke bottoms.'

He looks at her sideways and, smoothing his chino pants with the palms of his artistic hands, he quickly catches on. Laughing hysterically, he cries out, 'Oh, darlink, you're so funny! I simply adore you! You guessed, yes, I'm a fucking fairy!'

'Well, darling, and now let me introduce you to Spiro. I don't think you attended Ursula's christening, did you?'

'Oh, yummy, I could crack a walnut with his arse; oh my God, it looks so deliciously tight.'

'Well, don't let me stop you,' laughs Mum.

Halva is served along with long trays of flaky filo pastry topped *bougatsa* sprinkled with fine icing sugar. As time transforms the muted light of the afternoon into a strawberry pink sky, the smell of cloves and olive wood smoke wafts through the air as fireflies flash, pulsating like tiny rapid heartbeats as the thump of discombobulated music prompts Mullet to stand up and cry out, 'Can youse stop the music please, just for a minute. I want to make a speech. I want to make a speech. *Skaste, skaste, shut up, shut up* everyone!'

Moments pass and then eventually there's a sort of Greek silence. Mullet gestures Ursula to move into the clearing and stand by his side. Leaning their bodies inward, they artfully position themselves so they are able to survey all their friends and family. Mullet clears his throat and with the usual topped-up glass in hand begins, 'I want to thank youse all for being here today for me and Ursula's special day. It means the world to us to have youse all here sharing in our wedding. As youse know, things started off a bit rocky, didn't they, Anna? Well, we won't get into too much detail about that now, will we? But I will say that was the morning I thought the gunshot I heard was you coming after me with a gun, but no, as it turned out that bullet was for poor old Byron, the billy goat.'

Mullet gives a relieved laugh as we watch on.

'Yep, it's been quite a journey for me and Ursula. I came into a bit of luck in London and, well, it turned me finances around for the better. When I knew I was financially secure I plucked up the courage to get the girl I love and that's of course me chick or I should say, me beautiful wife, Ursula. Contrary to popular belief, there's never been anyone else for me. I reckon I'm dead set lucky she said yes! I'd especially like to thank me Mum and Aunty for coming all the way from Australia to be here.'

The audience stay quiet as Mullet looks over and smiles with genuine gratitude at his mother and aunt before he continues. 'And, of course, Jo and David for kindly allowing us to use the grounds of their stunning villa for today's events. You and all your family, Father George, George, Anna, Stick and Took ... youse have been the best friends a man, or woman could ever have. So, I'd like youse all to raise your glasses. We look forward to having youse all in our life here on Corfu for many years to come. Now, before I sit down, I just want to add Ursula and I are flying to Athens in half an hour to start our honeymoon. I know a lot of youse will be disappointed about this but how can I have Ursula in me life without showing her where I come from? So, tomorrow morning we will be in Syntagma Square having a few drinks before we depart on a Qantas flight for Sydney tomorrow night. Now before you all book flights to join us … I hear all the flights tonight are full so we can't take an entourage with us. Sorry about that, folks. So, I'll say our farewells as Ursula and I have to leave now. So, everybody cheers and *yia sas*!'

As Ursula peers dreamily into Mullet's bloodshot eyes we all respectfully raise our glasses to the newlyweds. But beneath this show of pleasantries, Irene is furious. She tightens the fist of one hand beneath the table until her knuckles turn white. Now she won't have the satisfaction of shaming Ursula tomorrow morning before the entire village with the bridal sheets. It's a master stoke by Mullet and the tensions between individuals for the present at least will remain subdued, veiled under the magical spell of a wedding day. A charmed aura is cast over the hilltop as if a silent ovation from the bending boughs of olive trees blesses this almost timeless scene.

Chapter 38

The Night of the Flying Typewriter

One of twelve Olympian gods, Aries is the Greek god of violence and war. There's a wildness and unpredictable element to this god when he's cranky. He engenders cruelty and isn't liked by most of the other gods. His noble birth in the hierarchy of Greek gods puts him right up amongst the most important ones. He is the son of Zeus and Hera. And, while it has been mentioned before, locals sometimes call upon the ancient gods for help from time to time, they are wary of asking Aries to intervene. They prefer to use prayer as they have marvellous results with Saint Spyridon. If that doesn't work there's always evil eyes to ward off trouble makers.

In Greece evil eyes are available for sale everywhere for this very reason. They are the physical manifestation of powers that are invisible, like Aries. But while Aries may not be visible like evil eyes, he's always hovering, waiting for the right moment to pounce.

My parents don't believe in God or gods even though Dad may talk about them. Father George once told me, believing in something beyond one's self puts a lid on the ego, a moral cork in the bottle. The existence of a higher power places a pause or hold button on temptation so we may reflect; even stop our potentially odious deeds. Where would we be without a place to pause and stop? A place to consider consequences and turn situations around?

As time moves on, as it inevitably does, Aries still lingers and, even though hope fills the hearts of the Greek people and dramatic change comes to the country over the next few months, the anger and anti-junta political crisis following the 'Polytechneio' incident does not sit well with the Greek people. It hangs in the air like a rotting carcass. There is also the very real fear of a full-on war with Turkey, brought on by tensions stirred up by Ioannidis' frenzied fervour for *'enosis'* and his attempt to politically crush Archbishop Makarios of Cyprus. Over the next few months, Makarios wakes to find Greek military tanks on his front lawn and this has led to the invasion of Cyprus by the Turks. What was essentially a national matter with anger expressed by the Greeks targeting the junta has now exploded into a very dangerous international crisis. As a matter of urgency, Constantinos Karamanlis is returned to Greece from self-imposed exile in France. He's seen as a potential saviour, a man capable of turning the political tide to calm international and national tensions. Halt an all-out war between Greece and Turkey but also restore democracy to Greece. Quite a task for any man.

He arrives in Athens to a hero's welcome. The junta is overthrown and over the next few intense months, we see a restoration of civil order and liberty. Greeks who had been exiled return, perhaps none more famous or loved by the world than Mikis Theodorakis. With his return to Greece, people blare his music from loudspeakers in cities and villages all over Greece as they dance through the streets. There's a new exuberance and excitement filled with reignited hope for a better future. A short time later, Greece is formally recognised both domestically and internationally as a democracy. Communism is legalised and a referendum is held, resulting in Greece becoming a republic. These are optimistic times for the Greeks – perhaps not the Greek royal family, however. Within days many of those who had been involved with the junta are imprisoned. Some face the death penalty but over time these sentences are soon changed to life imprisonment. Rapidly the political world around us is filled with a new, stable and revitalised sense of renewal and optimism.

I live in hope. I hope that Dad pauses whatever is going on in his head and writes his book and that my parents stop arguing. But the dream is dying just as surely as the light fades at the end of each day. As the years continue to roll by and even with his teeth in, the tension between my parents jumps from niggly to explosive. Money is the problem. It's always the elephant in the room. I damn the drachmae and our lack of it. Inflation escalates in Greece. We are handcuffed here, unable to work because of our residency status. To get out of this mess, we need some kind of a financial miracle. The Greek authorities, irrespective of the restoration of democracy, say either you can afford to live in Greece or you can't and I get their point. They're right of course, and to a large degree control our ability to stay or go.

Each year as our Residents' Visas run out, Dad convinces the still very 'alien' Alien Police that we have enough money to stay. How he manages to do this is a mystery. Perhaps it's the way he stands as a warrior defending our stranded tribe, the way he stoically takes one for the team, fronting up at police headquarters irrespective of the fact that he is treated like a recalcitrant child. Dad explains to us, 'We expats all grumble among ourselves, of course, but we are powerless to complain to the authorities in case we are deported. It doesn't matter who's in power … so the lot of us sit outside his office resembling Sisyphus rolling the old stone up the hill every day only to have to do the same thing with the same stone for the rest of eternity.'

Anxiety drapes Dad's bright blue eyes as he describes how every detail of our lives is scrutinised by that unsmiling official. It's the same for foreign property owners, unless you are among the very wealthy foreign elites. Bank statements, passports are checked again and again. Questions, relentless questions. Yet, year after year, Dad convinces them we can afford to live in Greece. Even when he's convinced them, where does that leave us? Unconvinced? We're broke and vulnerable. And my parent's dream of an enchanting Greek odyssey – what of that?

Now we exist between myth and reality, tempered by my parents' consumption of alcohol and shallow reassurances. Our evening meals together under the fluorescent stars feel like tsunamis building force but tonight feels more ominous: a storm is definitely brewing. These long-time proponents of beans, bread and tomatoes jab at the lean pickings on tonight's menu. We kid's clown to ease the tension.

On an instinctive urge, I sense it's my turn to fan the sparks of strain in some other direction, release its grip on any lingering combustible material meandering between my parents. I pipe up, 'Katerina tells me an eccentric foreign woman who has moved in down the road soaks her vegetables in her bidet. Can you imagine? Last week Katarina said the old duck had her undies soaking in it ... now her cucumbers and tomatoes sit submerged in the stained and discoloured ceramic. Not only that but she uses her bidet like the French ... you know ... never uses loo paper. Talk about a multifunctional bidet.'

I hear expressions of 'tut-tut' as I'm tossed looks of eyebrow-lifting horror. Delighted I've eased the tension momentarily, I continue. 'She sleeps with potatoes seeding under her bed. Perhaps their sinewy roots will penetrate her mattress? Can you imagine if she woke up one morning and found herself wrapped in potato roots and couldn't free herself so she rotted to death in her bed, the roots sucking the life out of her? Katerina says she's even got putrid braids of rotting garlic and onions hanging along her dark, mouldy bedroom walls. There's barrels of olives and tall tins of olive oil used as furniture … she's topped them with planks of wood. Katerina says her room smells like the back of Thanasi's slaughterhouse on a hot day. She takes her lovers in there, into that room of hers. Villagers say some never leave! I wonder what's happened to them? Is she pickling body parts? Maybe she feeds them to her potatoes? Spooky, huh?'

The silence between my parents intensifies so I keep rattling on. 'When I asked Katerina why the woman stores her food in her bedroom, she said, "In case there's another war." In case the junta returns. If they do, she'll grab her food stash, run into the mountains and hide it down an old empty well she's staked out. Not only that, to save water she bathes in the same water she's used to mop her floors. Do you think there's going to be a world war if Turkey and Greece can't become friends?'

I'm not only thinking about the tensions in Cyprus, Athens and the Middle East as I sit and wait for an answer that doesn't need answering. Of course, and it's going to be right here and any minute now. The war between my parents. Mum's been stirring for hours and asks 'the' question with tilting sarcasm, the one she knows irritates Dad the most. It's a question she's asked many times before. This time however, time has moved on and our situation is desperate. She's had too many wines. Cruelly pressing the sides of an overripe honey dew melon with her nails, she strikes:

'How's the author coming along? You've grown a beard to look like a writer: hah, instead, your goatee resembles Byron the bygone, bah, bah. You're pathetic. Man, time is ticking,

ticking like a fucking time bomb. Bills are piling. The kids are sick of asking for credit … so am I!'

She lights a cigarette and inhales as if gulping a drink then continues to goad him. 'You haven't got the balls to write, have you? Bah, bah ….'

More drinks are poured. I wonder if this is for courage or it's a futile attempt to still the moment, dissipate the dark remanences of her mocking song. Perhaps any of these. Like my question about war, her question sits unanswered, menacing the air. Moments pass. I feel sick because I sense something ominous is coming, then I panic because I can't find a way to save this moment from its looming, unpredictable outcome. I search my mind but it's too late.

'Come on, where's your bloody book … you hopeless dud? Bah, bah black sheep have you any books?'

Dad's composure recedes at last like a tide before a tsunami as Mum stretches the lyrics of the nursery rhyme into a drunken lingering slur, cigarette in one hand, glass of wine in the other, meals left untouched. In a flash, the military man, that ghost I remember so well but have chosen to forget from the Melbourne days, re-emerges with a shout that scares the hell out of me. The serpent within him is aroused and with meticulous precision, he aims then fires, haunting words I can't forget from the past. Words retrieved from his well-stocked armoury of sayings once reserved for us, his subordinates …

'I kick where I see a head. I will always attack my enemies first because it's the best form of defence. You don't call me Dad; you call me sir when addressing an officer!'

Yes, these old well-worn words, terms and expressions most possibly used in military strategies but were chucked like incendiary devices into arguments and our hearts.

He yells, 'You wanted to leave Australia; you couldn't wait

to get away. Why? Why did you push so hard to leave? To come here? You ignored everyone's warnings. This was your fucking idea, you bitch. I'm no writer. You knew that all along. We've lost everything – our home – our friends – the children's education – all because you wanted to leave. Not me! Now most of our kids are stuck working illegally and scattered all over Europe. They could be arrested at any moment. I did all this to please you. Now we're stuck here in this vanquishing Greek nirvana. So, don't come the raw prawn and blame me. We're stuck-up shit creek in a barbed wire canoe without fucking oars because of you!'

Stumbling over her slurring words she's determined to impress us, her audience, show her virtue and shift the blame. 'You prick! Me? You hold me responsible! Oh, please! You wanted to get your sons out of Australia before they were drafted. You gutless shit, it's okay to send other people's kids to Vietnam but not your sons. Oh, no! You're just an old drunk ... look at you. A failure. Half a man! A dud. We moved here so you could fill up on cheap grog and suck on fags all day! Piss our lives up against a white-washed wall. That's the truth! You and your hedonistic dream ... I want to be a writer!'

Again, she mocks him laughingly. Half-consciously, she discards her plate as if following his actions and fills her wine glass again.

He releases a look that could scare horses, and devilish rods of ill-intent protrude outward on forks into the night light. I can't move.

He shoots back, 'You bitch! Once in a while you could think about calling me sir! I'm a military officer after all! A war hero. People respected me. But no, you don't. You never have. Our sons would have dodged the draft. The war's been finished for years. And you put me down in front of our children like I'm some piece of worthless shit! You and your panoply of demands. And there you go again, always the supportive muse! Anything I write you criticize. I've had enough of this bullshit. I'm no writer and you've always known it, you bitch!'

There's never a good time for a quarrel. They are always ill-timed, not just for the mutilated civilians on the sidelines but the soldiers too. I'm sitting in the cockpit of one unholy cockup with no place to dissolve into. And there's no way out. Then, in a late eruption of a word storm, adjectives fly back and forth as we kids sit unmoved, sweating in the night heat like unwilling spectators to something akin to a mean battle between sworn enemies. Could these two have ever been lovers?

Resembling a rumbling bull, he looks along the table for an object to hurl; his target: Mum. She's flouted enough cannon fodder to get him going. His red rage gains momentum.

About to discharge his charge at first, I think he's going to chuck a handful of olives or his uneaten plate of food, but no. My grandfather's typewriter sits beside him. In a flash fused by a fury likened to strikes of lightning firing from his gaze, he grabs the heavy machine and abruptly stands; hurls it across the tired outdoor table. It's on course for Mum's head.

Time stands still as the gravity of what's happening stuns us. She sees the typewriter's flying armour, letters a-jumble. Flashing in the fused air, the projectile resembles an aeronautical black battleship as it soars across the table towards her. She, in a quick jittery juggle with her wine-infected wits, manages to move aside, but only enough for the full impact of the object to hurtle past. The side of the typewriter strikes, clipping the edge of her forehead.

I feel sick. In this heated Hitchcock moment head and machine momentarily fuse. It could kill her! Even yet, her injury might kill her. Seconds later the typewriter continues on its course then crashes to the ground behind her head. Agile as a boxer egging for a fight, she rises to her feet, goading, seemingly untouched, victorious, spurring him on with hands and words, her eyes filled with mocking pointed hatred. It's as if she hasn't been hit.

I sit astounded, watching as the horror of the moment escalates before me. Scarlet liquid emerges, dribbling downward along the line of her contorted face, making her stop abruptly to wipe the gooey trickle. Her hand sweeps along its length, following its seeping path. She pauses from jeering for a moment to examine it. It's covered in blood. I release a muffled scream. Resembling an abstract by Picasso, her facial lines distort with red paint.

Horrified by what he has done, Dad stands to move toward her, pain infusing his face but he quickly changes his mind and backs away. Gutless, he's repelled by his actions and her hurling a new round of insults. Defeated, emasculated and unequivocally ashamed, he stumbles into the darkness heading for the villa. With shoulders and head slumped, his back becomes a shock-absorber warding off more of her insults. My father is a defeated man. But she's still thrusting swords into him like a vindictive victorious matador, the power of the moment gone to her head. The bloodied face that gave it all away is now a symbol of my father's weakness and of his ability to be evil and violent. As if expecting cheers from her adoring, mesmerised fans she's disappointed because she receives none. There will be no garlands or chaplets of laurels in her honour or his.

Attempting to further her cause, she screams out into the night after him, 'You fool! You're a pathetic loser. You were born a dud and you will always be a dud. You see, kids, this is your father – the man I stupidly married. A cruel and violent bastard! Couldn't organise a bloody chook raffle and now look where we are? Oh, Christ, kids ... look what your bastard of a father has done to us!'

Silence falls and Mum pushes me aside, away from helping her settle, wash and bandage her head. I sit under the stars for a while, shell-shocked by a night stripped of hope. In that mocking laugh of hers that tears like piercing barbed wire, something was spoiled. For the rest of my life, I believe her mocking laughter will be everywhere and in everything I think or ever do.

Chapter 39

In the Hands of *Hebe*

No one talks about the night of the flying typewriter the next day or any other day. It is as if it never happened. When I ask Mum how she is she replies irritably, 'I don't know what you are talking about?' as if the crusty blood-clotted wound on her head isn't there.

I repeat my question, 'Last night, Mum your head ... I can see it. Where Dad hit you with the typewriter, are you okay?'

With the sun up and first wine for the day in hand, she replies, 'I don't know what you are talking about .... you need to stop making up stories and causing trouble. In fact, I will rattle your chain, Missy, when I want you to bark. You are the reason I drink ... never forget that, you little shit. Now piss off.' Limply waving her hand as if dismissing me like a discharged servant, she gives me a look that convinces me that I am indeed the problem.

As enraged as I am because what I'd seen is denied, I don't challenge her. How can I? After all, my reality is shaky. Should I count the days assembled around unsteady moments like this? Denials ... lots of denials have messed with my head. It's a rocky and unstable ground upon which a child can build and shape a life. I say no more about her injury because what would be the point? I am frightened and singed by her vindictive moods and wounding words. What she will do next with our half measured, strained and clotted relationship. She's like a soldier marching out of step with my head and I rage inside because no one does anything about it. Least of all me.

I follow her instructions: 'piss off' and sit with my loyal dog Patch on the side of the hill in the supportive arms of a warm Corfu morning and glance toward Corfu's Prison Island feeling as much a prisoner as the men held captive on that speck of an island near the *Neo Limarni*. I wonder: am I going mad? The elephant in the room has come to sit beside me as my guts tighten. Did last night even happen? I recall seeing the film *Gaslight* and how that young woman was almost driven insane because her husband kept telling her she was imagining things, all the while he willfully and deliberately undermined her world. If this is what is happening to me, then why do I feel trussed like a Christmas turkey wrapped in guilt? Am I really the source, the culprit of Mum's drinking? If I am not, then why is Mum saying I am? I wonder what *Hebe*, the goddess of youth, would think of these scorched days of my childhood? Does she have the powers to restore moments in a child's life that are blatantly contradictory, confusing and profoundly disturbing? She serves nectar and ambrosia to Olympians; she's the restorer of youth so might she do the same for me before my youth fades with the rapid passing of time?

Maybe these moments of sadness and insecurity could have been avoided if my parents adopted the miraculous orbs of worry beads instead of cognac, ouzo or whatever's on tap. Now that's a thought! Yes, worry beads rather than pointing the bone at me like the Aborigines when they want someone to die of guilt. I die many times over in my heart, distilling the things that are said and done, and other violent experiences best left in the past. Perhaps when we initially crossed the northern frontier borders and entered sun-filled Greece and gone shopping for the first time, could worry beads with their smooth texture, and rhythmic ways have shooed away their worries? Yes, those nebulous mythologised stringy adult soothers. Those tiny Greek heroes of a sort, perhaps they could have come in handy if only my parents, like the wise Greeks, had given them a fair go instead of tossing them away. Dad's beads eventually ended up in the *Nou Nou Gala* cardboard box in the kitchen along with the rest of his rejected words and failed book attempts, life's opportunities thrown in a Greek milk box of a bin only to be incinerated in the back garden.

After a storm it might seem as if nothing can be salvaged from the ruins but in the aftermath of any terrifying gale, there is an unnerving calm. Things settle and that's what emerged after the night of the flying typewriter, a persistent unsettling stillness. My parents' relationship morphed into what it had always been, only now the heat was turned up just that bit higher as a constrained form of functional tolerance straddled the gaping fault lines. There were, of course, the occasional shots of sarcasm targeted like sporadic gunfire at one another, at all of us. But for the most part what sat unresolved in the days and years that followed was avoided as a deferred reality sat unnervingly suspended, waiting for enough pressure to build up and explode again. But, like all the other arguments that had gone before irrespective of how traumatising they had been, they'd always be denied or dismissed as simply farts in a windstorm, followed by warnings to never speak of them again.

We moved from Villa Kapodistria a year or so later into a very comfortable villa in Perama. What we'd lost in terms of charm, grandeur and character, we gained in extra bathrooms, modern conveniences in the kitchen and a new part of the island to explore. In the meantime, I slipped away from Corfu for a while. On the face of it, it seemed like a good idea to follow some of my older siblings to Dublin and so, at the age of fifteen, I moved to Ireland. I worked in the fashion industry before I returned to Corfu a year later. I'd missed Greece and back on Corfu I managed to work under the radar of the Greek authorities as a tour guide, but the wages were shocking; in fact, not much better than Dublin's.

Another year or so passes and from Perama we rented a small apartment in Corfu town. It was here in this noisy apartment with its hard cold surfaces, steep steps and tiny box-like rooms that our lives were stripped of those wonderful views of the Albanian mountains or *Pontikonisi, Mouse Island* and we were reduced yet again to an even more basic level of survival.

The idea of returning to Australia was still out of the question, and I recall an aunt arriving from Australia much to my mother's horror. Screaming and shouting, Mum let us know that as far as she was concerned her sister's arrival couldn't have occurred at a worse time. Why hadn't she visited when we lived on the stunning Ipsos coast or Villa Kapodistria, just not this poky, sterile and characterless, noisy cheap flat? The awkwardness of the situation was not helped by the fact that the two women were never close, or so Mum said. But her sister cared enough to want us all to go back to Melbourne where my mother could get proper treatment for her eyesight which was becoming a serious problem. I could go back to school or find a reasonable job. We could go back to our family. But as much as she begged my parents to leave Greece, they insisted on remaining on Corfu.

This small uninspiring modest flat would be my last home on the island. In the end, I had to release Corfu and all the hopes that went with it, along with the friends I had made over the years. As it turned out with life's strange twists of fate, many friends I'd never see again. With this acceptance that my Corfu days were over, so went the many things that I loved about it. What is it about the mundane moments that we take for granted and why do they cling indelibly? – those simple familiar everyday rituals and experiences that separate Greek life from any other life: the sound of Greek radio in the morning pumping out the national anthem; news readers speaking *katharevousa*, a language I could never quite get my head around but loved anyway and now *Demotiki*; the rich aromatic smell of strong Greek coffee, toasted village bread, marble counters, *terrazzo* floors, chaos and anarchy, the slower pace of life and most of all, the opportunity to debate everything because everything is of interest to the Greeks. They are a race with opinions and they don't hold back on them. How wonderful ...

But sadly, I left my friends sitting in a tiny café by the harbour on a rainy morning, the chill kept at bay by the warmth of their comforting words and assurances that we'd all meet again. Somehow, I wasn't convinced. It's easy to pretend and smile on such occasions but the truth as I understood it was that lots of people come and go with the ebb and flow of the tourist seasons on this island, and with the struggles most of my expat friends experienced over the years. Corfu was a place very few foreigners stay forever; the odds are stacked against them.

Mullet and Ursula made the early morning trip in from Saint Marcos to say goodbye as did Dimitri from Gouvia. He'd wanted to leave with me, or so he said. Picking me up at the town flat, I bid my goodbyes to my parents – they didn't like farewells so didn't come down to the port. As for Dimitri, I knew he'd never be able to leave the island and it wasn't only because there was an impending court case hovering in the not-too-distant future for him. There had been an accident at his furniture factory, a young apprentice arriving early in the morning had slipped while cleaning sawdust from one of his huge woodcutting machines. The boy had lost his balance; his foot knocked the start button of the saw, the roar of its engine deaf to the boy's cries, it did what it does every day and began slicing. That same day Dimitri rushed to tell us, his face white with shock and horror knowing only too well that under Greek law, he would face charges, considered guilty as the owner of the factory until proven innocent. He could now not predict his future.

Once at the harbour, he stood distracted, counting my few bags over and over again, making sure I hadn't left anything in his car while Mullet and Ursula ordered ouzos and had them lined up in a row on the white marble table top among the jumble of bodies, luggage and the disarray of tables in the small cafe. I joined in knocking them back like tequila slammers, probably as many as they did. I don't remember. But I do remember I didn't want to leave my friends, but there was no other way. My head swayed like the shifting boats and ferries tossing at the edges of the new port opposite.

Soon, with the sound of heavy clanking chains and ferry horns filling the air, my friends and Corfu faded into the distance as the morning light shifted to reveal a dark ominous sky. A flotilla of white-winged seagulls rose sharply through the salty mist and cried into a cold wind and then it was all gone.

I moved back to the busy heartland of Dublin's inner city where the retail shop floors, sounds and smells of urban life shaped the next five years of my working life. As kind and wonderful as the Irish people were, it felt like a half measure of a life. Warmth appeared in the smiles of my Irish friends or beside firesides – apart from that it was a cold place. How many times had I put washing on the clothesline to dry but by the next morning my clothes had mutated into something more akin to frozen surfboards of various colours and sizes? In those moments I'd unconsciously reflect fondly on the Corfu days, those now extinguished years on that beautiful sun-filled island. A humming Marietta would come to mind, her laughter and the smell of the sheets, sun-kissed and fragrant, perfumed by a mix of lemon and orange blossoms. It dawned on me that we'd only been living in Greece for a couple of years when, as a family, our spell at Pyrgi proved to be the last time we'd all be together as a family. Corfu had unwittingly been the setting for our unintended but necessary fragmentation. Who could have imagined that this would happen when we set sail from Port Melbourne full of nervous anticipation about the future as we pulled out to sea bound for Southampton? Dad and Mum stayed on Corfu for eight years before they moved to Dublin to take up residence in my sister's artisan cottage in the Liberties. After living in Europe for eleven years, I returned to Australia. Once back home, it took a while but eventually, I discovered a few tragic truths about my mother.

Chapter 40

Giving Up the Ghost

It wasn't easy learning about Mum's past but eventually those pieces of information spilled out, but only by accident. Only then could I give up her ghost and begin to understand her hostility toward me, toward the world. Ironic that the truth was leaked out by a close family member over far too many drinks – a recurring scenario in my family – to another close relative. Once out, the news ricocheted down the line of siblings faster than a hungry Aussie chasing the only lamb chop at a BBQ, identifying those who had known for years. These were the relatives who had, over time, morphed into virtual strangers.

Upon reflection, it explained in my mind, why for a decade my immediate family (I had married and had a daughter by this time) experienced exclusions from family get-togethers for there were those who were invited and those who were not, based on who knew. I suppose it was inevitable with the disclosure of the truth and the post-mortem that followed, it would do little more than tragically fragment any remaining trust that had held our scattered family together for all those years.

When I eventually found out the truth, I struggled to catch my breath. I wept for my mother and wanted answers. By the same token, I was also outraged by her hypocrisy. Who was the woman I'd grown up with? All those years of bullying and shaming me, her above-reproach and clean-cut image which she'd projected so convincingly to the world now seemed jarringly outrageous in hindsight. Even so, disappointingly not all the puzzle was able to be explained because too many years had passed. However, the reason why Mum pushed so hard to leave Australia now seemed obvious. Well to me, anyway.

Anonymity.

But as luck would have it, by the time I discovered the truth both my parents had died. Now I could never sit quietly with either of them and talk about what happened. If a way to the truth had been opened before Mum died, I believe things could have been very different. But most of all, I think it would have made her life less traumatic. She could have finished her days in peace surrounded by love, but I don't think Mum could risk sharing her pain. Upon reflection, there is not a single moment when I would not have wanted to find out what happened to her instead of wondering for most of my life what was distressing her.

Perhaps Mum thought people would reject her if they knew about her complex past; leave her meandering like an outcast. If only she'd have had the courage to unlock and let go of her fears; join the club and admit she was human; less than perfect like the rest of us. Maybe then she'd have had a chance to be happy in her few remaining years; perhaps even repair our cracked Humpty Dumpty family and put it all back together again.

But it seems to me that Mum is a product of history having lived through a time when shame and fear quenched the thirsts of the bigoted hypocrites in authority, the medical institutions, churches and a narrow-minded society that had the control and authority to interfere in vulnerable women's lives. In Mum's era, people didn't talk about a lot of things, especially the taboo subject of illegitimacy. In fact, even now much silence surrounds this part of Australian history. Today people now openly talk of the Stolen Generations of Aboriginal children who were so tragically and wrongfully ripped from their mothers and families. However, few people speak of the many "Stolen White Australian Children".

The trauma experienced by single mothers who were coerced and forced to give their babies away can never be fully understood by those who have not experienced this loss. It has come to light that many of these women experienced long-term trauma. Some were drugged, shackled to beds, had their breasts bound, told their children had died and were medicated in order to stop them from lactating. Many were humiliated, lied to, not informed of their legal rights. Numerous women experienced toxic coercion and were demonized, labelled as sinners and evil for being unmarried and pregnant. The paralysing effect of such a traumatic forfeiture for these women from the loss of their children must have been devastating because in so many cases, the unresolved and repressed impact of this loss was left to ruthlessly meander unchecked through their lives and those of their families because of the secrecy and shame surrounding these policies.

Like a complex jigsaw puzzle, I've tried to piece as best I can the events surrounding some of my mother's past and what caused her depression and erratic moods and actions. This has not been easy because those who might know will not tell or are genuine in their ignorance. However, emerging from the past are three brothers – three brothers I didn't know I had. They were born between 1947 and 1951. Were two of my brothers removed soon after birth under Australia's "Removal Policy," taken rather than relinquished by my unmarried mother and subsequently adopted? I have come to understand that up to 250,000 white babies were adopted under Australia's brutal, unethical and coercive practices that were endured by mothers impacted by these forced adoption and removal policies between 1940-1982. (Hannan. L, *Sydney Morning Herald* 2010). These policies of "Forced Removal" have, in many cases, indelibly affected unmarried mothers, fathers, adoptees and their siblings. Such incidents of "Forced Removal" are now often referred to as Australia's "Stolen White Generations."

The long-lasting trauma for these women and girls often manifested into post-traumatic stress disorder, pathological, inhibited, traumatic, disenfranchised or delayed grief, their pain minimalised, hidden. Some women were unable to share their pain because of shame or in case they thought they wouldn't be believed. The impact on women's mental and physical health, the result of these policies, was often chronic and is now recognised, along with other periods in Australia's history, as one of our nation's most shameful eras.

Because of the mystery surrounding the births of my two eldest brothers, and my New Zealand brother, did my mother suffer from cumulative grief, the result of multiple losses? To my knowledge, she never had professional counselling. Did this result in a form of long-term, silent and painful unresolvable grief? I believe it's very likely that the consequences of this type of grief had, at various times, adversely impacted the relationships between all my family members. I cannot but wonder how many daughters' lives have been unintentionally plundered by their traumatised mothers' obsessive fears, bullying and abuse, ensuring that they don't have the same experiences as their mothers. How many of these traumatised women consciously or unconsciously passed on their trauma to the next generation? Its harm is deep and often incalculable.

Life very likely descended into a living hell for many unmarried women in similar circumstances to my mother, confronted as they were with society's demonising attitudes towards them. Victim blaming back then was something akin to a national pastime, and it proved to be tragic for our relationship. Her trauma projected into the very heart of our relationship with her slanted perception of women and girls, raving on about all females being inferior to men, born dirty, shameful, sinful and immoral creatures. I can now see why so much of my childhood innocence was torn to shreds by her unfounded accusations, slurs and disturbing behaviour.

Tragically, Australia's "Removal Policies" continued through into the early 1980s when over the years eventually the laws changed in each state. These women, after the loss of their children, were simply told to get on with it ... their gouged-out lives. Sadly, by virtue of circumstances, I will never be able to stitch the few fragments that remain of this patchwork of my mother's life back together.

Having had two baby boys removed under these policies in Victoria between 1947 and 1949, my mother, then still single, found herself pregnant again in 1950. She met my father and shortly after the two of them decided to leave Australia. They'd made the hasty decision for Dad to join the New Zealand and UN air force. Shortly after their arrival in New Zealand, they married. He was away serving in the war in South Korea during most of Mum's third pregnancy and when my third brother was born. Dad had left for Korea only two weeks after they'd married so Mum was left alone in New Zealand.

Mum would tell my father and an aunt that the child she was carrying had died, saying she'd had an ectopic pregnancy. My father thought it was his child who had died in New Zealand in 1951. However, without my father's knowledge, my mother secretly had this boy adopted. Years later, in the 1990s and after our return to Australia, this child, now a grown man, would come looking for her. He would find her and Mum would deny to my father that this person standing on the doorstep was her son, irrespective of the fact that the adoption papers had her signature on them. Her son was told to go and never come back.

It would not be until 2011, after my parents' deaths, that I learnt I had two brothers in Victoria and a brother in New Zealand. My brothers in the eastern states eventually made contact with me but details about my New Zealand brother were kept from me by a sibling who had met him the day he'd turned up on my parent's front doorstep years earlier. Once I found out about my New Zealand brother, I was hurt by the secrecy surrounding his existence, and endeavoured to find him through the New Zealand courts.

With the assistance of a social worker in Auckland helping me navigate my way through their legal system, I was eventually given access to my brother's adoption papers. I was however, given no information about where he lived. This I had to discover myself by going over his birth and adoption records and using the only information my sister had about this brother. In a Eureka moment, I eventually found my New Zealand brother and was able to speak to him. In a very emotional conversation, he told me he'd been trying to find me for years. At one stage he'd even hired a private detective but my married name was the stumbling block.

Regarding my two Australian brothers born between 1947-1949, these boys were most likely taken from my mother by force shortly after birth. Of course, I don't know exactly what happened as mum is dead now and so much time has passed. Tragically there is still too much silence surrounding these policies and what happened inside these hospitals and institutions. However, when Mum gave birth to her first three children, she would have been told that the adoption laws would not allow her to be identified as the mother of these children ... ever. This heartbreaking confirmation would have given her a chance to get on with her life and try and heal her pain. She'd have been assured of anonymity. However, this was not to be. In the mid-1960s pressure was building for Australian State and Federal Governments to change the forced adoption laws and allow adoptees to find their birth mothers, and mothers to find their children. Petitions for this increased throughout the 1970s until it finally became law in the late 1970s and 80s. New Zealand would also change its laws.

As the years went by did Mum panic in case her identity was revealed to her first three sons? Would they try and find her? As much as she may have wanted them back in her life, did this fill her with crippling fear and dread? What would Dad say? Another concern for her would have been that her maiden name varied by only one letter from her married name. However, I have jumped ahead of myself, for these things I would not discover for many more years.

In the meantime, in the early 1950s after the secret adoption of her third son, Mum had gone on and created a new life for herself with my father; moved back to Melbourne from New Zealand and had five children with Dad. Throughout the 1960s, was Mum then filled with dread when she heard the news about the adoption laws being reviewed? Did this weigh heavily on her? Was this why she wanted to get away from Australia in the late 1960s as fast as she could? Australia was in the mood for a change of government; Whitlam was becoming increasingly popular with what seemed like new, even radical ideas after twenty-three years of conservative government. Mum hated the Labor government and their ambitious policies.

After we left Australia in December 1969, Whitlam, once

elected in 1972, introduced a raft of policies for women, including the single mother's benefit; removed sales tax on the pill and installed an advisor of Women's affairs to the Prime Minister. Was Whitlam going to change the adoption laws too?

For Mum, did Greece seem the perfect solution? It was a cheap place to live on Dad's pension once he'd retired. Indeed, no sane person would come looking for her. With a politically combustible situation that could turn into a civil war, indeed it was a dangerous strategy for our family, let alone anyone else. And then later in Greece, dealing with her fears about our often-desperate financial circumstances, the volatile military junta struggling to maintain power and Greece on the brink of war with Turkey over the Cyprus conflict, her vulnerable mental state, could she, this wounded phoenix, ever hope to rise above the tragic ashes of her past?

After their years in Greece, my parents, like me, also moved to Dublin and then a few years later returned to Australia. In Dublin, my sister was selling up so they could no longer remain in her artisan cottage in the Liberties and renting elsewhere in Ireland was far too expensive. My parents had no other choice, they finally relented, deciding to go back to Australia. Mum was furious about this; she did not want to return to Australia. But with no other choice, upon their return to Australia from Ireland, my parents made Perth home rather than Melbourne, which was a surprising move given that all our relatives were in Melbourne. Could my parents have been uncomfortable about the failure of their Greek island dream, Dad not producing a book, the return of the prodigals so to speak, or was it because in Victoria, changes to the adoption laws were racing ahead?

Mum's first-born sons could still be living there. Yes, even though my parents came home to Australia with little more than a suitcase each and a few tea-chests of personal items, Melbourne seemingly was not an option and Perth became their new home.

These were difficult times for my parents as they were too old to re-start their careers. Anyway, shortly after their arrival back in Australia, Mum would be considered legally blind. It seemed to me ridiculous that they didn't reunite with family in Melbourne, yet after a few wines, weirdly plausible. After more wines, completely plausible, their dislodged lives so often precariously allied with and seen through the distorted prism of a glass.

But then too my childhood had been steeped in strange, weirdly plausible reasons for why all sorts of things happened. The weird weirdly enough morphs into the norm after a while. So firmly did I, even as an adult, hold on to their peculiar explanations about all sorts of things, believing I was not being misled. I had to hold onto something. Or was I imagining it all? After all, my self-belief had gone through the wringer on more than a few occasions. The truth is, I'd blame myself rather than entertain the idea that my parents were covering something up. This I put down to the unconditional trust and belief vulnerable children and young teenagers have in their parents, especially if they find themselves threatened with being abandoned alone in Europe. They may turn inwards, as I did, and learn to dislike themselves and not necessarily their parents. My mother's acts of marginalising and treating me mean kept me keen and it lasted our entire relationship. I blamed myself back then because I ached for her love and approval, desperately clinging, wanting to fit in.

Upon their return to Australia, my parents didn't rectify the mistakes on my birth certificate with the authorities even though I pleaded with them to do so. For me, the mystery remained and, over the years, it compounded my crippling fear of abandonment. However, irrespective of the confusion and fear I felt, I knew it wasn't normal. I was determined to find its corrosive root cause in order to understand myself as much as my mother. When my daughter started school, I decided to go back to school, finish where I'd left off at the age of twelve. After successfully completing a university entrance course, I went onto to complete two degrees.

In the meantime, and in my parents' final lonely years in Perth and struggling again with their finances and poor health, I know they'd yearned for Greece even though their lives on Corfu had been complex and difficult. They missed the holiday lifestyle of the island, the continuous flow of interesting people coming and going, the cheap grog and cigarettes. They felt the Perth seaside suburbs somewhat soulless compared with the deeply seductive coastlines of the Ionian islands, dull compared to the throbbing excitement and sound of the bouzouki beckoning from a nearby smoky Corfu *kafeneon* or a stroll along the romantically captivating *Liston*. And what of the narcotic pull of air bursting with the fragrant perfumes of Greek spices and herbs floating on the breeze through the narrow, ancient Venetian laneways to the sun-kissed *agoras* in Corfu town? They even missed the simple things like their morning banter on the Pyrgi waterfront with old Yannis, the fisherman, those conversations always animated and open to hilarious misinterpretations. There in Dad's top spot to jot beneath the gentle dappled dipping drapes of the ancient olive trees in our garden with a *Maestro* breeze coming in from the west, and like a cool fabric, wrapping itself around my parents' bodies on a summer's day.

With a runaway mind in those final lonely days of their lives, they hungered for the glorious spectacle of the changing colours of the mainland mountains of Albania and Greece as the light shades shift inevitably, giving way to the day as time invariably moves on. And Dad with his memories of Mum with her arms wrapped around his neck in a rare expression of affection, peering curiously, hopefully over his bent shoulders as he typed under the olive trees. I wonder … did this shapeshifting of images in their minds release, momentarily at least, the valve that held back the pain and torment that so overwhelmed their failing hearts? Did Dad realise Mum had lied to him about the adoption of the child in New Zealand? Did this break his heart? Did he know about her other two sons, not far away?

When she was dying, he didn't want to see her in hospital, nor did he attend her funeral. Perhaps these doubts lingered deeper than we can ever imagine. At the time, I didn't understand Dad's coldness toward her. In my parents' efforts to emulate the lives of George Johnson and Charmaine Clift in Greece, did Dad see more painful parallels with their lives than he could ever have imagined even though he never became a novelist?

In 2013, on the 21st of March, long after my parents' deaths, Prime Minister Julia Gillard delivered a groundbreaking speech in the Australian Parliament. It was a National Apology on behalf of the Australian government to those impacted by the forced and shamefully brutal adoption or removal policies and the pain and suffering these caused. It's heart breaking that Mum never lived long enough to hear this long overdue apology. It's incredible that it took a Labor government to do it, a political party my mother hated her entire life.

Chapter 41

Pebbles from Pyrgi

'Come to the edge,' he said.
They said: 'we are afraid.'
'Come to the edge,' he said.
They came.
He pushed them ...
and they flew

(Guillaume Apollinaire)

Today, I'm on Corfu and amble along Pyrgi Beach feeling the swaying shift of smooth, sun-bleached pebbles loosely shuffling beneath my feet. The sky is blue and as cloudless as I remember from all those years past. I recognise the sound of the familiar liquid lap of the rhythmic summer tide and recall in these same waves my childhood flowing in and out like living breaths released from this forever shoreline. I think of my family. How we once lived in this beautiful place so far from what might have been a conventional and perhaps predictable life in the Melbourne suburbs.

Oh, what a life we had in this simple yet majestic place. We are immortalised forever for few, if any, other Australians shared our unique world beside Pyrgi's waters amidst such political instability, family tensions and entanglements in those early years of the 1970s.

As we anchored ourselves into the multi-facetted spheres of hamlet and village life, the local folk unfurled their arms welcoming us as only Greeks know how through the ancient promise of *filoxenia*. Perhaps at a subconscious level goodwill was ensured because of the Australian soldiers who had served, as both my grandfathers had done, fighting against the Turks in WWI, or the many others in Greece against the Germans and Italians in WWII. It may also have been because of the numerous Greeks who had prospered and settled happily in Australia. Whatever the reason, we were accepted along with our joint peculiarities and eccentricities.

As time went on, we were often affectionately referred to as the *"Ta kali, ala trelie Australasous, the good, but mad Australians"*, for Greece by its very complex nature has the power to challenge you to the edge with all its daily crazy twists, frustrations and joys. But for all this too, I have enormous affection for the Corfiot people.

I glance along the beach where the Bogdanos Hotel used to be. Now a repurposed building, I remember as a child I'd sit on the bleached bench in that kitchen and chat to the animated kitchenhands in the daily chaos of them preparing meals for their mostly British package-deal hotel guests. Some days a live wet octopus, at first tickled and teased, was pulled fearlessly from a watery bucket squirming with other pulsating octopi. Grabbed by its rubbery neck, the creature's eyes were calmly sucked from its head as it withered helplessly in the kitchenhand's gripping hands. I'd sit fascinated as the hard centre of the creature's eye was spat like a missile into the air, ricocheting off the tiled kitchen walls to the amusement of the rest of the kitchen staff. Black ink trickled down the side of the kitchenhand's smiling mouth as she too joined in the fits of laughter. Teeth-stained fluid black; it was as if she'd eaten too much soft licorice. Then she'd suck out its other eye.

Now a safe distance from those squirming octopi, I can smile at these flashbacks from a vanished past.

It's whispered through what is left of the old village that the hotel has been transformed into the exclusive private residence of a Middle Eastern sheik. I'm not surprised. Around the many postcard bays below Mount Pantocrator live countless rich and famous people in this stunning setting. Yet, the roads through the mountain range where the groves meet the ocean are still pitted with deep cracks and holes. That's the irony of Corfu: some things never change. Yet, this is considered an exclusive part of the island. It's not the inexpensive part my parents hoped it would be all those years ago. Beauty sets its own price.

Back along the beach, I move to the spot where undulating rocks arranged in a horseshoe shape provide a small secure sanctum where rowboats are moored and leisurely venture back and forth with the rhythmic tide. This is where we once kept Hercules and where Yannis the fisherman with his twirl of a cheeky black moustache, showed me how to expertly gut fish with one finger. On other days he'd thump and slap octopi to tenderise their tentacles on a long ago nominated round shaped rock. This rock is now as smooth as polished marble by centuries of belting and bashing fidgeting tentacled flesh from surrounding waters.

But he's gone – kind old Yannis – that tall lovable figure on the beach with his patched rolled-up baggy blue trousers, crooked captain's hat and enormous toothy smile. He now lies in a graveyard somewhere on Corfu pushing up daisies with my other friends – Marietta, Anna, Helen, Frosso, Hoppy, Theo, Katerina's parents and so many others. Even old Ajax the donkey has gone, buried somewhere along with my lamb and dog Patch. Dimitri's factory also lies empty, its doors bolted and the building left to deteriorate at the entrance of Mandooki. I don't know what happened to him and I heard Ursula and Mullet moved on. They didn't put down roots after all but decided to rent out the villa at Saint Markos and begin a new life somewhere in Sweden. Katerina too has moved on but she and her sister have developed their parents' land by the bay into rooms for lease to holidaymakers. Her parents' humble home where we spent so many happy hours now stands dilapidated and abandoned at the rear.

Pausing for a moment to bend on the beach opposite her villa, I select a smooth pale pebble from the familiar tide-line and greedily clasp it tightly in my fist, drawing it close to my heart. I'm seeking something. In squeezing it tight, I hope against hope that once upon a time each member of my family and all my friends had stepped upon or touched it and now I'm holding a fragment of them. I steal the precious trophy into my pocket for safekeeping, a touchstone to preserve forever. It will secure my papers as I write, in the same way a similar pebble held secure the pages of my father's words in letters home to Australia as he sat under the now uprooted olive trees in our old garden across the road. They, like the verve that ran through the veins of our Pyrgi villa, are gone. Helen's olive grove too – that place where Mum saw my grandmother's distorted face in the spooky shape of the ancient olive tree's grey trunk. All swept aside now making way for progress; just like Anna and Helen's villas. Much like Mum's reverie about Dad becoming a writer. Now all gone.

Is there a place along this coastline where time hasn't disfigured those beloved places from my childhood, like our old villa and the ancient grove that had stood for centuries on the block next door? Of course, there is. Here … all along this hauntingly beautiful shoreline. It's here I feel the presence and very essence of an enduring past. I confess it's hard to hold back feelings of melancholy as my eyes trace the pier where we as children careered off its bleached creaky end, performing bombs and excruciating belly-whackers.

I remember how we rose up through the Ionian like jubilant young dolphins breathless for air and laughing. Imitating Neptune's offspring, we'd burst through a hail of water, our bodies armoured, wrapped in liquid. Up we'd go merging with a brilliant symphony of sunlight. We'd be dazzled by the vast mountains of Albania, the peaks of *Pantocrator*, and a blue, blue sky that seemed to go on forever. But with every summer comes its end along with our childhood days. Like today will soon end.

As I amble toward what remains of Pyrgi village, I pause before the small roadside shrine. Miraculously it's still here. I make a mental note of how many times I had passed it as a child as I carried shopping home from Hoppy's *kafeneo* eating my small sweet reward. Through the shrine's small hazy glass window, I see an ancient olive oil lamp winging flickering light onto an old icon. It is as if it is sending forth a final farewell to my mother's secrets. It's a poignant moment as I send forth a prayer for Mum's first child, the brother that died just as we found one another, but sadly never met.

The wise old all-seeing and knowing *Pantocrator* up there on the mountain juggling for primacy with the other gods knew this all along. He understood that one day Mum's story would see the light of day. I believe he must have known that one day I'd understand her inner torment, especially why she held the brothers I grew up with so tightly, pushing me away in favour of them. Truly for her it must have been in those dark cavernous moments of inner torment that she believed they too could be torn from her arms. I see now that the truth was always in those deep, sad green orbs of her eyes.

Today on Corfu, my only wish is that my recently discovered brothers could have been here to enjoy the best of those days with us, especially with their mother. What I wouldn't give for them to have been where freedom spreads its wings along this shoreline and to have moved in motion with the heartbeat of this captivating island when we were children; this playground of beauty in all its alluring manifestations. All refracted now on this wonderous Matisse blue canvas of stirring waves before me. If only Mum could have held on to my brothers; if only they could have known the Greek people as I do. And for all of us to be set adrift in a pool of joy upon this sublime sun-lit pallet. These thoughts will always remain in my dreams for I can only wonder at the incredible memories we'd have shared.

The End

About the Author

Elizabeth Pappas was born in Melbourne and now lives in Perth, Western Australia. Her family moved to Corfu in April of 1970 during the peak years of the Greek Junta, right-wing military dictatorship. Some of her family returned to Australia in 1981 after a brief spell in Dublin. On Corfu, Elizabeth's formal education ended abruptly at the age of twelve, but she continued her studies in Australia in her thirties. Becoming an anthropologist and sociologist, she worked with tertiary students who were studying Indigenous Health and Community Management and Development at Curtin University. Pursuing her postgraduate thesis research into Byzantine and post-Byzantine icons, Elizabeth has lectured extensively on these topics, curated exhibitions, founded, and was President of the Icon Society of Australia Inc. for nine years.

In pursuing her passion for writing, in 2017 Elizabeth founded Chapters for creative writers where she facilitates this fun and talented group. Chapters published its first anthology in 2021. She is a member of the Society of Women Writers WA and has won two literary awards, including the Bronze Quill Award in 2019. Both honours were awarded for stories in this autobiography. She is also a member of Curtin Universities' Golden Key International Honour Society.

While Corfu on my Mind is Elizabeth's first autobiographical novel, she has published widely. Elizabeth is also an artist and playwright having written a comedy for stage. Set on a Greek island, the play is titled 'Let's Talk About Sex, Baby'. Elizabeth also enjoys travel, gardening, and writing poetry.

Passionate about social justice, and following the shocking revelations surrounding her mother's life, she encourages 'truth telling' to help heal the past.

Elizabeth has never lost her affection for Greece or its people. In 1985 she fell in love with a man of Kastellorizian heritage. They married on the island in 1986. She and her family return to the stunning sundrenched shores of 'Kazzie' and her beloved Corfu, whenever possible.

www.ingramcontent.com/pod-product-compliance
Lightning Source LLC
Chambersburg PA
CBHW020135130526
44590CB00039B/169